The All New
Official AOL UK Tourguide

Including Version 4.0i

by Michael Hewitt

The All New Official AOL UK Tourguide Including Version 4.0i
Copyright © The Coriolis Group, 1999

The Coriolis Group, Inc.
An International Thomson Publishing Company
14455 N. Hayden Road, Suite 220
Scottsdale, Arizona 85260

602/483-0192
FAX 602/483-0193
http://www.coriolis.com

Printed in the United States of America
ISBN   1-57610-385-4
10 9 8 7 6 5 4 3 2 1

Publisher
Keith Weiskamp

Acquisitions Editor
Stephanie Wall

Marketing Specialist
Gary Hull

Project Editor
Toni Zuccarini

Production Coordinator
Meg E. Turecek

Cover Design
Anthony Stock

Layout Design
April Nielsen

an International Thomson Publishing company

Albany, NY • Belmont, CA • Bonn • Boston • Cincinnati • Detroit • Johannesburg • London • Madrid
Melbourne • Mexico City • New York • Paris • Singapore • Tokyo • Toronto • Washington

About The Author

Michael Hewitt is a freelance journalist who writes about "anything and everything," from topics such as technology, travel, and the arts, to health and fitness. His work appears regularly in such publications as *The Times*, *The Daily Telegraph*, *The Evening Standard*, and the UK's leading technology monthly, *Personal Computer World*, to which he contributes the "Sounding Off" column. He has been using online services since the days of 300bps modems and is currently investigating whether his finances will extend to the installation of an ISDN link. Other books he has written in the area of online services include *Travels with a Laptop*, published by International Thomson Computer Press.

Acknowledgments

AOL would like to thank Arlene Wszalek for her contribution in editing this edition of the *AOL UK Tourguide*. Her unparalleled knowledge of AOL means that members can now benefit from the most comprehensive and informative AOL UK guide ever published.

Michael Hewitt offers thanks to his brothers David and Peter, and to Peter's wife, Pam, for agreeing to binmail graphics, generate samples of email, and take part in chat sessions—often with no notice whatsoever and sometimes at very unsociable hours—simply so that he could grab appropriate screenshots.

Foreword

We started AOL UK in 1996 with a hearty band of beta testers, a small but dedicated staff, and an excellent product. Just two short years later, AOL is the leading Internet online service in the UK. Why's that? I was hoping you would ask. :)

One reason is that when you join AOL, you're not alone out there in the World Wide Web. Sure, you can surf the Net to your heart's content, and this book will show you how to get started, but AOL is much, much more than the Internet. As an AOL member, you're part of a community of half a million members here in the UK, and over 12 million members around the world.

What are the benefits of being a member of this community? For just about every interest—including computing, sport, education, shopping, news, entertainment, finance, travel, games, and even romance—we offer Chat rooms, message boards, file libraries, feature articles, and other resources. We do all the work to bring you the very best and most current information, all just a mouse click away.

Email is one of the most popular features on AOL. You can exchange email with anyone in the world who has an email address. Your AOL account includes five email addresses; you can use them to separate your work and personal correspondence, for example, or assign one name to each member of the family.

As I mentioned earlier, with AOL you also get full, fast Internet access, at a local calling rate, no matter where you are in the UK. AOL software includes the powerful Microsoft Internet Explorer Web browser to help you get the most out of the Net. Do you want to be a part of the Internet, and not just look at it? Each AOL account gets 10MB of free Web space, and we'll even show you how to build your page.

Family and friends are an important part of AOL, just as they are in any community. With your AOL Buddy List you can invite friends to a Chat room, start an Instant Message conversation, or locate your friends online. Parents will want to take advantage of our Parental Controls, which let members manage their child's online experience.

Because we're a community, AOL and your fellow members are here to help. If you've got a question this book doesn't answer, we have fast, friendly, and free phone support. We've also got an interactive Tech Chat room, extensive online and offline Help files, and a dedicated team of volunteer Guides and Hosts to help you along.

AOL is such an extensive service, even I'm constantly discovering new features and content. If you're an AOL subscriber, this book will help you make the most of your AOL experience and have you navigating the service like a pro in no time. Even AOL veterans will probably pick up a few new tips and tricks from the chapters that follow. If you're not already one of our members, I hope this book will persuade you to join us!

Jonathan Bulkeley
Managing Director
October 1998

Contents At A Glance

Table Of Contents

Chapter 1

What Is AOL?

What is AOL? When the first edition of this book came out nearly three years ago, that's what most people were asking. An overnight courier service? Millwall's new Argentinian midfielder, perhaps? Back in 1996, AOL was the new kid on the U.K. block. Today, however, it's become the biggest of its kind—not just in the U.K., but in the whole world.

"The biggest what?" you're probably asking.

To put it quite simply, AOL is an online computer information service *and* an Internet service provider. You fire up the software on your PC and dial in via your modem. You can then send and receive email, participate in online conferences, buy goods from online stores, meet your future wife or husband in a Lonely Hearts section, access virtually all the information on the planet via the World Wide Web, and so on. Quite straightforward, really.

One of the reasons AOL has become the biggest and most successful service of its kind is equally straightforward: It's better designed and easier to use than all the others. There's nothing at all intimidating or complicated about AOL. It's aimed at perfectly normal, nontechnical human beings who don't want to be impeded by technical language dreamt up by computer geeks in anoraks. The folks who use AOL range from toddlers barely out of nappies to centenarian great-grandmothers.

Simplicity is AOL's essence, and I hope it's the essence of this book as well. If you want detailed discussions on asynchronous data exchange or modem protocols, I'm afraid you won't find them here.

If you want a fair analogy of what AOL is and what it does, think of it as being a superior version of teletext. With teletext, you can key in 101 and get the news headlines, 300 brings you sports information, 200 is finance, and so on. Indeed, there's virtually everything on there, from share quotes to fashion, from horoscopes to the latest weather forecast. All you need to do is punch in the right page number on your remote control.

AOL, which runs on a standard home PC rather than a television set, is an information service like teletext, but it offers much, much more. Furthermore, it's easier to use, and it's presented in a far more graphical, user-friendly format. You don't key in numbers to get to different areas; you use your mouse to click on icons and pictures. Or you can take shortcuts straight into specific areas by typing in Keywords. **NEWS**, for example, takes you directly to the day's headlines, complete with photographs and links to online newspapers.

The biggest difference between AOL and teletext is that AOL is a two-way, interactive service, whereas teletext is just one-way. When you key in, say, 113 on teletext to read a story about the latest scandal surrounding a cabinet minister, that's all you can do—read it. But on AOL, you're part of an online community, which means you can interact with other AOL members in all sorts of ways. For example, the news sections— nearly all sections, for that matter—have message boards, which are somewhat like Letters to the Editor pages. So, you can read a news item, and then contribute your opinion, which can in turn be read and responded to by other AOL members. Major online debates, arguments, and even friendships start this way.

Just as you can contribute posts to message boards, you can send letters directly to other people—not only to other AOL members, but also to anyone, anywhere in the world who has a connection to the Internet. This is called *email*, and it's perhaps one of AOL's most widely used features. Its advantages over the Royal Mail are many. Deliveries are 24 hours a day, 7 days a week, including Christmas Day. There's no risk of the letter being lost in the post or of the postman (or his letters) being chewed by a dog. Multipage documents can be sent in seconds, not just to locations in the U.K., but around the world. And email, even international email, costs less to send than a first-class stamp (and you don't have to lick the stamp).

But I'm getting ahead of myself. It's probably best if I give a brief description of one of my typical AOL sessions, which should help illustrate just a few of the things that you can get out of the system. Then I'll move on to hardware and software requirements and, finally, the signing-on procedure. At this point, you can try the service for yourself—if sheer curiosity hasn't already compelled you to do so.

A Typical Online Session

Ordinarily, I sign on to AOL three or four times a day. In the morning and afternoon, I'm usually on for just five minutes. This is sufficient time to check my email and, if it's urgent, compose a reply there and then. It's usually in the evenings, however, once dinner has been digested and there's a leisurely bottle of wine to hand, that I become a "power user" and take advantage of a fuller repertoire of AOL's features.

A couple of years ago, I introduced my two brothers to AOL. They're now fanatics, and you'll find them online most evenings. One of them lives up north, near Manchester. The other lives either in Athens or in a hotel in whichever city in the world his company has sent him to on that particular day. (AOL, as you'll discover in more detail in Chapter 14, is one of the few truly international online services, allowing you to connect from virtually anywhere on the planet that has a phone.) AOL has therefore become an invaluable way for us to keep in contact without having to depend upon the vagaries of airmail and without racking up massive long-distance telephone bills.

Here, briefly, is how it works.

I sign on, and hear a woman's voice declaring, "You've got Post!" This means there's new email waiting for me. Its subject, I see, is "Hello from Tel Aviv." It's obviously from my globe-trotting brother. I notice that he has attached a picture to his email. He does this rather a lot these days, ever since he bought his digital camera. He takes a picture on the spot, transfers it to his laptop computer, and then sends it as email. It's just like sending a postcard, really, except it gets to its destination almost instantaneously. In this case, the destination is me. I click on the picture to view it. There he is, reclining in the bar of his Tel Aviv hotel, sipping a piña colada while the sun sets over Jaffa in the distance. I suppose I could counter by sending him a picture of me sitting in a pub. However, "This is me drinking bitter in the saloon bar of the Marquis of Granby" doesn't really compare. Instead, I just read what he has to say: "Meet tonight at 8.00 P.M., your time, for a chat."

"How can we meet for a chat when he's over 2,000 miles away?" you're asking. Bear with me.

It's 7.45 P.M., so I've still got 15 minutes to go. In the meantime, then, I'll have a look at a few more things—the News, for instance. AOL's news service is like a combination of a newspaper and television news. There are regular stories and photographs, as in a newspaper, but they're continually updated, as they are on TV. One of the headlines, for this week's Wimbledon tournament, reads, "Confident Henman In Bullish Mood Before Semifinal." (In hindsight, it was too much to hope for, but it looked good at the time!)

I'll go off to amuse myself at the movies instead. What shall I see this weekend? I go to the This Is London film guide and check out reviews of all this week's new releases. *Sliding Doors*, with the American actress Gwyneth Paltrow, is in theatres now. Paltrow did OK with a period British accent in *Emma*—can she master a contemporary version this time? Maybe I'll check it out on Saturday.

OK. What's the weather going to be like tomorrow for a trip up to the West End? I go into the AOL Weather area and find a map of the U.K.; it's covered with sun and cloud symbols. I click on the cloud above me, in Epsom, and I see that for the southeast of England, the Met men reckon tomorrow's going to be dry with sunny spells. I better get the umbrella out....

Suddenly, Ping! "Come into Room HewittTA1," says the Instant Message. It's my brother in Tel Aviv, asking me to join him in a private chat room. Off I go.

When I arrive, my Manchester-based brother is in there, too. It isn't a real room, of course. This is what you would call a *virtual* room. Basically, it's a private area in AOL where people can get together and have a "chat" without being overheard or disturbed by anyone else. (There are public chat rooms too, where anyone can speak to anyone else, but I'll deal with those later.) It's a bit like a telephone conference call, except instead of speaking, the various participants type their messages. My brother in Manchester says he has just put in a new fireplace. To prove it, he emails us both a photograph. My brother in Tel Aviv says he has spent the afternoon on the beach, and now he is sunburnt. I tell him I've spent the afternoon on the Downs, and I'm wind-swept.

If we had to telephone one another—from Manchester to Tel Aviv and Epsom, from Tel Aviv to Manchester and Epsom, and so on—it would cost a fortune. As it is, we're all three of us only paying for a local telephone call plus our AOL bills, neither of which is going to break anyone's bank.

Anyhow, after half an hour or so, when we've said everything that needed saying, we go our separate ways. My northern brother works in computers, so he'll likely be off to AOL's computing area to check what's new in technology (which he has probably been doing the whole time we were chatting, anyway). My jet-setting brother is attempting to reengineer his love life, so I suspect he'll be off to one of AOL's singles areas. Me, I've got a new AOL manual to write, so I sign off and get on with that.

And it's all as simple as that.

Oh, Really?

Yes, really. "Simple for you, Mike," you're saying, "because you're already familiar with AOL. But how long is it going to take a newcomer like me to master all the intricacies of the service and get to the stage where I can just breeze through it?" To be truthful, not very long at all!

You've probably already got a basic understanding of how Windows, your PC's operating system, works. (Those of you on a Mac, indulge us here. Besides, you've got Chapter 12 all to yourselves.) If not, you'll find that there isn't much to it. Everything is rather obvious. If you want to fire up, say, Solitaire, you simply click on the Solitaire icon. If you want to use Word for Windows, you do the same with the Word icon. All of these functions are menu driven and virtually idiot proof. To save a file, for instance, you click on the little disk icon or go to the File menu and click on Save. To print it, go to the File menu and click on Print or click on the print icon.

So it is with AOL. Yes, there are online services that *do* require you to be a rocket scientist or a Nobel laureate in order to use them. Thankfully, AOL isn't one of them. If you can point and click, you're 90 percent of the way there. This book will help take you the remaining 10 per cent.

The rest of this chapter describes how to install the AOL software and make the first connection with AOL itself. If you already have an AOL account, feel free to skim the next bit or skip ahead to the next chapter.

Hardware Requirements

Before we get to the main feature—"Signing On For The First Time"— a word about hardware requirements. In other words, let's find out if you can run AOL on your existing PC. The official line is this: If you've got *at least* a 486DX 66 computer with a minimum of 8MB of RAM, a VGA monitor, a mouse, and a modem, then, yes, off you go; you can use AOL.

To be sure. And if you've got a Model T Ford with a two-stroke engine and half a tank of petrol, you can drive up Route 66. It's just that you won't get far, and you won't get far very slowly. Likewise, AOL *will* run on the sort of antediluvian machine I just described, but it will do so like a tortoise wading through treacle.

To be perfectly honest, to run AOL optimally, you need a Pentium PC with at least 16MB of RAM and an SVGA monitor. But, to be perfectly honest again, outside of an antique shop, you would be hard-pressed to find a machine *less* powerful than that. Today, even the basic starter models sold in places such as PC World and Dixons are Pentium multi-media PCs with 32MB of RAM and cavernous hard disks. So you'll have no problems if you're buying new.

If you've got an older or less-powerful machine, do consider upgrading. You can often do so for just a few hundred pounds. And it's not just AOL's performance that will improve. You'll notice an appreciable improvement in the way all your other programs run too.

So much for the PC itself. The other indispensable item is a modem. What is it? The word is derived from its function: *modulator/demodulator*. A modem turns your computer data, which is digital, into a series of squawks and hisses (analogue data—it's the sound a fax makes) that can be transmitted, in the same way as your voice, over a conventional telephone line to AOL. Once these modulated squawks and hisses reach the other end, AOL's modem turns them back into digital data (demodulates them, in other words) and feeds the information into its own computer.

If you're buying new, virtually all PCs come with built-in modems, so you needn't bother yourself there. You *do* need to bother yourself if your PC *doesn't* come equipped with a modem. But it isn't that much bother. You can pick one up for less than £100—nearer £50 if you shop around—in most stores that sell computers. There are two types of modem: internal and external. The former, as their name suggests, hide themselves away inside your PC and can't be seen, whereas the latter are attached to the back of your computer by a lead.

Which you choose is up to you. External modems have lots of flashing lights on the outside. That's about their only virtue—that and the fact that they're slightly easier to install than an internal modem, which requires you to open up your PC in order to install it. Even here, though, the shop will usually do it for you should you feel yourself overly perplexed.

A final word on the subject of modems relates to their speed of data throughput (in English, how fast they can physically shift computer information over the telephone line). AOL can handle all speeds up to 56,000bps, or V.90 as computer nerds call it. You'll find these figures on the side of the modem box. It therefore makes sense to have a modem at your end that runs at the same speed. It's not that a slower one won't work. It will, but AOL's modem will have to slow down to make allowances for the tardiness of yours.

Don't buy anything slower than a 28,800bps modem (V.34), even though it might be going cheap. It would be a false economy. One thing that distinguishes AOL from other online services is the quality and sheer number of its graphics. Graphics, by their very nature, tend to be fairly large computer files. So if you have a slow modem, it will take forever to download AOL's graphics to your computer and could cost you a small fortune in online time and telephone charges.

But that said, as with a 486 DX PC, you're going to have a hard job finding anything slower than a V.34 modem these days. Even V.34 bis— or 33,600bps—is looking a bit passé now. V.90 will soon be the norm.

Signing On For The First Time

OK, let's go for it; but before we do, a quick word. The registration procedure *should* look as it does in this section's figures. If you notice any significant differences, please turn to Chapter 14 for help.

I should point out at this stage that AOL will, for want of a better word, handhold you through the entire installation and signing-on process. So don't worry about anything here. Besides, there's offline help (click on Help on the menu bar), or you can phone a freephone number at 0800 376 5432, which will put you through to the AOL Customer Call Centre, based in Dublin. There, a helpful technician will be happy to take your call and talk you through any problems. If, however, it all goes smoothly—and there's no reason to suppose otherwise—this whole procedure should take about 10 minutes. There are a few things to do first, though:

▲ Will you install AOL from the sign-on program that came with your new PC? If so, you'll need to find where it is. Usually, it's located in a folder called Online Services. If in doubt, look in your PC manual or ring the manufacturer. If, on the other hand, you're installing from a CD-ROM, simply stick it in your PC's CD-ROM drive and follow the setup instructions.

▲ Have your credit card handy. AOL requires that you enter the details before it will allow you to access the service. (If you don't have a credit card, ring up the freephone number and find out if AOL has introduced any other methods of payment recently.)

▲ Keep a piece of paper and a pen by the side of your PC to take any notes.

▲ Make sure your modem is actually plugged into the phone socket.

▲ If you have a BT "Star" service, such as Call Waiting, disable it (#43#). Sudden interruptions on the line during the logging-on procedure will likely cause AOL to hang up.

▲ Keep the printed AOL certificate number and password that came with it to hand. You may be asked to enter them when you register.

Signing On

Signing on is a totally painless procedure; simply follow these steps:

1. First, you have to install the software. If the setup program has been preloaded on your new PC, find the AOL symbol—as I said earlier, it's usually in a folder called Online Services—and double-click on it. If, on the other hand, you're installing from a CD-ROM, the setup program should load automatically and come up with an AOL icon when you close your CD-ROM drive. If it doesn't, simply go to the Start menu, select Run, and type "D:\Setup95" (assuming D: is your designated CD-ROM drive; if it isn't, amend accordingly).

2. At this point, the setup program announces itself and begins to analyse your computer configuration (see Figure 1.1). This could take a few minutes. What it's doing during this time, among other things, is checking to make sure there's enough hard disk space, that you have a modem, that it's plugged in, what COM port it's on (i.e., which socket in the back of the PC it's attached to), and its speed. It also unpacks other ancillary programs, such as Microsoft's Internet Explorer (of which, more anon). Anyhow, just sit back and enjoy while everything happens.

3. If all is in order, a second screen appears. Click on Install.

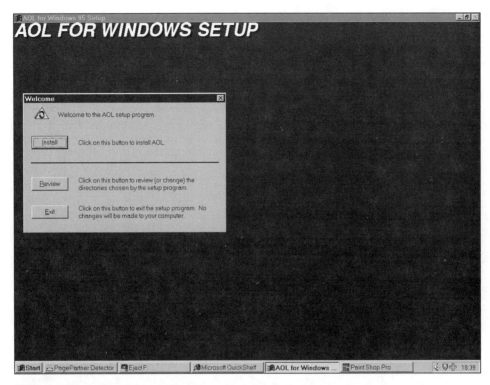

Figure 1.1
The setup program automatically analyses your computer's configuration.

4. Next, you are asked if you want to create an AOL shortcut from your Windows 95 Start menu. Why not? Click on OK. The program announces cheerily, "You're ready to use AOL," and suggests that you click on OK and then the AOL icon.

5. Behind the scenes, an AOL shortcut icon is added to the Windows 95 desktop and an AOL folder is created. Please note: If you're upgrading from a previous version of the AOL software, your old copy will remain untouched, in a different folder.

6. After you have double-clicked on the AOL icon (Step 4), AOL advises you that the show's about to begin (Figure 1.2). It assumes that:

▲ You don't need to dial 9 to get an outside line.

▲ Your modem is where the installation program thinks it is (in this case, on COM4). Yours will probably be different—COM2 or

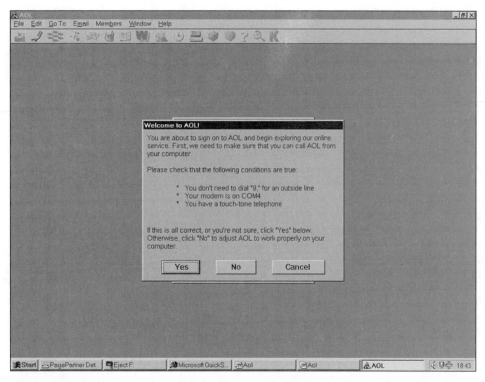

Figure 1.2
Almost ready. Here, AOL assumes you have a direct phone line to the outside world and that you use tone dialing.

COM3—than what is shown in Figure 1.2 because I have a rather weird setup.

▲ You have a touch-tone telephone.

But what if any of these conditions are untrue? Suppose, for example, you're using AOL from an office. You may well have to dial 9 to get an outside line. Also, it could be that your telephone exchange is of the old rotary, or Strowger, variety, as they're called. It that case, you can't use tone dialing. You'll have to use pulse.

7. Select No if any of the conditions in Step 6 aren't met. This takes you into an additional dialogue box (Figure 1.3). Here, click on the Use The Following Prefix To Reach An Outside Line box. An X will appear to show it's active. You'll note the number 9 followed by a comma. If by chance you need a different number (0, for instance) to

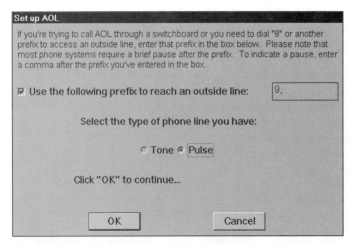

Figure 1.3
If you have to dial the exchange to get an outside line, you'll need to fill in an additional dialogue box.

dial outside the building, amend this accordingly but leave the comma there. The comma tells the internal exchange to pause for a second after the 9 is selected, giving the system a chance to connect properly to your telephone provider. If your telephone system is pulse dial, select that option. Finally, click on OK.

8. When you click on OK, the install program takes you into a COM port selection dialogue box (Figure 1.4). AOL might have been confused into thinking that your modem was on COM2 when in fact it's on COM4. If so, let it know the error of its ways and select the correct port. It's only a computer program, after all, so you do have to make a few allowances. At this stage, you can also define exactly what make of modem you're using. However, unless you really know what you're doing, you should let this be for the time being and plough on. Click on OK.

9. "Welcome to AOL!" says the window (Figure 1.5). New members are advised to have their AOL registration certificate number and password and their credit card to hand. Existing members just need their screen name and password. Click on OK.

10. The program selects a nationwide local rate number for AOL. When it's done so, click on OK.

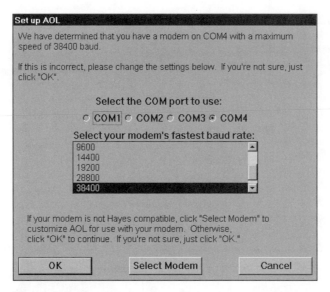

Figure 1.4
Which COM port is your modem on?

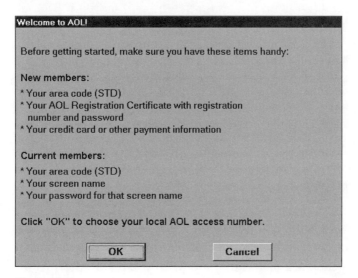

Figure 1.5
Have your registration number and credit card to the ready; you're about to
sign on for the first time.

11. The nationwide local access number is displayed (Figure 1.6). Now
    it's time to actually make contact. Select Sign On To AOL.

12. At this point, the initialisation screen pops up (Figure 1.7). When
    your PC makes contact with the modem and tells it to wake up

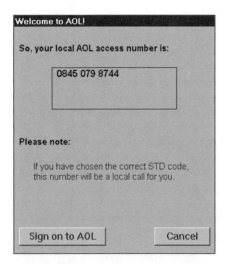

Figure 1.6
Time to sign on.

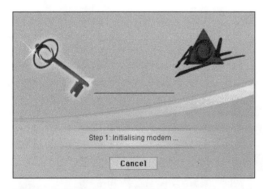

Figure 1.7
AOL's initialisation screen.

and start dialing, the first picture, that of a key, is illuminated. Assuming your modem's speaker is on, you'll hear the dialing tones being generated, just as they are when you make a normal telephone call. There may then be a wait of a few seconds while AOL performs an identity check. Once that is completed, the AOL symbol is illuminated. Congratulations—you're in.

13. The Welcome To AOL screen appears (Figure 1.8). If you're asked to do so, enter the registration number and password that came with your AOL program disk. In my case, the registration number is

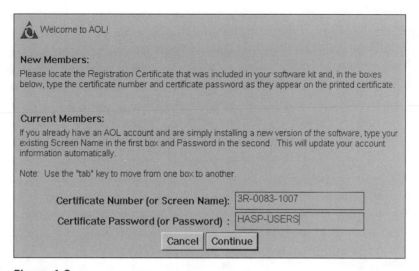

New Members:
Please locate the Registration Certificate that was included in your software kit and, in the boxes below, type the certificate number and certificate password as they appear on the printed certificate.

Current Members:
If you already have an AOL account and are simply installing a new version of the software, type your existing Screen Name in the first box and Password in the second. This will update your account information automatically.

Note: Use the "tab" key to move from one box to another.

Certificate Number (or Screen Name): 3R-0083-1007
Certificate Password (or Password) : HASP-USERS

Cancel | Continue

Figure 1.8
You must enter your registration number and password exactly as they appear on the form that accompanies your program disk.

3R-0083-1007 and the password is HASP-USERS. To move from the top box to the bottom box, press the Tab key or click in the box with your mouse. If you make a mistake anywhere, just click on the box containing the error, press the backspace or delete keys to erase, and then correct your error. When you've finished, click on Continue.

14. Now you're into the address info screen (Figure 1.9). Move from one box to the next by pressing the Tab key. The address details must be filled in accurately. If they're not, AOL might not accept your credit card. When you've filled everything in here, click on Continue.

15. The Welcome To AOL screen comes up next. This is just to let you know that you've got a certain number of free hours online before AOL start charging you. You can get to know the system without doing any major damage to your credit card. Once you've read the welcome message, click on Continue.

16. AOL tells you that Visa, Access/MasterCard, and American Express will all do very nicely. Select as appropriate, and the screen for entering your credit card details comes up (Figure 1.10). Enter the details exactly. Incidentally, if, perish the thought, you should be feeling in a

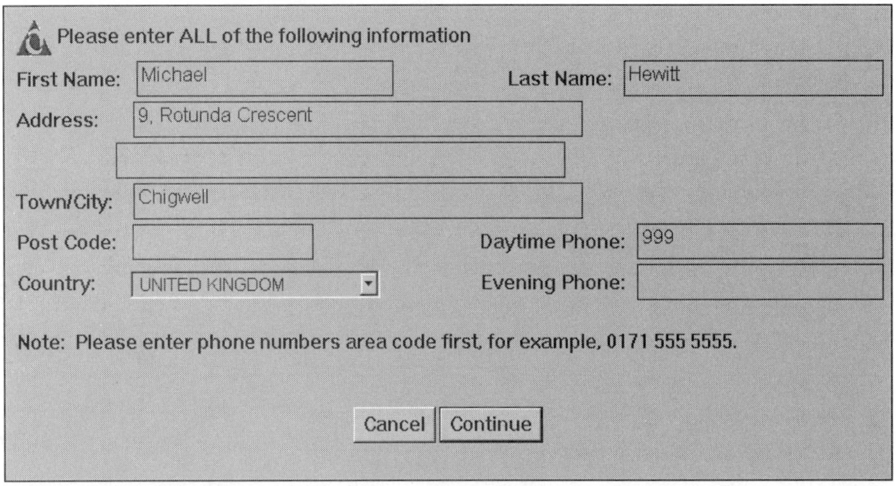

Figure 1.9
Your address details must be entered accurately to ensure that AOL accepts your credit card.

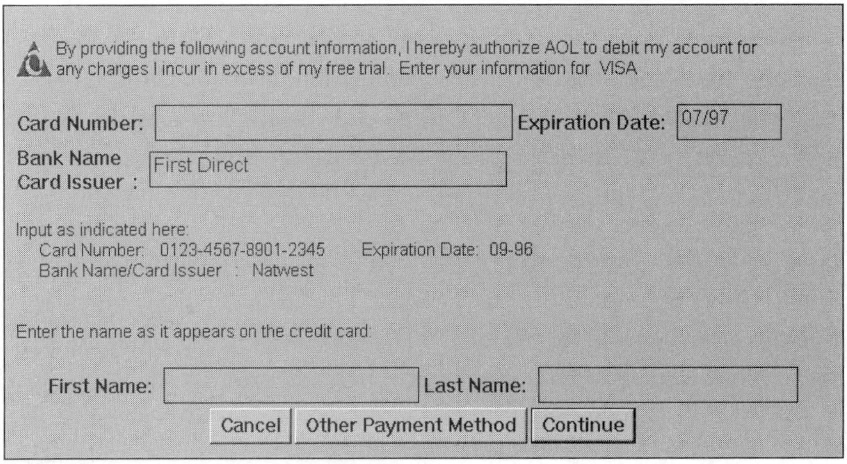

Figure 1.10
Make sure you enter your credit card details exactly.

nefarious mood and try to enter dodgy credit card information, AOL will know instantly. It's able to match credit card numbers to addresses. If they don't match, you won't get in. I just mention that in passing. When everything is filled in, click on Continue once again.

17. You're then presented with a screen displaying the conditions of service (Figure 1.11). It says that you use the service at your own risk,

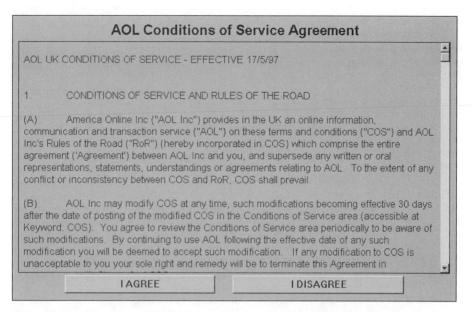

AOL Conditions of Service Agreement

AOL UK CONDITIONS OF SERVICE - EFFECTIVE 17/5/97

1.   CONDITIONS OF SERVICE AND RULES OF THE ROAD

(A)   America Online Inc ("AOL Inc") provides in the UK an online information, communication and transaction service ("AOL") on these terms and conditions ("COS") and AOL Inc's Rules of the Road ("RoR") (hereby incorporated in COS) which comprise the entire agreement ('Agreement') between AOL Inc and you, and supersede any written or oral representations, statements, understandings or agreements relating to AOL. To the extent of any conflict or inconsistency between COS and RoR, COS shall prevail.

(B)   AOL Inc may modify COS at any time, such modifications becoming effective 30 days after the date of posting of the modified COS in the Conditions of Service area (accessible at Keyword: COS). You agree to review the Conditions of Service area periodically to be aware of such modifications. By continuing to use AOL following the effective date of any such modification you will be deemed to accept such modification. If any modification to COS is unacceptable to you your sole right and remedy will be to terminate this Agreement in

| I AGREE | I DISAGREE |

Figure 1.11
AOL's Terms and Conditions. Read them carefully.

you promise not to harass people, you won't transmit obscene material, and the usual. If you agree, select I Agree. If you don't, the sign-on procedure will immediately be terminated.

18. You're now advised on choosing your initial screen name. You can have up to five screen names, so members of your family or your friends can use the account, too. But the initial, or *Master*, screen name is the one by which AOL will identify you for future reference and for all official email. Once selected, it can't be changed, so don't think up anything too ridiculous. The name has to be at least 3 characters long, but no more than 10. It can be any combination of numbers and letters—MH12K8, for instance.

There are several million people using AOL, so likely as not, you'll find that your first preference for your screen name will already be taken. For instance, I went for Hewitt (Figure 1.12), but AOL said it was already being used. So I tried Michael. No again. It then tried to be helpful and suggested MHewitt773 as an alternative (Figure 1.13). I suppose that will do.

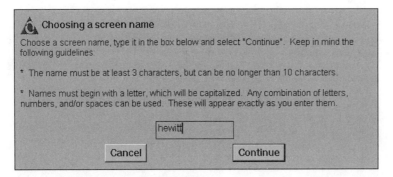

Figure 1.12
Because AOL has so many members, it's quite possible that your first choice of screen name has already been taken.

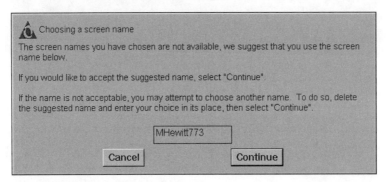

Figure 1.13
MHewitt773 doesn't exactly trip off the tongue, but it will do.

The first character of your screen name must be a letter, and it will automatically be capitalised. You can choose whether the remaining letters are in upper- or lowercase. If it makes an aesthetic difference to you, keep that in mind when you devise your name. Once you've entered it, you can't change uppercase to lowercase and vice versa. When you've come up with a name that's mutually acceptable, both to you and to AOL, click on Continue.

19. AOL confirms my choice of screen name (Figure 1.14). MHewitt773 is how other AOL members will know me, and mhewitt773@aol.com is how I can be contacted from the Internet and from services outside AOL. (On Internet email it doesn't matter, by the way, whether you use upper- or lowercase letters.) Click on Continue.

Figure 1.14
When you and AOL have finally agreed on a screen name, AOL confirms it.

20. Now it's time to choose a password (Figure 1.15). This is important because it ensures that no one else can get into your account and use it at your expense. Don't tell anyone else what your password is, and don't choose something that others might be able to guess easily. Examples of risky passwords include your husband's or wife's name, your birthday, and any single word found in a dictionary. Basically, treat your password as you would the PIN number on your cash card. Reveal it to no one. (And remember, no one from AOL will ever ask you for your password or billing information!)

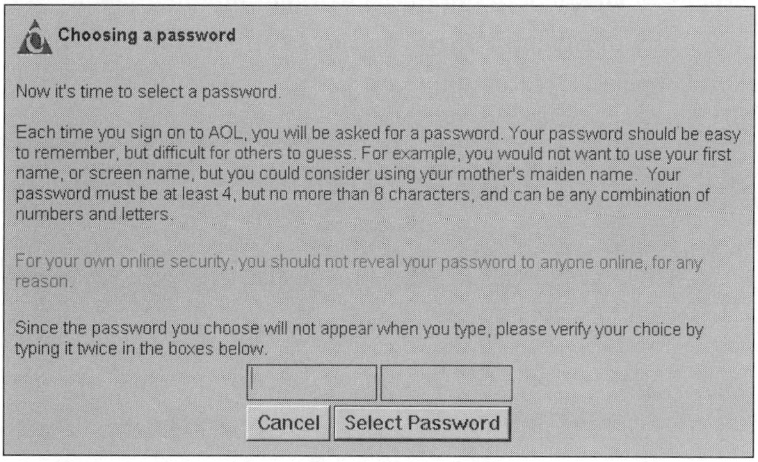

Figure 1.15
Choose your password carefully because it protects the security of your AOL account. Don't choose one that's too obvious.

Your password has to be at least four characters long and no more than eight and, like your screen name, can be any combination of numbers and letters. (In fact, AOL *recommends* that it be a combination of letters and numbers; those kinds of passwords are harder for other people to guess.) When you type it into the box, asterisks will appear in place of letters. This is just in case someone is looking over your shoulder. Press the Tab key to move to the next box and type it again for verification. Then note the password down somewhere and don't forget it. Next, click on Select Password.

21. At this point, you'll move through a series of welcoming screens that tell you the sort of things AOL has on offer and give details about its online help service. Click through them until you get to the final Welcome To AOL screen (Figure 1.16). This is the last of the preambles. Click on Enter AOL.

If you have a sound card—and most likely, you do—you'll hear a sultry female voice say "Welcome!" Does she sound familiar? Yes, it *is* Joanna Lumley. Next, the Welcome screen comes up (Figure 1.17). There could be a delay of a second or two while your computer downloads various pieces of artwork from AOL, including an icon for the day's top news story and three other icons that change regularly, promoting some of the many services that AOL has on offer. In this case, we've got info on mortgage advice, what's hot in the world of mountain bikes, and an opportunity to sign up a friend and win a trip to Vienna. While all of this is happening, Joanna pipes up again. "You've got Post!" she says, ever

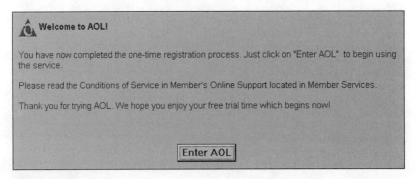

Figure 1.16
Welcome to AOL! At last.

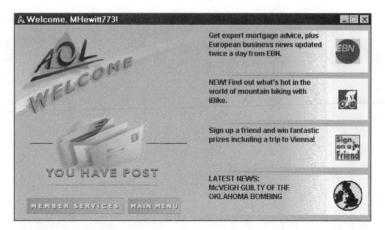

Figure 1.17
AOL's Welcome screen.

so enthusiastically. (By the way, if you can't abide Joanna Lumley, you can change her to anything you want, as you'll find out in Chapter 10.)

Congratulations, these are your first pieces of email. To see what you've got, click on the You Have Post icon, and they're listed (Figure 1.18). You've received a welcoming letter from Jonathan Bulkeley, Managing Director of AOL, and another from Una Mullarkey, Member Services Manager. To read them, just double-click on them (Figure 1.19). These are the kinds of emails you might want to read again later. If you do, you can find them in your Personal Filing Cabinet by clicking on the Toolbar's file cabinet icon. (More on managing your email in the next chapter.)

From this point onward, you can start exploring the system. Don't try to do too much all at once, though. Bear in mind that those first free hours

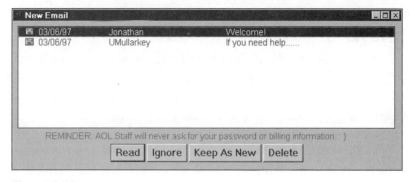

Figure 1.18
Your first email messages, welcoming you to AOL.

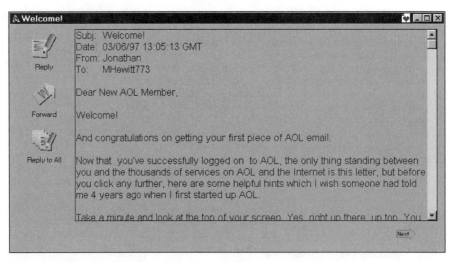

Figure 1.19
To read your email, double-click on the message.

can soon speed by. To exit, simply click on Exit under the File menu or click on the little x box in the upper right corner of your screen.

Pricing

AOL has three pricing plans: unlimited usage, light usage, and annual. By default, all newcomers are charged for the light-usage plan. To find out more about pricing plans or to change plans, please turn to Chapter 14.

Of course, another expense you'll generate by using AOL is your phone bill. If you plan on using AOL a lot, it may be worthwhile to see if your telephone provider has any special offers for heavy usage (for example, BT has the Friends and Family and PremierLine schemes).

What Have I Just Connected To?

Although you may be dialing in to AOL from London or Cardiff or Glasgow (or wherever), you're actually getting through to a series of minicomputers about the size of Hoover twin tubs, based in a place called Vienna, Virginia, just outside Washington, D.C.

When you dial in to AOL here in the U.K., it relays your computer data over a fixed transatlantic line to the U.S. So when, for instance, I send a piece of email from here in Epsom to my brother in Manchester, it goes first to London and then to a computer in the U.S., where it resides until my brother in Manchester dials in to a local number and accesses it. It's the pass-the-beanbag principle, which is the basis of all online services. All AOL data—be it message board information, graphics, email, or even the day's news headlines—is stored on servers in the U.S. and read remotely.

So why Vienna, Virginia? This is the head office location of one of AOL's parent companies, America Online. Since the service was founded in 1989, it has grown to become the world's biggest online service, with upward of 12 million members. AOL was founded in the U.K. in 1995 as a joint venture between American Online Inc. and Bertelsmann AG. Currently, America Online also has services in Australia, Austria, Canada, France, Germany, Japan, Sweden, and Switzerland, and it continues to expand around the world.

Although one of its parent companies is American, don't presume that AOL is simply America Online trying to affect a British accent, like Dick Van Dyke in *Mary Poppins*. It's actually a separate service in its own right, serving distinctly U.K. interests and activities. At the same time, however, it provides access to the American and other international AOLs, with all the resources and information they offer. So basically, you have the best of all worlds.

In the end, what really sets AOL apart is people—the online community to which I referred earlier. The dictionary defines "community" as "an interacting population of various kinds of individuals in a common location," and that's as good a definition as you can get for AOL. AOL members come from all over the U.K. and from all walks of life to interact online. That's what AOL is all about, and it's good to keep that in mind even as you become a sophisticated online veteran.

In the following chapters, I'll discuss the sorts of services and features that are available on AOL. This book can only be a rough guide, though. AOL grows and changes by the week, continually adding features and services. The best and only way to stay up-to-date is to sign on and explore it yourself.

Now let's look at the basics, such as email and navigation.

Chapter 2

Trouble Avoidance, Email, Mail Controls,™ Navigation, Chat, And Message Boards

Now that you're signed on, you'll want to get to know AOL as quickly as possible. One of the first things you'll see each time you sign on is the Main Menu (Figure 2.1). The Main Menu window features 14 icons shaped rather like pop-art rugby balls. They represent what AOL calls its Channels, and you can use them (in addition to several other methods, which I'll get to in a bit) to navigate around the system. AOL Channels are even better than television channels because each one is dedicated to the subject at hand, be it shopping, entertainment, finance, or whatever. So if you go to the Travel Channel, you won't be distracted by material on cookery or pensions. Try clicking on each icon and see where it takes you. I'll talk about the Channels in greater detail in Chapter 7.

Perhaps more important than getting to know AOL itself, you'll want to get to know your fellow AOL members. I'll start, however, with a quick mention of some fellow AOL members who, for obvious reasons, you won't want to know. Then I'll move on to more serious matters. First, I'll discuss email—near instantaneous communication between you and the rest of the wired world. Next, I'll talk about navigating your way around the system, using the Toolbar, Keywords, and Find. And I'll conclude, briefly, with an introduction to Chat and message boards.

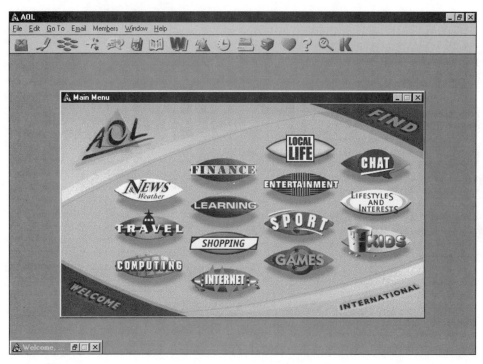

Figure 2.1
AOL's Main Menu.

Trouble

It would flatter me enormously to believe that you were hanging on my every word and that you wouldn't consider using any part of AOL before I explained what was in there and how it worked. However, I must reconcile myself to the fact that, as far as you're concerned, this book is more like one of those tourist guides in St Paul's Cathedral, waving his red umbrella in the air more in hope than expectation. He's encouraging you to gather round and have a look at Wren's grave. But you've already headed upstairs because you're more interested in seeing the Whispering Gallery or having a panoramic view of London—or whatever else takes your fancy.

Fine. That's how it should be. But before you do a Livingstone and explore *too* much of AOL's uncharted territories on your own, let me give you a word of warning.

Mostly, the online community is well behaved, and the people you meet will be perfectly pleasant. *Mostly*. Sadly, all online services, not simply AOL, have their fair share of miscreants, just as the real world does. They prey especially on newcomers who haven't yet found their virtual feet.

The sort of people you must particularly be on your guard against are those, like the character in Figure 2.2, who send you an Instant Message or email in an attempt to discuss your account details. They often pose as AOL staff members and try to sound as official as possible, using phrases like "Important: account verification" or "Your account is due to be terminated." All they're doing is trying to fool you into giving them your password or credit card details. Ignore them.

TIP *Warning!*

Never give your password or credit card details to anyone, whomever he or she claims to be. No one from AOL will ever ask you for this information online. Revealing your password is like going public with your PIN number.

If this sort of thing happens, or if you encounter any hassle whatsoever, go to Keyword: **TROUBLE**. Keywords, as I'll explain shortly, are short-cuts for navigating to different sections of AOL. Press the Control button and then the letter "K." Type the word "Trouble" into the screen that appears, as shown in Figure 2.3, and then click on Go.

Figure 2.2
An online villain after my password.

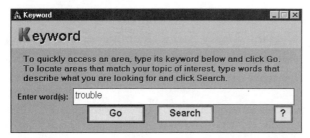

Figure 2.3
Summoning help from one of AOL's online troubleshooters.

Within seconds, sometimes faster, you'll be taken to AOL's Notify AOL screen (Figure 2.4). From here, you can select the appropriate button to, well, notify AOL about people who are after your password, send you dodgy email, behave abusively, or otherwise violate AOL's Conditions of Service (COS). It is AOL's COS staff who will most often deal with your complaint. If you're having trouble in a chat room, however, AOL will dispatch one of their Ambassadors (an online Guide) to quickly deal with the offender and put your mind at rest.

Online Guides And Hosts

This is a good time to introduce Hosts and Guides, actually. They are online volunteers who help newcomers and those with online difficulties. If you're perplexed by the workings of AOL, for instance, they'll try to

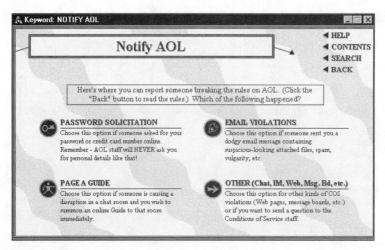

Figure 2.4
Seek help via AOL's Notify AOL screen.

answer your every question. If they can't, they know a man (or woman) who can. Where and when do you find them? Luckily, one or more of them is online around the clock.

AOL's Guides all have screen names that start with the prefix "GuideUK." They're online generalists and roam from one chat room to another within AOL. If you want to track one down, you'll normally find them in the New Members Lobby or in main AOL chat rooms, answering questions and cracking jokes.

Guides serve a twofold function. First, they answer questions about using AOL. If they can't do so themselves, they'll direct AOL members to people or places that can. Their second role is to deal with troublemakers in chat rooms, such as the person you saw in Figure 2.2.

Hosts can also be identified by their screen names, which begin with the prefix "UKHost" (UKHostMike, for example). A Host is a specialist affiliated with a specific area on AOL. The Diadem area, for instance, has two Hosts who look after its message boards. You'll often find them in the Diadem chat room. Because they *are* associated with specific sections on AOL, you would normally approach a Host with questions that are specific to that section. It doesn't mean he or she is woefully ignorant of everything else, mind you. For example, asking a Host in the Computing channel about the Chelsea Flower Show might not be too productive. In such a case, the Host will put you on to someone more qualified.

A final word on potential trouble: Don't worry about it. Basically, dealing with it is just common sense, like locking your door when you leave the house and remembering to cancel the milk and newspapers when you go on holiday. The *vast* majority of the online community—and please notice that I've italicised "vast" in order to labour the point—are friendly, welcoming, and helpful.

Email

What is email?

Email is post that's created on one computer and transferred to another via some sort of intermediate network. The other computer could be next to you in the same office or 10,000 miles away on the opposite side of the world. It doesn't matter. In either case, the electronic missives that pass between them are called email. AOL handles over 200 email messages *each second*.

Why is AOL's email more efficient than both the Royal Mail (or snail mail, as many techies call it) and the fax? Its advantages over a first-class letter should be obvious. It gets to its destination almost instantaneously and doesn't cost nearly as much to send. But what about email versus fax?

I have a fax machine, myself. I quite like it. It sits very nicely alongside my 1930s wind-up gramophone and my antique cash register, which is where, in my opinion, it belongs. A fax machine is outdated technology.

Let's make an analogy. Suppose you go to The Ivy restaurant in London W1. (I highly recommend it—around £60 for two, including wine, unless you go for some of the vintage stuff, then prices start getting silly.) Having studied the menu, you ask the waiter for a juicy half-pound steak with the usual herbs and seasoning. *"D'accord, monsieur,"* he says, and departs. Twenty minutes later, with a flourish, he presents you with something resembling a McDonald's Quarter Pounder. Would you object? I'm sure you would.

To create a burger, you take a perfectly serviceable steak, mince it up, add herbs, spices, and seasoning, and then, basically, stick it back together again. Similarly, when you send a fax, it scans whatever you're sending and turns it into a series of thousands of dots, or a *bitmap*, as those in the know call it. This results in a massive file, which is sent, comparatively slowly, over a telephone line. When it eventually reaches the other end, it has to be reconstituted back into the original document.

I often sit by my fax machine as documents slowly whir through, wondering why the sender is bothering. And when someone faxes me something the size of *War and Peace*—especially if it's faxed from abroad and international telephone rates apply—I calculate how many dinners at The Ivy the sender *could* have enjoyed if he had simply emailed the document to me instead.

Email sent via AOL costs only the price of a local telephone call plus online charges. Even together, they don't come to the cost of a first-class stamp. With AOL, it only takes a few seconds to send a document (even one consisting of several hundred pages) to anywhere in the world, and you can send it for, basically, peanuts.

Sending Email

To send email, follow these steps:

1. Sign on to AOL and wait for Joanna to do her stuff. When she's finished, you have two options. You can select Compose Email from the Email menu, or you can click on the pencil icon on the Toolbar. What's the Toolbar? Look directly underneath the menus and you'll see it; it's a series of small icons. The Compose Email icon—a little picture of a pencil—is the second one along from the left. I'll cover the Toolbar in more detail in a few pages, so please bear with me for the time being.

2. Whichever route you go, you'll eventually end up in the Write Email screen (Figure 2.5). As you can see, there are four boxes: To, CC, Subject, and the box for the message text itself. The cursor will be blinking in the To box. This is where you enter the address of the person to whom you're writing. In this case, I'm emailing an Italian friend, Rafaella. I type her AOL name, galbricci.

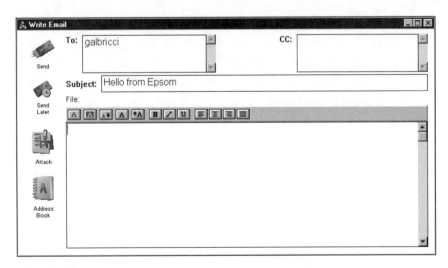

Figure 2.5
Compose your missive in the Write Email screen just as you would in a word processor.

I'll digress ever so slightly at this point. What happens if you want to send a single email message to several people? You can do so by including all the relevant screen names (and/or Internet addresses) in the To field, separated by a comma and a space—for example: galbricci, mhewitt102, joeslavko. You can enter several hundred names here if you wish. But then, of course, you do risk receiving several hundred replies in return.

Do you want to send a carbon copy of your message? You have probably seen business letters with cc: (which originally meant "carbon copy") typed at the bottom and followed by a list of the other recipients. AOL email works in exactly the same way. Just enter the screen name(s) of the intended recipient(s) in the CC box.

On the other hand, you might want to send a copy of an email message to another person without the addressee knowing that you've done so. This is called a *blind* carbon copy. To send one, enter the recipient's screen name into the CC box *enclosed in brackets*, that is, (galbricci). Then no one but the recipient of the blind carbon copy will know of your duplicity.

Whether you're sending a message to multiple addresses, sending a carbon copy, or just sending a message to one person, the next step is to fill in the Subject box.

3. Go to the Subject box by clicking in it or using the Tab key. Let's get back to my mail message to Rafaella. I type in "Hello from Epsom" in the Subject field simply because it's the first thing that comes to mind. You can't leave the subject field blank, incidentally. This can be a pain, but it forces you to declare to the recipient what the mail is about.

4. Next, I go to the message text area (or use the Tab key) and type my message (Figure 2.6). Having done so, I click on the Send icon and the email is sent.

What happens if you've made a mistake and misspelled the recipient's name? Or suppose, just for the fun of it, you enter a totally fictitious name. (Be careful here—AOL has so many members that it's quite possible that the name, however outlandish, might in fact exist.) AOL

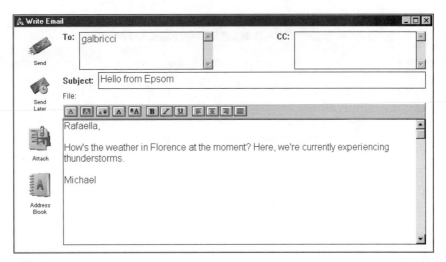

Figure 2.6
Fill in the subject and the body of the message and click on Send to speed it on its way.

will simply come back at you with an error message saying that the screen name doesn't exist. This is another advantage of AOL's email service over the Royal Mail. If I incorrectly address a conventional letter or send it to a non-existent person, it will take the post office weeks to discover the fact and inform me. With AOL, it's instantaneous (unless you're sending Internet mail, as I'll explain later).

5. When you click on Send, the Write Email screen disappears and a little information box appears in its place telling you that the letter has been sent. Note that this is true unless you've deselected the option to confirm mail after it's been sent.

6. At her end, once she's signed on, of course, Rafaella hears Joanna Lumley's voice saying, "You've got Post!" At the same time, she'll note that the You've Got Post icon (the envelope on the far left side of the Toolbar), which was previously greyed-out with an X across it, has now lit up and has acquired a tick. She then clicks on the You've Got Post icon or on the New Mail icon and finds my letter listed in the New Mail screen (Figure 2.7). As you can see, the information bar tells her when it was sent, who sent it, and the subject matter.

Figure 2.7
The New Mail screen shows all the new email messages you've received.

7. To read the mail, she double-clicks anywhere on the bar or on the Read button at the bottom of the New Mail screen. This brings up the letter itself (Figure 2.8). The other three options, in addition to Read, are Ignore, Keep As New, and Delete. I'll get to these anon.

What I've just described is how to send mail while you're online. But this is only really practical with very short messages. Remember, if you're on the Light Access pricing plan, the meter is ticking from the moment your password is accepted at Sign-on. And regardless of your AOL pricing plan, your telephone provider will be charging you as long as you're online. So unless your lottery numbers have come up and money is no object, you probably won't want to compose a letter—especially a long

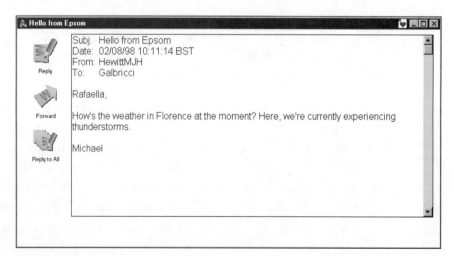

Figure 2.8
My letter to Rafaella Galbricci, safely delivered.

one—while you're signed on to AOL. Instead, be kind to the credit card and compose it offline. The same goes for *reading* long email messages. This, too, is more economically done offline.

To find out how to compose and read mail offline, please turn to Chapter 6, where I talk about maximising your online time. After all, it's your money.

TIP   *Handling Very Large Emails*

AOL's limit on the size of an email message is around 30K, which, in layman's terms, equals about 15 pages of closely spaced A4. So if your email message is going to be longer than this, you have two options. First, you can cut it into smaller pieces and send each piece separately. Call them, for example, Mail1 and Mail2 to avoid confusion at the other end. Alternatively, you could send a multipage message in a file as an *attachment* to your email. More on this in Chapter 5.

Has Your Email Been Read?

If I send someone a conventional letter or fax, I won't know for certain whether or not it's been read until I receive a reply. The recipient might be out of the country for all I know. However, if her or she is a fellow AOL member, AOL not only tells me whether my email has been read—or (horrors) ignored or deleted—it also tells me exactly when. Unfortunately, this doesn't work with email sent to someone on the Internet.

To find out if your mail has been read, follow these steps:

1. Select Check Email You've Sent from the Email menu. The Outgoing Mail window opens (Figure 2.9). AOL retains all outgoing and incoming mail messages for at least two days (in the figure, you can see some I've sent over the past few days).

2. To check a message, highlight it and click on the Show Status button. The status window for that particular email message comes up (Figure 2.10). When I check the message I've just sent to Rafaella, which is the first in the list, the status window tells me that the message was sent at 10:11 BST and read a minute later, at 10:12.

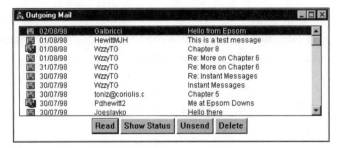

Figure 2.9
The Outgoing Mail window maintains a list of your most recently sent email messages.

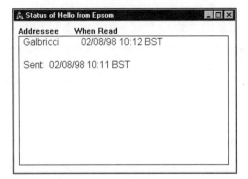

Figure 2.10
The status window tells you if and when your AOL email has been read. It doesn't work with email sent to Internet addresses, however.

Unsending Email

Why would you want to unsend email? There are any number of reasons. Lots of times, for example, I've sent letters and wished I hadn't: "Congratulations on your 40th birthday," say, when she was only 38, or "Happy wedding anniversary" to a couple going through the divorce courts. With conventional mail or a fax, once it's gone, it's a *fait accompli*. With AOL's email, however, you needn't worry unduly. As long as the intended recipient hasn't actually read the email you've sent, you can unsend it.

Just click on unsend mail from the Outgoing Mail window and it's sorted. Unless, as I said, the recipient or anyone else to whom you may have sent the same email *has* already read it. Then you really do have problems.

▲ The Delete Button

The Delete button does exactly as you would suppose. Basically, it's a housekeeping feature. All it does is remove the selected email message from your Outgoing Email list. AOL still delivers it. People who send several dozen email messages a day will find this feature useful because it helps keep Check Email You've Sent lists short and manageable.

By the way, email sent over the Internet, which means to people other than AOL members, can't be unsent. Once it leaves AOL's gateway for the vast reaches of the Internet, AOL can't fetch it back for you.

Reading New Email

As you've already seen, you can read email while you're logged on simply by clicking on the You've Got Post icon or the New Mail icon on the Toolbar. This brings up the New Mail screen (shown earlier in Figure 2.7). If you've received more than one piece of email, the messages will be listed from the top in chronological order. What happens next depends on which of the four buttons at the bottom of the New Mail window you decide to select:

▲ *Read*—Displays the highlighted email message. Alternatively, just double-click on the message itself.

▲ *Ignore*—Copies the email message into the Old Email list without your having to read it. Be warned, though, that if people do a Show Status check on their outgoing email, they'll see the word "Ignored" next to the message in the Outgoing Mail window. If it happens too often, they could start getting a persecution complex.

▲ *Keep As New*—Returns a message that you've already read to your New Mail list. So every time you sign on to AOL, it will show up as new mail. This function will prove useful as a memory jogger. If, for example, you've received a particularly important message that must have an urgent reply, you can select Keep As New to make sure you don't forget it. However, if the sender does a status check on it, it will be marked as read in his or her Outgoing Email window.

▲ *Delete*—Deletes the highlighted message. This option is useful for those of us who are plagued by junk email trying to flog insurance, get-rich-quick schemes, and the like. Normally, this sort of stuff comes from external Internet sites, not from AOL, with subject lines such as "Exciting Business Opportunity" or "An Offer You Just Cannot Afford To Miss." If you feel you *can* miss it, click on Delete. It's like taking a piece of junk mail that's landed on your doormat and transferring it straight to the bin. It disappears from your New Mail list, and it isn't transferred to the Old Email list either. If it came from another AOL member, their status check will display the word "Deleted." It's gone. Zapped. And you can't undelete it.

For more, read "Mail Controls™" later in this chapter.

Suppose You Don't Read It?

Unread email is retained by AOL for around 27 days, after which it's deleted automatically. So if you're doing a Phileas Fogg, break off every three weeks or so, if you can, in order to check your email. Or simply inform all your friends beforehand that, for the next 80 days, you'll be incommunicado. Or, if you'll have access to the Internet but not AOL, think about using AOL's new NetMail, which I'll come to shortly.

Replying To Email

Composing a reply is essentially the same as composing any other email message. Turn back to Figure 2.8, which shows a newly arrived missive. You'll see three symbols by the side: Reply, Forward, and Reply To All:

▲ Select Reply and the Reply window appears (Figure 2.11). You'll notice that the subject line is preserved, except this time it's prefixed with "Re:" Also, the To field is already filled in because, as this is a reply, AOL knows exactly where it's going. Compose your witty riposte and click on Send. Off it goes.

▲ You might also want to forward the email message to someone else. Click on Forward and a slightly modified Write Email screen appears with the header prefixed by "Fwd:". Enter the address of the person to whom you're forwarding the email in the To field and type your message into the text box in the usual way. Send the email. Your recipient ends up with a hybrid of the original message and your comment (Figure 2.12). A line separates the two.

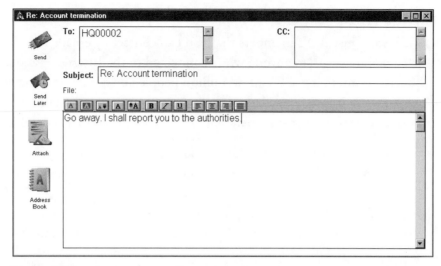

Figure 2.11
The Reply window.

Figure 2.12
A forwarded email message is an amalgamation of your message and the original message.

▲ The Reply button will generate a reply only to the original sender of your incoming email. However, if he or she addressed the email to multiple recipients—there might be several names in the To or CC boxes, for instance—you can reply to all of them at once by clicking on the Reply To All button.

Internet Mail

It's not just AOL members that you can contact by email. You can send email messages to anyone who's connected to the Internet—and at the last count, that was about 60 million people and rising—as long as you know their Internet address. I don't use only AOL, so I've got other email addresses on other systems. For example, **M_HEWITT@delphi.com**.

As you can see, Internet addresses aren't subject to the 10-character limit that AOL addresses are. They therefore tend to be long and eminently forgettable. Then again, so is 44, Acacia Avenue, Worbleton, Sunford SX17 6TT. Why don't people complain about the length and complexity of snail mail addresses, too? Because, if you get a postal address slightly wrong—you use the wrong post code, for instance, or misspell the addressee's name—the post office will nevertheless probably still be able to get the letter to its destination. Whereas if you misspell an Internet address by as little as one letter, it won't be delivered. What does all the gibberish mean?

Everything to the left of the ampersand is the user's ID; everything to the right is the name of the service where that ID is registered. So take, for example, **hewitt@cix.compulink.co.uk**; this is my address on a UK-based conferencing system called CiX.

Then there's my AOL Internet address. If someone on AOL wants to mail me, it's simply **mhewitt102**, which is my main screen name. However, if someone on the Internet wants to send email to my AOL account, then both my screen name and AOL's network name, which happens to be aol.com, must be included. Together, that adds up to **mhewitt102@aol.com**.

Unfortunately, no one has yet produced the equivalent of a comprehensive member directory for the Internet. There are just too many separate networks. And with 60 million users, it would be a very big book indeed. So unless you know a person's Internet address from the outset, you could have a hard time tracking him or her down.

Sending Email Over The Internet

Actually, the process of sending email over the Internet is identical to sending AOL email. The only difference is that the addresses are longer.

If you want to mail me on CiX, you just put **hewitt@cix.compulink.co.uk** in the To field in the Write Email screen.

When you receive email from an Internet address, it will look almost identical to incoming AOL email (Figure 2.13). Joanna Lumley will react in exactly the same way to Internet mail as she does to AOL email. The only difference is that the address in the From field is so much longer for Internet mail. Otherwise, you treat it just as you would a piece of AOL email: reply, delete, ignore, forward, or whatever.

Just a couple of points to remember. Email sent between AOL users arrives almost instantaneously. Email sent to an external Internet address can sometimes take a bit longer. On very rare occasions, delays of up to eight hours have been reported. Also, unlike AOL email, Internet email can't be unsent. So take care what you write.

As you've seen, many Internet addresses can be impossibly long and therefore easy to get wrong. So what happens if you do make an error? Something called a Mailer-Daemon (a Unix program that lurks in the background on computer networks) sends you a message with "Returned Mail: User Unknown" in the subject line. Included in the mail is a copy of your undeliverable email. When your email message has been returned,

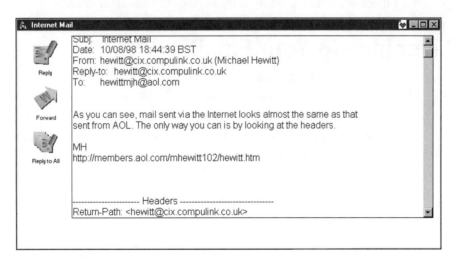

Figure 2.13
Internet mail received via AOL looks just like normal AOL mail, except for the return address.

it has been *bounced*. The delay between sending and bouncing can be as short as a few seconds, or it can take a couple of days. There's no telling.

Of course, there are no such problems with AOL email. If the recipient doesn't exist or you get his name wrong, the mail simply won't go. Instead, you'll get a rather curt error message from AOL saying, "This is not a known AOL user."

AOL NetMail™

This section is just a plug for a forthcoming AOL attraction, NetMail, which will no doubt have come by the time this book appears.

Let's suppose you're visiting with some unwise individual who's on the Internet but doesn't have an AOL account. Or suppose you suddenly find yourself in a cybercafé without AOL software on its computers. Amazingly, these things happen. In days of yore, if you were in one of those situations and wanted to check your AOL email, you would be pretty much stuffed. Today, however, thanks to AOL NetMail, you can use whichever browser you have to hand to check it over the Internet. You can send and receive messages, attach files, and all the usual.

I'll cover AOL NetMail in more detail in the next chapter.

Livening Up Your Email

I mean livening up your email visually, of course. (How boring you make the content is your own business.) In the Write Email screen, between the Subject field and the text body area, you'll see a set of small buttons. If you use a Windows word processor, you'll probably find that it features similar icons. They allow you to do such things as increase the size of your text, change the background or foreground colour, use text attributes such as bold and italics, and justify text.

Why would you want to? Because conventional text-only email has all the grace and lightness of a tax demand. But by tarting it up slightly, you can imbue it with a bit of personality. Don't go overboard, though. If you mix too many font sizes together, it will look like a ransom note. Also, lay off the more garish background colours. Your recipient might be suffering from a hangover.

Figure 2.14 shows the sorts of things you can do. In addition, you can add hypertext links to your email so your recipients can just click on a link and be instantly transported to a specific AOL or Internet site. Or to a site from your Favourite Places list. But that's all to come in Chapter 6.

TIP *Note Well*

Only your fellow AOL members can view these email "special effects." If you send an email with text enhancements to someone on the Internet, they'll just see a mixture of plain text and control tags. Best, therefore, to only send plain text in the first place.

TIP *Note Well, As Well*

You can also send computer files and pictures via email. It's very simple. I'll tell you how to do so in Chapter 5 if you haven't already worked it out for yourself by then.

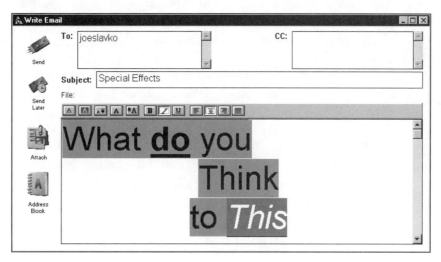

Figure 2.14
Email doesn't have to be boring. AOL allows you to change the typeface, the size, and the colour.

Mail Controls™

I was going to talk about the Address Book at this point. However, I've just received two items of junk mail, and my blood pressure is rather high as a result. If you'll forgive me, I'll lay into the problem right now.

Junk email, the plague of the Internet, is also known as *spam*, from the Monty Python sketch. Basically, junk email consists of the usual collection of improbable "chance of a lifetime" and "amazing bargain" offers. They're from companies and private individuals—most of them based in the United States—who take advantage of the fact that it costs virtually nothing to email hundreds or even thousands of different people simultaneously over the Internet. So even if 999 people out of 1,000 aren't interested in their offer, the one person who is, and who buys what they're flogging, makes it all worthwhile.

How do they know where to find you in the first place? The answer is that they can find you automatically. There are programs around that surreptitiously monitor everyone who visits a particular Web site or participates in certain chat areas. They can therefore get a rough idea of what your interests might be and whether or not you're likely to be amenable to their offers. These programs then compile lists of likely email addresses, and the junk bombardment commences.

So if, Heaven forbid, you happened to be a regular in some of the less salubrious "girly" sites, you could find yourself regularly inundated with "Live SeXXXX" and "Pin-up of the month" ads. So I'm told, anyway.

All online systems are susceptible to this sort of thing, AOL perhaps more than most because it's the biggest. However, unlike many of the other online services, which generally maintain a *laissez-faire* attitude toward it, AOL actively takes countermeasures against junk email. They compile lists of the worst junk email offenders and make sure that their emails are automatically filtered out before they reach you. Also, they've taken several spammers to court in the States and have convinced them to desist under threat of imprisonment.

Unfortunately, despite AOL's best efforts, some junk email will inevitably reach you. So it's at this stage that *you* can do something about it yourself. Enter AOL's Mail Control commands.

For security reasons, blocking and unblocking of email can only be carried out by the Master Account screen name. That's the permanent screen name you created when you first signed on to AOL. In my case, it's HewittMJH.

To block email, follow these steps:

1. Select AOL Post Room from the Email menu; this brings up (surprise) the Post Room. Click on Mail Controls.

2. You're then presented with a screen that gives the prompt "Please select a screen name whose Mail Controls you wish to modify" (Figure 2.15). The screen lists all the screen names in your AOL account, assuming you have more than one. You can modify all of them if you wish. For example, you might not want your youngest son or daughter to receive binary files, such as pictures or programs, attached to emails. (For more on this, refer to "Parental Control" in Chapter 10.)

3. Select a screen name and click on Edit. This takes you into Mail Controls (Figure 2.16). As you can see, by default, Allow All Mail is checked, meaning *all* mail is allowed. But if you don't like this state of affairs, you can do the following:

   ▲ *Allow mail from AOL members and addresses listed.* In other words, the member receives mail from any AOL member plus approved Internet email. To set up the approved addresses, type them into

Figure 2.15
The Master Account holder can selectively block email to and from certain addresses for all names in the account. This is useful for filtering undesirables.

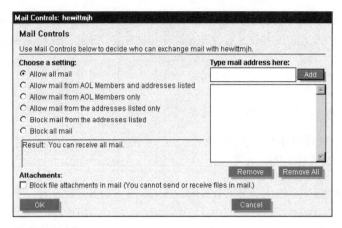

Figure 2.16
Mail Controls can be used to block email messages from (or to) people you don't approve of.

the Type Mail Address Here box and click on Add. The name(s) will then appear in the list.

▲ *Allow mail from AOL members only.* This option is self-explanatory. The member will only be able to receive email from fellow AOL members, not from anyone outside the system.

▲ *Allow mail from the addresses listed only.* If you only want the member to receive email from the addresses you approve—AOL addresses or Internet addresses—type them into the box and click on Add.

▲ *Block mail from the addresses listed.* Perhaps there are a couple of email addresses you're not comfortable with, whereas all the others are OK. In this case, proscribe those that offend thee in the box. This done, the member can receive all email messages *except* those from the addresses you've specified.

▲ *Block all mail.* This option is the Ultimate Weapon. The member can receive no email at all. Note: The member will not be able to *send* any mail, either.

▲ *Block file attachments in mail.* With this option checked, the member will neither be able to send nor receive binary files, such as programs and pictures, with email. I'll talk more about sending and receiving files with email in Chapter 5.

4. When you've finished updating the Mail Controls for each screen name, click on OK to save your modified settings.

What happens if you try to email a person who's blocked you? When you click on the Send button in the Write Email screen, the message "This AOL member is currently not accepting email from your account" appears, letting you know *exactly* where you stand.

The Address Book

Now, let's get back on track after that little interlude.

You can, if you like, manually type the recipient's name in the To field each time you send email. However, it's not only time-consuming, but there's always the possibility that you might misspell the address. This is where AOL's Address Book comes in. You can spend all night getting an Internet address letter-perfect and then store it in the Address Book. You never have to write it out again because it's transferred to the email To field with a click of the mouse button. And, of course, AOL email addresses are stored here as well. Let's set one up:

1. Select Edit Address Book from the Email menu. The Address Book appears (Figure 2.17) with the names listed in the order in which they were originally entered. Click on a name to see additional information.

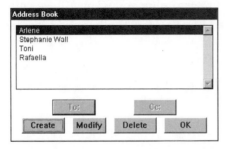

Figure 2.17
Save time by adding all your friends' names to AOL's Address Book.

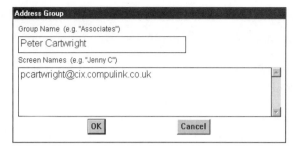

Figure 2.18
The Address Group window.

2. To enter a new name, select Create. The Address Group window appears (Figure 2.18). Enter the person's actual name into the top box and his or her AOL screen name or Internet address in the bottom box. (In this case, I've added the address for a friend who's on CiX.) Click on OK or press Enter. The new name is then added to the bottom of the list.

3. Now you can use the Address Book whenever you compose email. Just click on the Address Book icon in the Write Email screen and the Address Book pops up. When it does, highlight a name and click on To or CC. That person's AOL or Internet email address will be transferred to the corresponding field in the Write Email screen.

Navigation: The Toolbar

The Toolbar consists of 16 icons for the things on AOL that you're most likely to want to access quickly (Figure 2.19). Of course, you could use the menus within AOL. But I'm assuming you want to save yourself time. If so, you should get used to using the Toolbar and memorising what each icon does.

Figure 2.19
The Toolbar allows you to navigate your way around AOL with just a click of your mouse.

The following list explains the icons on the Toolbar from left to right:

▲ *The envelope icon*—We've already encountered the You've Got Post/ No Post icon (when I talked about email). Clicking on it takes you directly to unread mail.

▲ *The pencil icon*—The Compose Email button. When you click on it, it brings up the Write Email screen.

▲ *The Channels icon*—Like a series of Smarties seen in profile. Clicking on this icon takes you to the Main Menu screen, which you see on start-up. The useful thing about this icon is that even if you've closed down the Main Menu, or it's hidden amongst a desktop full of other windows, you can always find it just by going back to the Toolbar and clicking on the icon.

▲ *The star icon*—Takes you to a page featuring AOL's newest features and services. AOL adds them all the time, so it's a good idea to check out this page regularly.

▲ *The chat icon*—Takes you to the main Chat Channel screen.

▲ *The floppy disks icon*—The collection of floppy disks is the Software Search icon. Do you want some free software? Then click on this. Among the programs you can download gratis (although, in the case of shareware, you'll be expected to pay once you've evaluated it) are Paint Shop Pro, WinZip, and a whole host of sound and graphic files.

▲ *The newspaper icon*—Takes you directly into the News area. Check out current headlines and online newspapers, amongst other things.

▲ *The W icon*—Takes you to the World Wide Web. From there, you can go to a URL (I'll explain URLs in the next chapter), a search engine, and much, much more.

▲ *The My AOL icon*—Allows you to personalise AOL to your particular tastes. For example, you can create an online profile and new screen names, change your password, or set up Parental Controls.

▲ *The clock icon*—Tells you the current time and how long you've been online this session.

▲ *The printer icon*—Prints out any text or graphic that is currently in an active window. Use it for getting a hard copy of email or online articles.

▲ *The drawer icon*—Takes you to your Personal Filing Cabinet, which I'll talk about in further detail in Chapter 5. This is where your email is stored, together with downloaded files and postings from news-groups and message boards.

▲ *The heart icon*—Brings up your Favourite Places list. You'll use this more and more as you get more experienced with AOL. It's similar to the *bookmarks* found in Microsoft Internet Explorer and other Web browsers. In most online areas, including Web sites, you'll find a little red heart icon in the upper right corner of the window. As you'll see, you can drag this heart around and put it into email, Instant Messages, and even your Windows 95 desktop. Or, just click on it and the associated page or section will be placed in your Favourite Places list. To revisit, all you need do is click on the Toolbar heart and select where you want to go from the list; you're taken right there instantly.

▲ *The question mark icon*—Takes you to the Member Services area. This is where to go if you want technical help, have questions about your account, want to reread the COS (must be a slow news day), and so forth.

▲ *The magnifying glass icon*—Takes you to Find, AOL's internal search engine. If you have a particular interest and you want to see if there's a section on AOL that covers it, enter a search term and AOL will go off to see if it's there. Find not only searches AOL itself, but also the Internet.

▲ *The K icon*—Using Keywords is one of the best ways to navigate around AOL because most areas have a Keyword associated with them.

Navigation: Keywords

You've seen how to get to certain areas by clicking on icons and menu buttons. But there is a quicker, far easier way: Keywords. A Keyword is like an index tab, allowing you to bypass menus and subscreens and go straight to an area. You'll find that most areas of AOL have their Keyword appended somewhere on the screen. There's no international standardisation, though. In American areas, for example, you'll tend to find the Keyword somewhere on the main screen, whereas the U.K. areas tend to display it on the window's title bar (the bar at the top of the window).

Once you know the Keyword, you can use it as a shortcut. Either click on the Toolbar's K symbol (or press Ctrl+K) and then enter the Keyword. How do you know what the Keyword is for any particular area? For that matter, how can you find out what sort of forums and message areas are available to you on AOL?

Easy. Just turn to the back of this book and you'll find a list of them. You should note, however, that the list is only current as of August 1998. Regularly updated Keyword lists are available on AOL at Keyword: **KEYWORD**.

Here are 20 of the most commonly used Keywords:

▲ *AAA*—All About AOL. Pretty self-explanatory, really.

▲ *ABOUT EMAIL*—Everything you wanted to know about email.

▲ *BILLING*—Online billing summary and account management.

▲ *DOWNLOAD101*—Everything you need to know about downloading files.

▲ *FLASHSESSION*—The setup screen for FlashSessions.

▲ *HELP*—Go directly to the AOL Member Services area.

▲ *KEYWORD*—For lists of AOL Keywords.

▲ *MEMBER DIRECTORY*—To find other AOL members with similar interests.

▲ *MY ADDRESS*—Check your email address.

▲ *MY PAGE*—To build your own home page on the Web.

▲ *NAMES*—To create and delete screen names on your account.

▲ *NEW HELP*—The most current online help files.

▲ *NEWSGROUPS*—To read or subscribe to Internet newsgroups.

▲ *PARENTAL CONTROLS*—To restrict access to certain areas of AOL.

▲ *PASSWORD*—To change your password.

▲ *PRICING*—To change your AOL pricing plan.

▲ *PROFILE*—To create or edit your online profile.

▲ *QUESTIONS*—The most frequently asked questions about AOL.

▲ *TOUR*—A self-paced tour through AOL's most popular areas.

▲ *TROUBLE*—To page an online Guide or report online hassle or abuse.

Navigation: Find

If you don't know in which Channel a particular area or topic of interest is located, use the Find tool. Click on either the Toolbar's magnifying glass icon or the Find triangle on the Main Menu. When you do so, the Find screen appears (Figure 2.20). Let's say, for example, that I'm

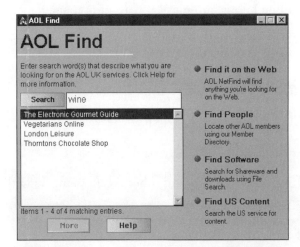

Figure 2.20
Looking for something? Try AOL's Find feature. If it isn't on AOL proper, the system will suggest you extend your search to the Internet where you're bound to find it.

something of a wine buff and I want to know if there's anywhere on AOL where people share my interests. I enter the word "wine" and click on Search. In a couple of seconds, it tells me that wine is discussed in the Electronic Gourmet Guide. To access that, I simply click on the highlighted words and I'm in.

If, however, AOL can't locate any such reference, it will tell me so and suggest that I either be more specific or extend my search to America Online or the Internet. If I can't find it there, I won't find it anywhere, as you'll see when you study the Internet a little more.

A Taster: Chat And Message Boards

Before we leave this chapter, let's have a short look at a couple of the delights awaiting you: Chat and message boards. Having just discussed Keywords, let's use one—Keyword: **CHAT**.

Almost at once, you're delivered into the main Chat screen (Figure 2.21). You'll see that it comes in two flavours: U.S. Chat and U.K. Chat. In this instance, click on U.K. Chat.

If you've recently joined AOL, clicking on U.K. Chat will deposit you, by default, into the New Members Lobby, which is a good place to start

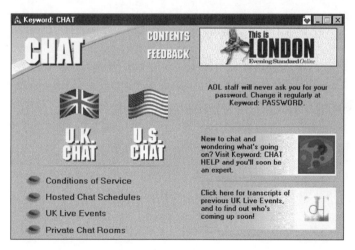

Figure 2.21
The main Chat screen with gateways to U.K. Chat and U.S. Chat.

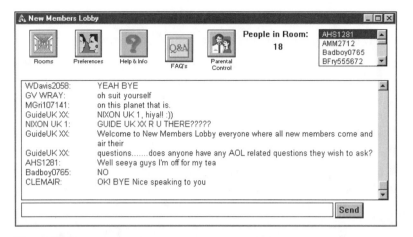

Figure 2.22
By default, AOL Chat first places you in the New Members Lobby, where you can meet fellow newcomers.

(Figure 2.22). If you're a veteran member, you can choose your destination from the U.K. Chat Areas menu. Upon entering the room, you'll see a heated debate in progress, or maybe a lukewarm one. It's now time to introduce yourself to the participants. To do so, just type what you want to say into the box at the bottom and click on Send. Instantly, your text appears along with the other comments. If anyone wants to respond to you, he or she will repeat the procedure by typing a reply into the same box and clicking on Send. Many online arguments, friendships, and relationships have been started in such a manner, as I'll explain in Chapter 8.

Another Chat-like function that's very useful is the Instant Message (IM). This is a private communiqué between you and someone else on AOL. No one else in the chat room can listen in. As I'll show in Chapter 8, you can use it either within a chat room or outside. You can even conduct more than one IM at once, if you dare.

But let's leave the debate in the New Members Lobby and go to Keyword: **DIADEM**. What's Diadem? I'm glad you asked. I'm not absolutely sure myself, but I know of a couple of thousand people who are. We'll meet a couple of them in Chapter 4.

What we're going to look at now is an AOL message board in action. What is a message board? It's a kind of electronic pinboard where you can exchange messages with other AOL members on any number of topics. In a message board devoted to cars, you would discuss cars; in one dealing with the news, you would talk about current events; and so forth. As you'll see, it's a bit like the Letters to the Editor section, except the "editor" and your fellow readers can answer back.

Here (Figure 2.23), we see the various topics in the Diadem message board: Any, Brainy, Funny, and Weird. This still doesn't tell me what Diadem is all about, though. So I'll ask in the Any topic. I click on Any and go to the list of earnest discussions (Figure 2.24). As I said, I want to find out what all this is about, so I'll click on the Create Subject button to do exactly that. And, lo and behold, a Post New Message window opens (Figure 2.25). Here, I pose my fundamental question and click on Send. Thereupon my new subject is added to all the rest.

So what's the reply going to be? What *is* Diadem? I'm afraid I'm going to leave you in suspense until we reach Chapter 4. It's time for the next chapter, where we'll be looking at the Internet, what's on it, how to browse it, how to search for things on it, and how to stop your children from doing the same.

Figure 2.23
Diadem's message boards, with the topics listed.

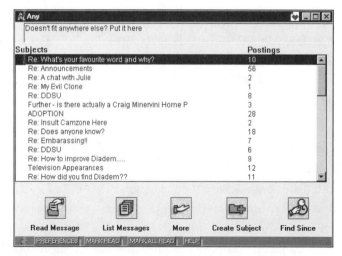

Figure 2.24
The list of current discussion in Diadem's Any topic.

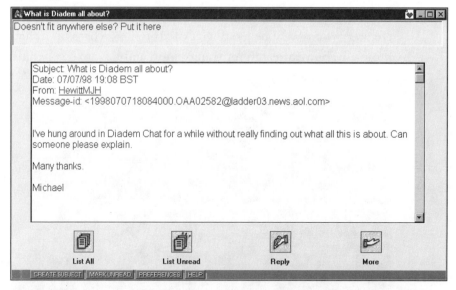

Figure 2.25
Posting a new message in Diadem. "What is Diadem all about?" I ask.

Chapter 3

The Internet

The Internet—also known to its friends as the Information Superhighway and the World Wide Web. In this chapter, I'll be dealing with what it is, how to use it, why you would want to use it in the first place, and how to search for things on it. Then there's a description of the new AOL NetMail™, which lets you access your AOL email via the Internet.

What Is The Internet?

Quite simply, the Internet consists of lots of computers all over the world joined together with millions of phone lines, optical fibres, and satellite links. If you were to look at a map of the world with the computers and connections drawn on it, you would see what looks like a rather messy spider's web pretty much covering the entire earth. Even the Antarctic has Internet addresses. So it's a kind of web that is as wide as the world, hence the term World Wide Web (WWW or just Web).

Anyway, the Internet is a big network of computers that can talk to each other by relaying messages around the filaments of the web. The network is designed so that if one filament snaps, the computers will try to redirect the message along a different route.

What Is The World Wide Web?

The Web refers to all the documents that are accessible on the Internet. Actually, the Internet is much more than the Web alone. There are, as you'll see, FTP sites, newsgroups, Telnet sites, and so forth. However, most people now use Web as a synonym for the Internet. Therefore, so will I.

This makes the Internet highly resilient. In fact, it grew up in the 1960s during the Cold War when the U.S. military realised that one or two big bombs could take out all their computer communications. Before the Internet, the computers were just linked end to end, like links in a chain. If you knocked out one link, the whole chain would break. But a web that allowed rerouting was much less susceptible to total failure. The military's network was called ARPANET.

So, what good is a nuke-proof network? Well, for one thing, it's immune to just about *any* kind of failure. Machines can break down, phone lines can be cut, servers can be stopped to take backups—but the broad integrity of the web goes on. So, beating their swords into ploughshares, the U.S. National Science Foundation built NSFNET and added it on to ARPANET.

Lots of additions later, we've got a storming mechanism for cheap data delivery around the world, accessed by millions of people. How many? Depends on who you believe. It's rather difficult to work out. Some people say 60 million; some people say more. Who are these millions of people? Scientists, librarians, students, CEOs, homemakers, MPs, academics, and computer nerds, amongst others—and, of course, you.

So given that it's so big and has so many active participants, what's actually on the Web?

Virtually everything these days. The sheer amount of material is over-whelming; 10 Downing Street is on there, and so is the Vatican, the Louvre, the British Library, NASA, the BBC, *Teletubbies* and *The Simpsons*, the *Financial Times*, the *Newcastle Echo*—you name it. You can download complete books, pictures, sound files, pin-ups, and even the Bible. You can track share prices, see realtime video of the latest natural disaster, or find your family tree.

"OK," you're saying to yourself, "If the Internet is so marvellous and there's a lifetime's repository of data and knowledge spread about its many computers, what am I doing bothering with AOL?"

If it were simply a matter of clicking on Button B to go directly to (for example) the *Newcastle Echo,* then I agree, there wouldn't be much point in using AOL to access the Internet. Unfortunately, as you'll discover, things aren't that easy. The Internet is so vast and spread out that you can liken it to a large ocean, littered with worthless flotsam and jetsam.

Amongst all the dross, but not all that easy to spot, is the occasional floating treasure chest.

Now, in searching for that chest, would you rather jump in headfirst, or would you prefer to make the journey in the QE2?

AOL effectively provides you with a five-star cruise through the Internet. But instead of onboard lecturers, there are lots of very clever computer programmers who've put up signposts to guide the novice traveller. Let's be guided by them.

Or you can jump in headfirst if you like. It's up to you.

So How Do I Get To The Internet?

If you've been heading out into AOL on your own, likely as not you've already been on the Internet and not really noticed. It can easily happen because AOL has been designed to seamlessly transport you there. How? Let's have a look at Figure 3.1.

You've probably observed that each time you sign on and the Welcome screen appears, one of the items—the bottom one, usually—is Main News. Clicking on this item takes you through to AOL's News & Weather Channel (or you can go to Keyword: **NEWS** if you prefer).

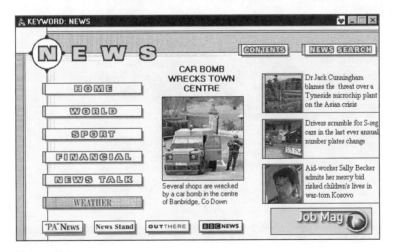

Figure 3.1
AOL's News & Weather Channel, with links both to AOL News areas and to news areas on the Internet.

The News Channel has lots of buttons on it: Home, World, Sport, and so on. These correspond, naturally, to the sort of news contained in each section, all courtesy of AOL. Notice along the bottom that you have a few more buttons. PA News you've no doubt heard of. The News Stand button will take you to a page with links to a myriad of Internet news sources. Next to that you'll find Out There news, which (in its own words) is news reportage "put together by a rabid worldwide network of fundamentalist hacks." The name on the fourth button—BBC News—you should certainly all be familiar with. Let's click on it and see what happens.

What does happen is that, eventually, the screen shown in Figure 3.2 appears: the front page of the BBC News. This isn't anything to do with AOL, however. This is the BBC News home page on the Internet. Easy or what?

Actually, en route you may have noticed a few dead giveaways that this *is* now the Internet proper and not AOL.

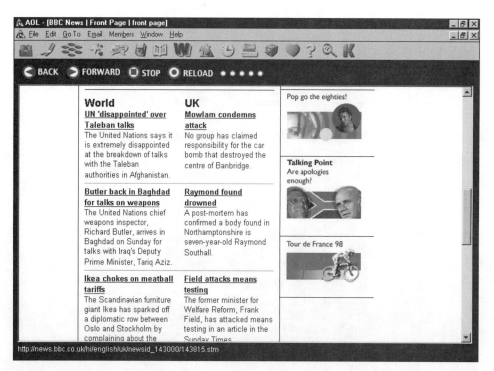

Figure 3.2
AOL can transport you directly to the BBC News Web site from its own News Channel.

The fact is, you've been pretty much cosseted on AOL. Whenever you click on an icon—Chat, for example—a couple of seconds later you'll be delivered safely into the corresponding area—in this case, the Chat area. Likewise with every other area on AOL: point, click, and you're there, if not instantaneously, then pretty quickly all the same. This is not always so with gateways to the Internet, unfortunately.

Occasionally, the Internet can be very, *very* slow. Look upon it as being like a close cousin of the M25. Round about midday, you can manage a good 70 mph in the outside lane. However, between 6.00 A.M. and 9.00 A.M., you'll be lucky to reach 20. That's if you move at all. The sheer weight of traffic at peak times of day can bring it to a near standstill.

Because there are so many Internet users trying to access so much information, the system can slow to a crawl at certain times of the day. This is particularly true during the afternoon in the U.K., when over the Atlantic all the millions of American Internet users wake up and sign on. So be prepared to wait, or simply avoid those times of day. And it can be particularly true for some of the more popular sites, regardless of the hour.

So how does this slowness manifest itself?

Let's return to the BBC News home page. The first thing you'll see when you click on the BBC News button is nothing but a new, blank window opening up. Soon you'll see that it's a *browser* window with Back, Forward, Stop, and Reload buttons along the top. At the same time, there'll be a message at the bottom saying, "Wait while site is contacted," or something similar. And to prove to you that it *is* working at it rather than just malingering or freezing you out, a row of dots on the upper right corner of the screen will flash on and off, like the LEDs on an external modem. Or, on some other screens, you'll see an AOL symbol spinning at speed.

Depending on the time of day and the speed of your modem, you could be sitting like this, navel-gazing, for several seconds or even several minutes.

When things eventually start moving, the message at the bottom of the screen changes to read, "Transferring document." Then the whole page starts to appear—in sections. Usually, the text appears first, and then the pictures, one after another. Many Internet screens display a progress bar along the bottom to give a visual and percentage indication of how much longer you'll have to wait. When, and only when, *all* the data has been downloaded, the progress bar will disappear and the dots will stop flashing.

As I said, it could be a long process. If you tire of it at any point, click on the Stop button at the upper left corner of your screen. This aborts the transfer. But that's a worst-case scenario. When I did the screenshot for the BBC News home page, it was all over and done with in about 30 seconds, which, I reckon, is about average.

Navigating A Web Page

Navigating a Web page is just like navigating AOL, really. For example, try moving your mouse about the screen. As the cursor moves over the buttons and highlighted areas, it changes from a pointer into the shape of a hand. This means that the underlying piece of text is a *hyperlink*.

Great...what's a hyperlink? Some people—those who write for computer magazines, mostly, and wouldn't know plain English if it bit them on the backside—would refer to hyperlinks as a hierarchical menuing system. Really, a hyperlink is much the same as the buttons and icons you've already encountered in AOL. For instance, click on Main News on AOL's Welcome screen and you're taken to a secondary menu—the News Channel—with buttons for the various other sections, like Home News. Keep clicking and you're taken further and further down.

Hyperlinks on a Web page work in exactly the same way. In the screen shown in Figure 3.2, the cursor becomes a hand if I move it over the various headlines. Scrolling down, I find the rather interesting headline, "Ikea Chokes on Meatball Tariffs." I can click on either the headline or the accompanying picture and reach the story about how the Swedish furniture company, Ikea, is, understandably, getting upset because of excise duty being imposed on their meatballs (Figure 3.3). Alongside that story, there are links to other pages that are related to it: the general situation in Scandinavia, for instance, or the Ikea home page itself. Clicking on those links takes me one level down to more stories and more links.

In fact, there's a whole lot more besides news stories that can be accessed from the BBC News front page. There's news comment, horoscopes,

Figure 3.3
Web pages are layered one under the other. Clicking on the headline for one takes you to the story beneath. And you can carry on clicking.

BBC weather, live video, live audio—you name it. Indeed, there's so much that I could write a whole chapter about just one Internet page and how it acts as a staging point for reaching all the rest of the Internet. But I don't have the space. Instead, click on the links and try it for yourself. This game is commonly known as *Net surfing*, by the way. Not only is it quite fun, it can also yield some highly rewarding gems, and you don't even have to get wet.

This is how *all* Web pages work, regardless of the software you're using to access them. It's just point, click, and wait. To get back to where you were immediately before, click on the Back button at the top of the screen. If you're bored with waiting for the screen to assemble itself, click on Stop and then on the Back button. Or Stop and then Reload sometimes does the trick. Alternatively, just wander AOL while your chosen Web page loads.

That's right. You don't have to just sit there, doing nothing. AOL allows you to get on with something else while functions such as file downloading and Web page assembly are going on in the bacground. So, while you're waiting, you could, for instance, be composing an email message, sending it, reading a news story, participating in Chat—anything.

The Internet Channel

Most sections of AOL have Internet links that are topic-specific. By this I mean that AOL's producers have done all the legwork on your behalf and sought out relevant sites on the Web, and then provided links to them from the corresponding AOL areas. So if you go into a section that's about, say, investment, all the Internet links there will be related to finance and money. You won't accidentally find yourself dumped into a motor racing page. Not only that, but those linked Internet sites will be those that, in the opinion of AOL and its members, are the very best that are available on the subject. They've separated the wheat from the chaff in advance.

Just to give one example of this elementary milling exercise, let us take a peek at Good Taste, AOL's gourmet area, which you can find at Key-word: **GOOD TASTE** (Figure 3.4). Here, clicking on the button Let's Cook brings up a resources page. Clicking on Weblinks at the bottom of

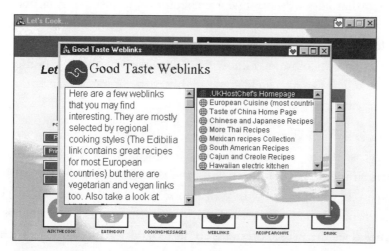

Figure 3.4
The food- and cookery-related links from AOL's gourmet area, Good Taste.

the resources page brings up a list of relevant Web sites. You can tell they're Web sites because they've got a globe symbol next to them. In other areas of AOL, the Web sites have a "W" symbol. This varies from page to page.

All well and good, but you don't want to have to hop around all over AOL to find all those linked sites, do you? Fortunately, you don't have to; AOL has gathered them all together in one place. That place is AOL's Internet Channel, which you can reach from the Main Menu or by going to Keyword: **INTERNET**. And when you do, the Internet Channel makes its debut (Figure 3.5).

The Internet Channel makes life easier by listing in one place some of the best Web sites around—nominated both by AOL members themselves and by AOL's own producers. And you won't have to remember URLs, either. The area includes links to companies, events, topical issues, Internet organisations, useful Internet software, top newsgroups, and other such gems. The Internet Channel also includes the Talking Point feature (a topical survey and discussion on a featured Internet issue) and plenty of help for getting the most out of the Internet.

Let's have a look at one example: "This Week's Hot Sites" (Figure 3.6). Here, as the name suggests, we have what's hot this week, displayed in the window in the middle. Down the left side, there are links to groups

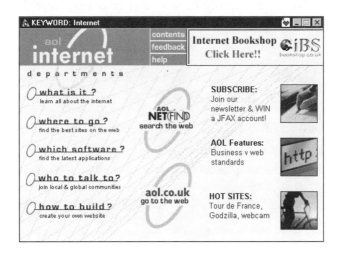

Figure 3.5
AOL's Internet Channel brings the best of the Internet together in one place.

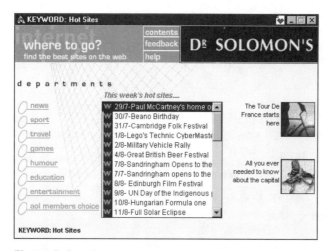

Figure 3.6
The hottest sites on the Web this week, gathered together by AOL.

of sites that, although they may have cooled down just a little in the interim, were themselves hot some weeks ago: news, humour, education, and so on. Let's have a look at humour. Up comes a list of all the best humour sites on the Internet. Among them are links to Father Ted's home page on Channel 4 (Figure 3.7).

You, of course, may feel that these sites aren't relevant to your needs. No matter—to each his own. Nevertheless, they act as good starting points for seeking out your own favourite sites. The Father Ted site, for instance, will link you to lots of other Father Ted sites, and beyond. So good hunting.

Internet Explorer

This is a good point at which to talk about AOL's browser.

In order to move out of AOL and on to the Internet, you need a separate program called a *Web browser*. When you access any site on the Web, the browser tells the target computer, "Excuse me. Chummy here wants to visit your site. Please send its data, including pictures, text, and whatever else you have, across to me here, and I'll assemble it onscreen in living colour. And snap to it, we haven't got all day."

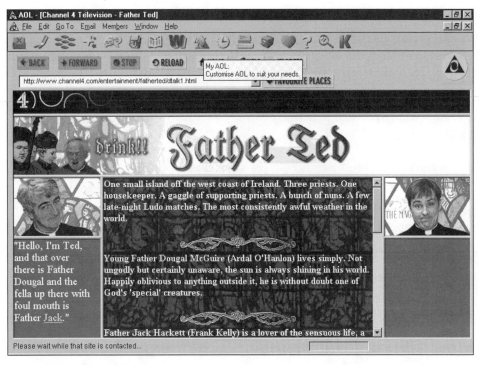

Figure 3.7
All you ever wanted to know about Father Ted Crilly, and more besides.

Not that you'll really notice that this is going on. It's all happening in the background. AOL software comes with the browser included. Handy, eh?

A browser can do other things, too, such as play audio and video clips. But sometimes in order to do so, you'll need to download peripheral programs called *plug-ins*. Adding a plug-in is equivalent to extending the functionality of your PC by installing a sound card or adding a scanner.

So where do you find these plug-ins and how do you download them? When you first visit a page that has audio or video capability, you'll be automatically prompted to download the requisite player. Depending on the speed of your modem and the state of network traffic, this download should take just a few minutes. Thereafter, the player is stored on your hard disk forever (or at least until you need to upgrade to a newer version, at which time you'll also be prompted automatically) and will automatically fire up and play audio every time you click on an audio application.

Probably the world's best-known Web browser is Microsoft's Internet Explorer. Would that the mere printed page could convey the whole range of special effects available with Internet Explorer, such as animation, moving headlines, interactive text boxes, realtime radio, live video relays, and so forth. Sounds exciting, doesn't it? I'll bet you're asking right now where you can pick up your very own copy of Internet Explorer.

Actually, you've already got it. It is now AOL's default Web browser, replacing the old belt-and-braces affair used in days of yore. Those of you who've had experience with the old browser and have just upgraded should notice an appreciable difference in speed and functionality. Faster and better, I mean. So where will you be able to find sites that best demonstrate all these new marvels?

You could do a lot worse than try **http://www.hot100.com**. As you can see from Figure 3.8, this is what's reckoned by some to be a repository of all things good on the Internet. Others may disagree. However, it can't be

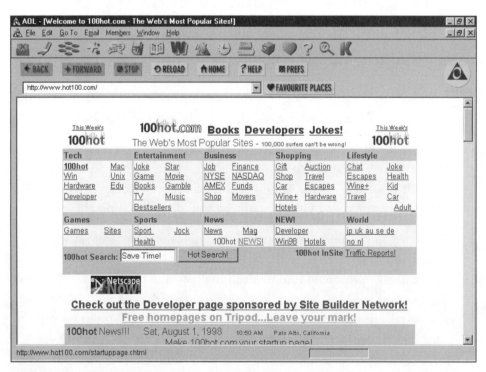

Figure 3.8
Some of the hottest sites on the Internet are gathered together in one place.

denied that here, at least, you'll find some of the snazziest sites in terms of video and audio content. For instance, on the home page of the British Aerospace Band (Figure 3.9), you can click on the Play button and listen in to such classics as the "RAF March Past," "Ruby Tuesday," and the theme from *The Dambusters*. OK, so you may not like marching bands, but this site at least demonstrates how RealAudio works.

Internet Explorer Preferences

Naturally enough, playing video and sound can add to the time it takes for individual Web pages to assemble themselves on your monitor. For those who haven't the patience to wait, you can disable all, or some, of these features by clicking on Internet Explorer's Preferences (Prefs) button (Figure 3.10). For example, you can tell the browser to display text only. It will look boring, mind you, but if text is all you need, you'll get it very quickly indeed.

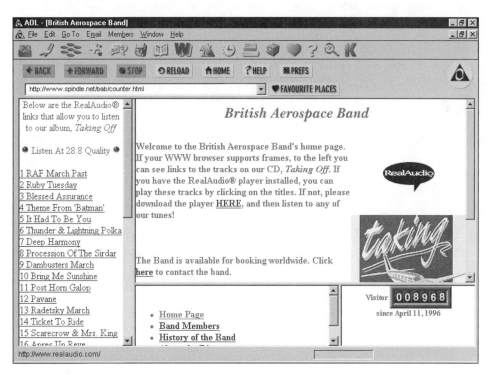

Figure 3.9
Listen to the British Aerospace Band, and many others, over the Internet.

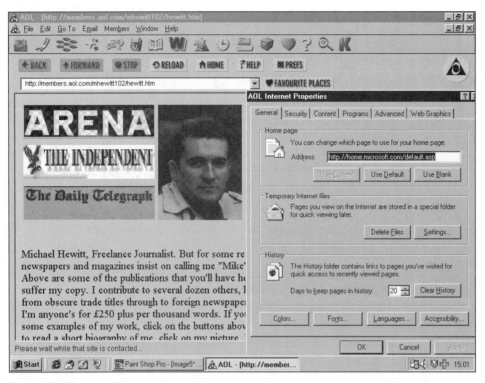

Figure 3.10
Click on the browser's Prefs button and you can customise many of its features.

You can also totally customise the way the browser looks and behaves by clicking on the Prefs button. And there are security features, too, allowing parents to prevent their children from accessing some of the more undesirable Internet sites. For more on Parental Controls, turn to Chapter 10.

 *Note Well*

Currently, there's a bit of a spat going on between Microsoft and the manufacturer of a rival browser, Netscape. AOL doesn't take any sides or try to claim that one browser is better than any other. If you don't like Internet Explorer, you don't have to use it. Instead, sign on to AOL, go to your Windows Start menu, and fire up the browser you *do* like.

AOL's Home Page

What with all this talk about Internet sites being good starting points for finding other good Internet sites, I ought to introduce you to AOL's own home page. You can get to it from the Internet Channel, of course. But remember in Chapter 2 when I preached the gospel of Keywords as a way to navigate around AOL? Just as you can flit about AOL with Keywords, you can use them for reaching Internet sites. In this case, the Internet site we want to visit has the address **http://www.aol.co.uk** (Figure 3.11).

What on earth is **http://www.aol.co.uk** you're asking? This piece of gobbledegook is the address line for the browser. It's called a URL—a Uniform Resource Locator. Basically, it's the site's address. It's the Web equivalent of saying: The Secretary's Department, 23, Acacia Avenue, Surbiton.

Anyhow, AOL's home page (Figure 3.12) has a number of different functions. First and foremost, like most corporate home pages, it helps to sell AOL itself. If you're not sure what the service is or does, here's where to find out. Should your appetite be whetted, you can download AOL's software from here. But if you know of someone who intends to try, warn him or her that it's a rather long download and that it would perhaps be better to send off for the free CD-ROM (or look for one of those computing magazines with AOL on their CD cover-mount).

AOL's home page is also a place to download add-ons such as those for AOL NetMail and AOL Instant Messenger, both of which I'll discuss presently. And, as you can see from the screenshot, AOL's Internet search engine, AOL NetFind, is here, too—more on that in a couple of paragraphs.

Just as on AOL proper, the various Internet sites are grouped together under separate subject buttons. So, for example, clicking on the hyperlink

Figure 3.11
You can use Keywords to get to any Internet site in the same way you can use them to get to areas of AOL.

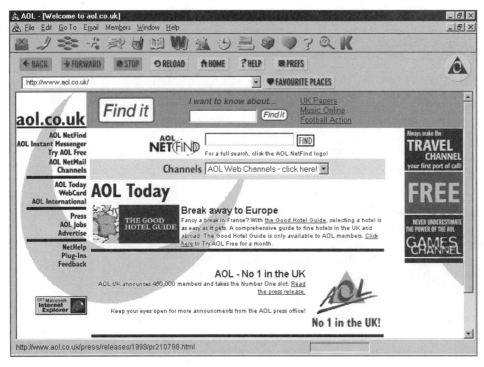

Figure 3.12
AOL U.K.'s home page is a useful repository of plug-ins as well as a good starting point to explore the rest of the Internet.

for News brings up a page with news and related sources, one of which is the ever-popular *Daily Mirror* (Figure 3.13).

Take a while to explore this page and its various links. I think you'll be quite impressed.

Finding It On The Internet: AOL NetFind™

We've established that AOL makes navigating the Internet a lot easier than rival systems do, thanks to its frequent use of the online equivalents of signs like "Turn left" and "Last trout farm before the motorway." It effectively plans your itinerary through the Internet in the way that a Suntours rep plans your package holiday. At Suntours, Day One is a trip to the old marketplace. On Day Two, they take you to the Roman ruins, with a stop-off at the local wine merchant where you can pick up a bottle or two at discounted prices. And so your holiday goes on, until the poolside barbecue at 8.00 P.M. However, after a while, seasoned travellers

Figure 3.13
The online edition of the *Daily Mirror* has the familiar look of its paper-based sibling.

feel they can do away with being chaperoned like this and decide to head out on their own. To do this, tourists will use a map. To explore the Internet, you'll probably want to use a search engine.

You already have some idea of how an AOL search engine works from the last chapter when I talked about the Find tool. There, I said that you could search for a particular subject within AOL by using a search term. So when I typed in "wine" and hit Enter, it brought up the Electronic Gourmet Guide. Internet search engines work in a similar way. They just tend to be somewhat slower because they have a lot more data to plough through.

AOL's very own Internet search engine is called AOL NetFind. You can get to it by going to Keyword: **NETFIND**, as well as from the Internet Channel or AOL's home page. There are a number of other Internet search engines you can access via the Internet: Yahoo!, AltaVista, Lycos, WebCrawler, and HotBot, to name but a few. Each has its own band of enthusiasts.

Is It Out There?

All search engines work in much the same way. The only real difference between them is in how much genuine information, or *hits*, they turn up. In my experience, NetFind turns up more than most. And it's somewhat easier to use than many.

Let's do a simple search, then. I've decided that I want some information about an old-style music hall that I once visited in London. The trouble is, I don't remember its name, nor do I remember where it was. The Yellow Pages is of no use to me because it doesn't have listing for music halls (and hasn't since about 1920). So I'm stuck with the Internet. Here's how it's done:

1. I go to Keyword: **NETFIND** (or **http://www.netfind.co.uk**) and up comes the NetFind search screen (Figure 3.14). In the search window, I enter my search terms: "music", "hall", and "London".

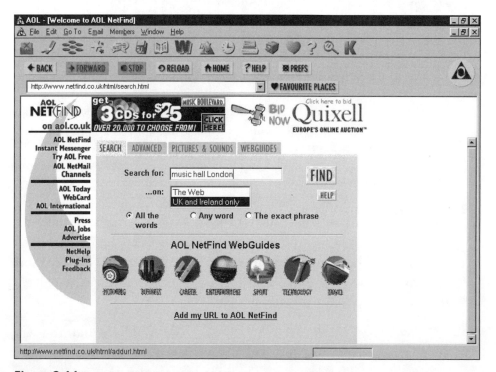

Figure 3.14
The NetFind search screen. Enter as many search terms as you can think of to increase your chances of a successful hit.

As a rule of thumb, the more search words you enter, the likelier your chance of a successful hit. For instance, if I had just used the word "London," NetFind would try to give me a list that includes every page on the Internet containing "London." Attempting to find music hall references amongst that lot would, I'm sure, be a major needle-in-a-haystack event. By the same token, however, if I entered "music" and "hall" but omitted "London," I could get references to every music hall in the world, including those in London.

2. In order to further restrict my search, I insist that my hits should include all the search terms. Hence All The Words is checked. Furthermore, I ask NetFind to search just those sites based in the United Kingdom and Ireland, not the entire World Wide Web.

3. I click on Find and sit back to hope for the best.

4. It looks as if I could be in luck here (Figure 3.15). NetFind has come up with 1,731 hits, ranked according to confidence. At the very top

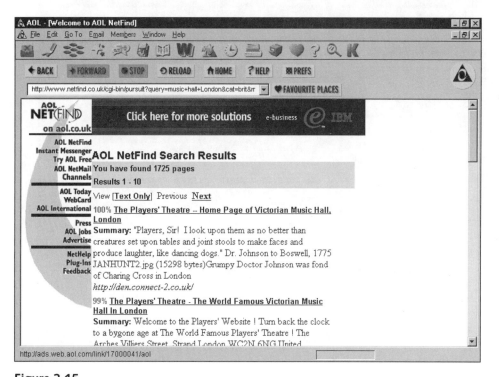

Figure 3.15
NetFind ranks the hits in order of confidence; in other words, exactly how likely it reckons the hits are the sites you're after.

of that list is "The Players' Theatre—Home Page of Victorian Music Hall, London." That sounds familiar. So I click on the header.

5. Success! This is indeed what I was after (Figure 3.16).

Of course, this was a very simple example. NetFind allows you to get a lot cleverer than that. You can, for instance, also use the so-called Boolean operators: AND, NOT, and OR. So here, the search term "fish AND finger" would bring up those documents that contained the words "fish" and "finger." The search term "fish AND finger NOT Findus", on the other hand, would produce all the documents containing "fish" and "finger" except for those that also contained the word "Findus."

As you can tell, it can get terribly complicated, and I don't propose boring you all with a long treatise on Boolean logic. Besides, the best way to learn how to search on the Internet isn't by reading a book—not even mine—but, curiously, by searching on the Internet. Enjoy.

Figure 3.16
The Players' Theatre, on The Strand, where the tradition of Victorian music hall is maintained.

AOL NetMail™

Before I leave this chapter and head out for pastures new(er), there's just one more Internet-related topic I'd like to discuss: AOL NetMail.

Newly available as a plug-in from the AOL home page, NetMail alleviates the understandable consternation felt by those who need to check their AOL email but, for whatever reason, temporarily find themselves at a computer without AOL software. Maybe they're abroad and can only get through from an Internet café. Or maybe they're staying with a friend who, inexplicably, has signed up with an Internet service provider other than AOL.

Whatever—now it doesn't matter. NetMail allows you to check your AOL email from any computer anywhere in the world that has Internet access. How so?

First, you've got to enable the computer's Web browser to use NetMail. To do this, go to **http://www.aol.co.uk**, click on the AOL NetMail button, and then follow the online instructions. Much as I would like to take you through this procedure step-by-step, at the time this book was being written, the product was still in beta (in other words, a sort of prototype, not an official release), so I can't. Suffice it to say, it's going to be very uncomplicated, like clicking on Download NetMail. So don't worry.

Let's assume you've done it and your browser is now NetMail enabled. Here's how it works (the following figures, by the way, are for the U.S. version of NetMail; it may look slightly different for the U.K. version, but not that much):

1. Click on the NetMail button on the AOL home page. This brings up the NetMail icon (Figure 3.17). Click away, as per usual.

2. The Sign On To NetMail screen appears (Figure 3.18), looking not unlike the AOL sign-on screen. Fill it in, using your AOL screen name and your password. Then click on Sign On.

3. If there's email waiting for you, a voice will pipe up "You've got Post!" It may be Joanna Lumley; it may be someone else. Nevertheless, regardless of who says it, if you've got email waiting for you in your AOL account, it will be displayed (Figure 3.19).

Figure 3.17
Click on the NetMail icon to access AOL NetMail.

Figure 3.18
Fill in your screen name and password exactly as you would on AOL.

4. Read your email. NetMail works in exactly the same way the email function in your AOL account proper works. If there's a file attached, you can download it to your host computer.

5. Reply to your email just as you normally do (Figure 3.20).

In fact, you can do most things from here that you normally do with AOL email: write, read, send attachments, forward, delete, and so on. The only

Figure 3.19
NetMail lists all new mail as well as email you've previously sent or received.

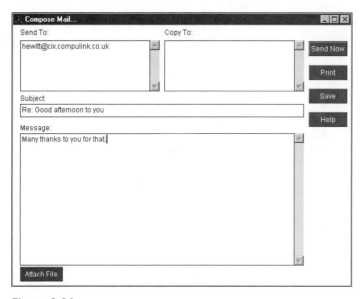

Figure 3.20
Reply to your email just as you normally do.

thing you should note is that if you *do* use NetMail to read or write email, the messages won't be stored to your Personal Filing Cabinet. They can't be because that only exists on your own PC. They will, however, still be listed under Email You've Sent and Email You've Read when you eventually sign on using your own computer. Nevertheless, I would recommend that if you do make a habit of reading your AOL mail via NetMail, you should click on Keep As New to save important messages. Then they'll all be waiting for you, "as new," when you next access AOL.

Please note that you can't use NetMail while you are signed on to AOL, even to check mail on an AOL account other than the one you've signed on with. NetMail is specifically designed for AOL members to check their AOL mail when they are using a computer that has Internet access but *not* the AOL software. If you do have access to an AOL account other than your own, you can sign on as Guest and check your email that way. Turn to Chapter 14 to find out how.

So much for accessing the Internet. In the next chapter, I'll talk about message boards and newsgroups.

Chapter 4

Message Boards
And Newsgroups

In this chapter, I'll be covering AOL's message boards, which are areas where AOL members can debate subjects of import with one another, inquire after information, or just sound off generally. Then it's on to newsgroups, the Internet equivalent of message boards. You'll find that just as the Internet is somewhat anarchic, so too is the kind of debate that goes on in its newsgroups.

Message Boards

What are message boards? They are a way of gathering information together, sharing your experiences with others, or just having a jolly good ruck with fellow AOL members.

They're called message boards because that's probably the closest real-world analogy. You remember them from your school days, no doubt. The teachers would post notices that they thought were important; for example, "There will be a fire drill at 11.00 A.M. tomorrow," or "Pupils and staff are ordered to assemble together to witness the caning of Tomkins Minor in the Main Hall at 3.00 P.M. Be punctual." Inevitably, people would append their own messages to these in pencil or crayon: "Why don't we have a *real* fire?" or "Tomkins Minor is innocent." And comments would be appended to those, too.

In a somewhat less anarchic and vastly more useful way, this is how AOL's message boards work. You post a message—a question or a comment on life—and someone responds to it; then someone responds to the response, and so on.

Where Are The Message Boards And How Do You Use Them?

Most AOL areas have their own resident message boards. So go to News, for instance, and you'll find message boards in which AOL members discuss the news and current events. Go to the Good Taste area and the message boards are full of people swapping recipes or debating the merits of various restaurants. Go to the Football area and they're all discussing—well, you know what they're all discussing.

So what's the practical use of a message board?

Let's assume you want to go to Florida on your holidays. You're on a budget, so you need to check out hotels and restaurants within your price range and decent places to visit that don't charge an arm and a leg for entrance. No problem. Locate a travel area or an area dealing with the U.S. or Florida, find its message boards, and ask in there. For instance, in the Florida or Walt Disney World message boards, you might post the question, "Can anyone recommend a good, inexpensive hotel within five minutes of the Magic Kingdom?"

Within a day of posting such a message, you'll probably find several helpful replies, either from people who've visited Florida themselves or from actual residents. This is one of the many virtues of AOL. It's such a large service, with so many members, that you're bound to come across people with similar interests or AOL members who are experts on particular subjects. In the majority of cases, they'll be more than willing to help you out. It's a very friendly place.

Posting A Message

Let's try posting that Florida message, shall we? I suggested posting it in the Florida or Walt Disney World message boards. How come I knew they existed in the first place, though? Because I looked for them. Herein:

1. I go to Keyword: **FLORIDA** and AOL presents me with a list of Florida-related areas (Figure 4.1). The obvious ones to go for are the Florida and Walt Disney World boards.

Figure 4.1
How do I find message boards related to Florida? Simple. I go to Keyword:
FLORIDA and up they come.

2. There are a number of message boards in here. One that is relevant is
   the board dealing with central Florida because, forest fires permitting,
   that's where Walt Disney World happens to be located. I double-
   click on the name of the board to list all its messages (Figure 4.2). Or
   else I can click on the List All Messages button.

3. I click on the Create Subject button to start off a new subject. Bear in
   mind that when you start a new subject, your subject line should be

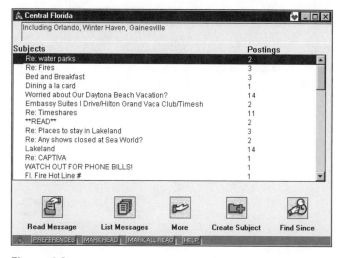

Figure 4.2
All the messages dealing with the central Florida area are maintained within a
separate Central Florida message board nested within the main board.

something that informs those browsing the message boards exactly what your post is about. "Help," for example, could attract a few good samaritans, but it isn't nearly as informative as "Inexpensive hotel within 5 minutes of Magic Kingdom?" (Figure 4.3). It says it all, really. Having written my message, I click on Send and off it goes.

 ## Text Enhancement In Message Boards

Please note that message boards have exactly the same text controls—colour, font size, and so on—as email messages. So use those controls if you don't like the idea of your thoughts just appearing as bland, unformatted letters and spaces—or ASCII characters as technical types would call them. But be careful: In addition to being a strain on the eye, overuse of mixed fonts and colours makes you look like a prat.

Reading And Replying To Messages

Chapter 2 ended with one of those Dick Barton-style cliff-hangers: I had just posted a message in the Diadem message board. But would there be an answer? If so, what? And from whom? Relax; all will now be revealed.

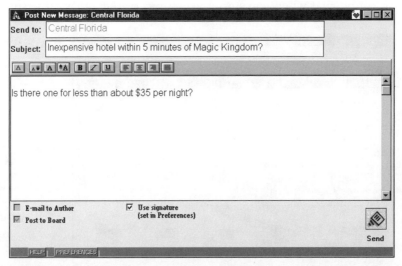

Figure 4.3
To help other AOL members and to ensure a swift response, always make sure your message header is as informative as possible.

I posted my message in the Any topic, if you recall. "What is Diadem all about?" I asked. A couple of days later, I return and find that, acornlike, my original message has now grown into 10 (Figure 4.4). In other words, I've either had nine responses to my original posting, or something that someone else has posted in reply to me has itself generated responses. Let's find out.

All you do to read the messages is double-click on the subject and then scroll through them by clicking on the Next Message button. Or, if that particular series of messages proves too boring or contentious for you, skip it altogether by clicking on the Next Subject button, which, as you might expect, takes you to the next subject. And, as you might expect, Previous Message and Previous Subject are the same, but in reverse.

Anyhow, message number 2 in response to mine is a rather lengthy one, and if set out here in full would probably add another 1,000 words or so to this chapter (Figure 4.5). Briefly, he says that Diadem is all about weirdness and a celebration of its diversity. At this point, online etiquette dictates that I should thank the author for taking the trouble to reply. This I do by clicking on the Reply button. When I do so, the reply screen appears and I make my thanks (Figure 4.6).

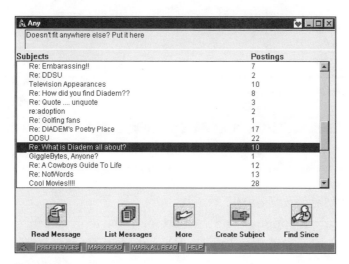

Figure 4.4
My message board posting, "What is Diadem all about?" has generated several replies.

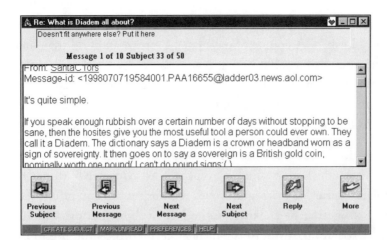

Figure 4.5
One of the responses to my original posting is rather long. No matter; it's the thought that counts.

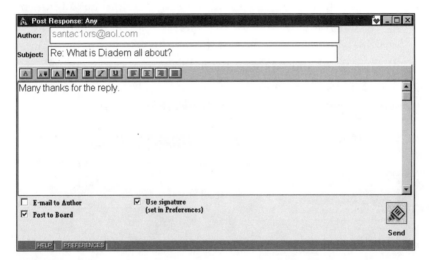

Figure 4.6
Replying to messages is as straightforward as posting them.

Mail Or Message Board?

Note the various options along the bottom of the reply screen, especially Email To Author and Post To Board. What are these for?

By default, the Post To Board box is checked. This means that your response will be posted on the message board for all to read. But if you check the E-mail To Author box as well, your reply will be emailed to the gentleman or lady whose post you're responding to *and* posted to the message board.

This, as we'll see shortly, is a convention borrowed from newsgroups. Time was that the Internet was so unreliable you couldn't be sure when (or even if) a reply to a newsgroup message would appear. To ensure that the author knew you had read his message (and for the sake of politeness, of course), it was customary to email your reply to him or her as well. If, on the other hand, you uncheck the Post To Board box but check E-mail To Author, your reply won't be posted on the message board. Instead, it will be sent as private email. Only the author will be able to read it.

Cutting The Messages Down To Size

Clicking on the Next Message button works well enough if the message board isn't particularly busy. Then it's easy to scroll through the various postings and find your original message and any replies. However, in a busy message board—News, for example, which regularly generates several hundred, if not thousands of messages per day—scrolling through the postings can be a time-consuming process. Just clicking on the subject line and then clicking on List Messages (or double-clicking on the subject line) does exactly that: It lists all the messages in that topic. That includes those that you've read before and new messages that have been added since your last visit.

Fortunately, AOL is well able to cope.

Let's take a look at the News message boards. Figure 4.7 shows those postings dealing with U.K. domestic news. There are hundreds of them spread over, possibly, several weeks. How do you find only the most recent postings? Or those that were posted between specific dates?

Easy, click on the Find Since button and, lo, the Find Since screen appears (Figure 4.8). Your first option here is to check the New (Since Last Visit) button, and then Find. When you do this, you're shown only those messages that have been posted since your last visit to the board. AOL is able to do this because, every time you access a message board, the system remembers the time and date.

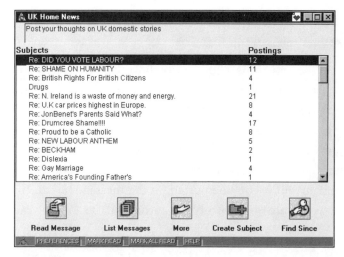

Figure 4.7
The News message boards are rather busy. You'll need help to find what you're looking for.

Figure 4.8
You don't want to read all the postings in the message board? Fine, read only those that have appeared since you were last here.

Another option is to tell AOL to go back a set number of days. For example, suppose I want to go back six days. So I enter "6" and click on Find, and AOL performs to spec.

On the other hand, it could be that you don't want to go back a set number of days, either. Maybe you've just spent six months in an igloo and haven't signed on to AOL in some time. Under these circumstances, selecting New (Since Last Visit) would be almost as bad as clicking on List Messages in terms of the sheer number of messages that would be waiting.

So instead, enter a date. To see if there was anything interesting said between, say, June 16 and June 18, check From, enter the relevant dates, and then only those messages posted between June 16 and June 18 will appear.

 Dating Yourself

By the way—and hopefully, this will soon be corrected, or will already have been corrected by the time this book comes out—you have to enter the date in the U.S. format. That's to say, month first, day second. So July 26 would be 7/26.

Finally, if you can't be bothered with any of this, please note the Mark Read and Mark All Read buttons hidden away on the base of the screen. If you highlight a message or group of messages and click on Mark Read, the message board pretends you've already read them. They'll therefore no longer be displayed. Mark All Read, on the other hand, is the Ultimate Deterrent. Click on it and AOL assumes you've read *all* that board's messages; none of them will be displayed. But if you foul up here, all is not lost. Simply go back to the Find Since screen, set the date to some time before your act of mass destruction, and like Arnold Schwarzenegger, they'll be back.

Message Board Preferences

Another button you may care to note is Preferences. Clicking on it results in the screen shown in Figure 4.9. From here, you can control how your messages are displayed. The options here are:

▲ *Oldest First*—In other words, you have to scroll from the top and down to get to the very latest.

▲ *Newest First*—As it implies, the newer messages are displayed up top. This is often a better idea, particularly if there are lots of messages and you don't dip in that often.

▲ *Alphabetical*—In other words, the messages are displayed as per the initial letter of their subject line. This is handy if you remember the subject of a message but not the date on which you read it.

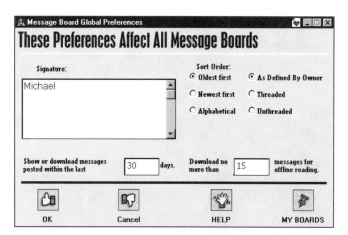

Figure 4.9
The Message Board Global Preferences screen allows you to assign the sort order of messages, as well as how many are displayed.

▲ *As Defined By Owner*—This means that you accept the default sort order as established by the person who "owns" or set up the board. They need to specify a sort order when the board is constructed.

▲ *Threaded*—This means that the various messages follow each other, not in the order in which they're posted, but by reference. So if, for example, there are six messages, and numbers 3 and 5 are both comments to message 1, then the order will be 1-3-5, followed perhaps by 2-4-6.

▲ *Unthreaded*—The messages are listed in the order in which they're posted.

Finally, you can set how many days' worth of messages you want to see displayed. By default, AOL retains messages posted in the previous 30 days. However, if you want to go back further, just amend the number accordingly; likewise when you're setting the number of messages for offline reading.

Offline reading? It's a good idea with message boards and, as you'll see, with newsgroups. Yes, you can type your messages and read them online while both BT's and AOL's meters tick away in the background. But surely there must be a more cost-effective way of doing this? There is.

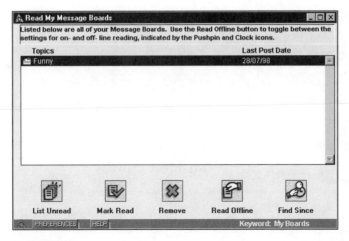

Figure 4.10
You don't have to read message boards online. Reading offline is a far more cost-effective alternative.

Click on the My Boards button, which brings up the screen in Figure 4.10. This shows one of my message boards that has been selected for offline reading. This means I can suck down all the unread messages, sign off from AOL, and then read and reply to those messages with the meter off. When I sign on again, AOL will automatically post those replies within a few seconds.

Intrigued? Stay so until Chapter 6.

Newsgroups

Newsgroups, which I mentioned briefly in Chapter 2, are the Internet's equivalent of message boards. They are, however, a bit more anarchic in character, which can sometimes be fun, but other times, it makes extracting meaningful information a bit of a pain.

You can access newsgroups from the Internet Channel, or you can go directly to Keyword: **NEWSGROUPS**, which brings up the main Newsgroups screen (Figure 4.11). I'm assuming at this stage that you're not knowingly a member of any newsgroups. You're therefore going to have to join (or *subscribe,* to use Internet parlance) one or several. But if you don't already know the name of a particular newsgroup, how do you know which to join, particularly since they all seem to have gibberish-looking

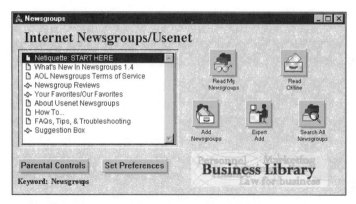

Figure 4.11
Newsgroups are the Internet's equivalent of message boards.

names like rec.music.classical.recordings instead of, say, Classical Music Discussion?

Finding A Newsgroup

Finding a newsgroup is an easy enough procedure:

1. Let's suppose you've got some vague idea of the sort of topics you're interested in. If so, the obvious first place to start is with the Search All Newsgroups button. This produces a search screen where you can enter a search word or combination of words (Figure 4.12).

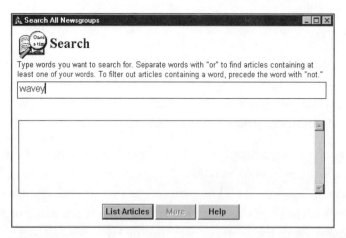

Figure 4.12
Enter the search terms into the Search screen to locate your desired newsgroup.

2. In my case, I'm looking to find a newsgroup that is dedicated to one of the legends of the Internet, one Wavey Davey. So I enter the word "Wavey" and click on List Articles.

3. The search engine rattles away for a second or two and finally yields a Search Results screen (Figure 4.13). It tells me that there's just one newsgroup dedicated to Wavey Davey: alt.fan.wavey.davey.

4. At this point, I can try to find out more by double-clicking on the name of the highlighted newsgroup. In more than 50 per cent of cases, however, this is a waste of time because not many people bother to add a description of their newsgroup (I told you the Internet was unregulated and anarchic), as indeed is the case here.

5. So, risking everything with one throw, I just double-click on Sub-scribe To Newsgroups alt.fan.wavey.davey. I have then subscribed to (or joined) the alt.fan.wavey.davey newsgroup. Had there been more than one newsgroup listed, I would have double-clicked on each of the highlighted choices to subscribe.

Browsing The Newsgroups

Given that there are in excess of 20,000 newsgroups, browsing the entire list will take a while. But if you insist, click on the Add Newsgroups

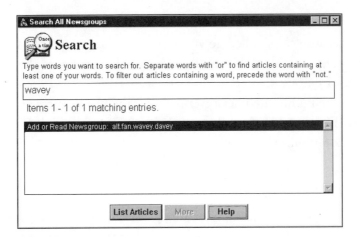

Figure 4.13
The newsgroup alt.fan.wavey.davey, the place to talk about Dave Winder—if you must.

button. This brings up a hierarchical menu of newsgroups sorted first by category, then by general subject area, then by topic. These are the main categories:

▲ *alt*—Alternative newsgroups, some of them of dubious subject matter, but some downright ordinary (for example, alt.morris.dancing)

▲ *biz*—Product announcements and the like

▲ *comp*—Discussion of and information relating to computers

▲ *misc*—Everything that doesn't fit anywhere else

▲ *news*—Discussion of current events

▲ *rec*—Recreational matters and hobbies

▲ *sci*—Science-related newsgroups

▲ *soc*—Discussions of sociology and psychology

▲ *talk*—Debate-oriented newsgroups on topics such as philosophy, politics, and religion

As I said, the newsgroups are listed hierarchically. So click on the alt groups, for example, and you'll get a list of all the groups in that category. These, too, can be subdivided.

If you're not sure and want to have a look, double-click on the newsgroup name. For example, I scrolled down those in the alt group until I came to alt.accounting. Then I double-clicked on it, which produced the screen in Figure 4.14—one lone newsgroup. To see its messages, I double-clicked on the highlighted newsgroup name, and all the messages were displayed (Figure 4.15). At this point, I can read them and, if I like what I read, click on Subscribe.

TIP *Joining "Dubious" Newsgroups*

AOL lists the vast majority, but not all, of newsgroups in existence. Some of the more...shall we say "salacious," as well as the more obscure, don't appear on the list. However, that doesn't mean you can't access them. See "A Roundup Of The Rest" later in this chapter to find out how.

Figure 4.14
A safe newsgroup in the alt series: alt.accounting.

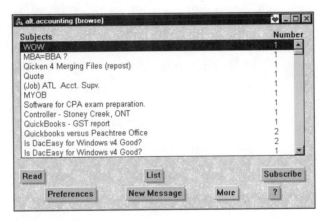

Figure 4.15
Double-click on the messages to read them or click on Subscribe to
join the newsgroup.

Posting Messages To Newsgroups

Go to the main Newsgroups page (shown earlier in Figure 4.11) and click
on Read My Newsgroups. A list of the newsgroups to which you're subscribed now appears, telling you how many messages are unread (Figure
4.16). Where did they all come from? Remember earlier when I said that
you're "not knowingly" a member of any newsgroups? Well, by default,
you're automatically subscribed to a few of AOL's own newsgroups.

If you don't like the look of this and decide you want to unsubscribe from
a newsgroup, highlight it and click on Remove. If you want to start reading, do so. If you're not interested, click on the Mark All Newsgroups

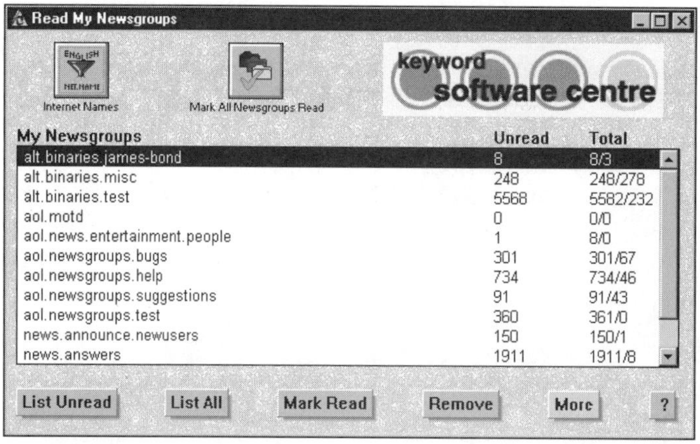

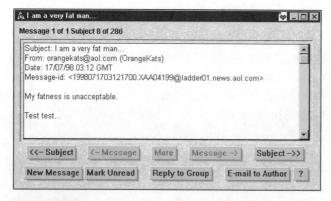

Figure 4.16
Click on Read My Newsgroups to find out which you're subscribed to—knowingly or not.

Read button. As with the similar button in the message boards, this fools AOL into thinking that you *have* read the messages, even though you haven't. In this case, I *am* interested, so I click on alt.newsgroups.test to display the unread messages. As its name suggests, this isn't a serious newsgroup. It's one set up by AOL for new members to hone their newsgroup skills before they try it for real.

Let's comment to one of the messages here:

1. "I am a very fat man" grabs my attention, so I click on it. This brings up the message. His fatness is unacceptable to him, he says (Figure 4.17).

Figure 4.17
A test message from the alt.newsgroups.test group. There's nothing serious here.

2. As with the message boards, I have the option of either replying to the author personally—E-mail To Author—or replying to the newsgroup as a whole—Reply To Group. In this case, I click on the latter.

3. The Post Response screen appears (Figure 4.18). You'll notice there are two windows here: one displaying the original message and one for my reply. Convention has it that when replying to newsgroup messages, one should either quote the whole message in the reply or quote its salient points. Here, I highlight the sentence, "My fatness is unacceptable." from the original message and click on the Quote button. This transfers the highlighted text to the Reply Window. The > arrow next to it means it is quoted text. To the quoted text, I append my comment: "Your fatness is unacceptable to me, too." I also add "test, test" just to show I'm not trying to give offence. Then I click on Send and it's posted. At this point, I could also click on CC: Author, in which case the author would get a copy of my reply in an email message, as in the message boards. And I can add a Sig to my post too (see "A Roundup Of The Rest" later in this chapter).

Now let's post an original message. To do this, simply click on the New Message button shown in Figure 4.17. This causes the Post New Message

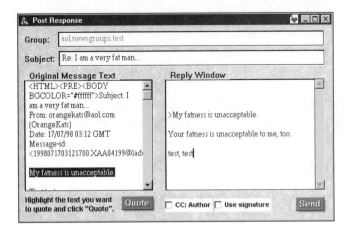

Figure 4.18
When you reply to a newsgroup message, it's customary to quote either part or all of it.

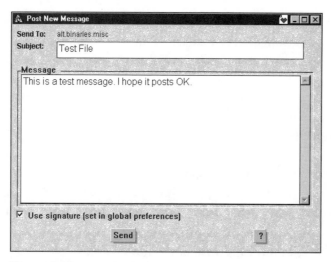

Figure 4.19
Posting a new message to a newsgroup.

screen to appear (Figure 4.19). In it I type something apposite and click
on Send. And off it goes.

Binary Files

Many newsgroups—they often have the word "binary" in their titles—
contain what are called *binary files*. This means that, strictly speaking, the
messages aren't text, but encoded computer files. These files could be
pictures, sound files, or even complete computer programs. However, to
be posted to the newsgroup, they had to be turned into a form of text.
Technically speaking, they've been *UUENCODED*.

To the naked eye, the message looks like complete gibberish, as if a cat
might have wandered across someone's keyboard. But AOL can identify
this gibberish as an encoded file. When it does so, you'll get a message
telling you the file is encoded and asking you if you want to download it.
You have three options:

▲ *Download File*—Download and decode.

▲ *Download Message*—Download the gibberish only. You'll decode it
later by using a special UUDECODE program.

▲ *Cancel*—No, you don't want to download the message at this time.

There's also a caveat about downloading files to your computer. Pay it heed. *If you don't know what the encoded file is or who it's from, it's often safer not to download it.* It could, for example, be a virus. I'll be talking more about viruses in the next chapter. If you *do* decide you want to download the file and click on Download File, AOL's Download Manager will prompt you for a folder in which to deposit it (Figure 4.20). I'll describe the Download Manager in more detail in Chapter 10.

A Roundup Of The Rest

The Parental Control button allows parents to ensure that their offspring don't get corrupted by potential nastiness on the Net and in newsgroups. Again, I'll talk about this in much greater detail in Chapter 10.

I mentioned earlier that not all the newsgroup names—the seedier ones, for example, or the more obscure—are listed. However, if I want to participate in the anonymous ones, I can—provided I know the name of the newsgroup to which I want to subscribe. This is where the Expert Add button can come in handy. Click on it, type in the complete newsgroup name, and click on Subscribe. The Latest Newsgroups button displays a list of those newsgroups that have been created since you last used the newsgroups area.

The Preferences button lets me determine how the newsgroups are going to be listed. As you can see from Figure 4.21, I can have them listed chronologically or alphabetically.

Figure 4.20
When you download a binary file from a newsgroup, AOL asks you which folder you want to put it in.

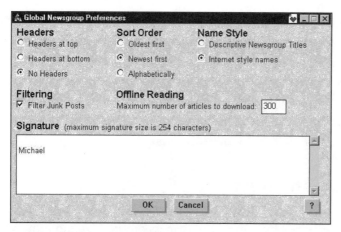

Figure 4.21
Global preferences that affect all newsgroups.

Also, I can have a Signature (better known in Internet circles as a *Sig*) automatically appended to the bottom of all my messages when I post them. It is considered a breach of netiquette to have a Sig longer than four lines, but it's a breach that you will see very often.

The Filtering button is supposed to exclude junk postings, which are the bane of many a newsgroup. It's dependent, however, on all newsgroup members agreeing to prefix their header messages with a prearranged symbol or set of characters. Those that don't aren't listed. It doesn't always work, though.

There's also an Offline Reading button. Turn to Chapter 6 for a lot more on that.

Netiquette On Newsgroups

A word on this is perhaps in order at this stage, although I shall reiterate later. *Netiquette* is the art of being polite and considerate of others on the Internet. If you follow the basic rules of polite interaction with others, your time on the Internet will be a happy one for you and for those with whom you come into contact. In order to participate productively, watch how a newsgroup operates for a while before you post to it, and read its FAQ (Frequently Asked Questions) if it has one.

Please confine your postings to the topic at hand. An article on gun control would not be appropriate in, say, a group that discusses classical music. The folks who subscribe to the classical music forum will appreciate your thoughtfulness and consideration if you do not post your armament musings to their group.

Posting a message that is a personal attack on someone, or one that is violently argumentative, is called *flaming* and is heartily discouraged. Disagreements are fine, of course, but please limit your responses to a discussion of the topic and avoid attacks upon the individual. Continued flaming usually results in a load of email complaints to the AOL Postmaster about you. It's also something you promised not to do when you agreed to AOL's Conditions of Service. So there.

So much for message boards and newsgroups. In the next chapter, we're going to be looking at files: how to attach them to email, how to send and receive them over the Internet, and where to find them in the first place. We'll also examine the concepts of shareware and freeware.

Chapter 5

Files And File Handling

Files can contain pictures, sounds, or even complete computer programs. Whatever they contain, AOL handles them all in much the same way. For example, you can attach them to email and send them to fellow AOL members or to others on the Internet. And if you're looking for specific files, AOL provides easy-to-use search engines that help seek them out.

Email File Attachments

They're called file attachments because that's exactly how it works. You simply *attach* a file to an email message and speed it on its way. Your recipient then *detaches* it. Here's how it works.

Receiving Files By Email

In Chapter 1, I described a typical online session during which my brother, who lives up north, was flaunting the fact that he had just put in a new fireplace. This he did by emailing me a picture of it. Here's what I did to view it (and what you can do to view any picture that's emailed to you, not just fireplaces):

1. I hear Joanna Lumley announcing that I've received post, so I click on the icon and view the incoming message. "Our New Fireplace," it says on the subject line (Figure 5.1).

   You'll notice that this email message is slightly different from those I've received before. Between the header information and the actual message AOL tells me there's a file attached: FIRE.JPG. Below that,

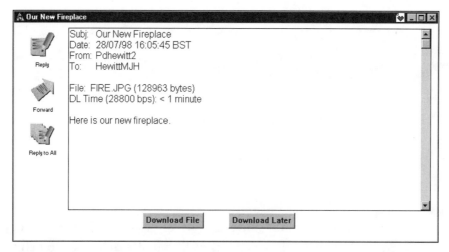

Figure 5.1
Email with an attached file displays the name of the file and information about how long it should take to download.

it tells me that, at 28,800bps, it should take less than a minute to download. And below the message are two buttons: Download File and Download Later. Both should be self-explanatory, although Download Later will, if you'll forgive me, "self-explain" itself in further detail in the next chapter.

2. For the moment, so eager am I to see this fireplace that I click on Download File. The basic Download Manager pops up (Figure 5.2). The Download Manager lets you tell AOL where to deposit files you download. By default, it places them in a subfolder called Download, which is nested inside your main AOL folder. You can change this destination directory and set it to any directory you would like to use, which I did. Mine is called Receive. (In Chapter 10, I'll tell you how to do this with another version of the Download Manager that has a few more bells and whistles.) Anyhow, the Download Manager says it's going to put a file called fire into my Receive folder. I click on Save and the process begins.

3. The picture appears on my monitor, piece by piece, in under a minute. And a very nice fireplace it is, too (Figure 5.3). I know it's fully arrived when Joanna Lumley announces, "File's finished."

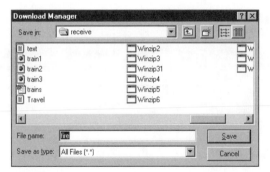

Figure 5.2
AOL's Download Manager tells you what the incoming file is called and asks you where on your computer's hard disk it should be deposited.

Figure 5.3
My brother's fireplace, delivered by email.

Sending Files By Email

Receiving a file by email was painless, wasn't it? Sending files by email is equally so.

Unfortunately, I don't have a fireplace of my own, so I can't respond to my brother in kind. What I *can* do, though, is send him a picture of me taken in one of my local pubs, The Albion. This is done as follows:

1. I click on the Reply button in the usual way and the Reply screen appears (Figure 5.4). "Here's a picture of me in the pub," I say. Notice

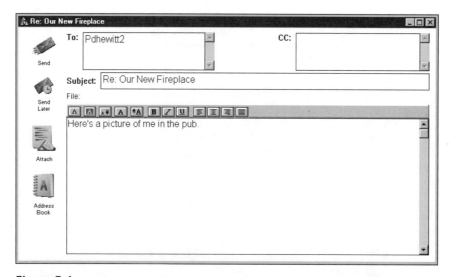

Figure 5.4
The Reply window. Note the Attach icon, which I'll use to attach the picture
file to my email.

the buttons to the left of the message window. The one I'm interested
in is the Attach icon, so I click on it. Upon doing so, the Attach File
window appears (Figure 5.5).

2. The Attach File window performs a function similar to that of the
Download Manager, but instead of telling AOL where I want to *put*
the file, I'm telling it the location from which I want to *send* it, in this
case, my Send folder. The file itself is called ME.JPG. Having

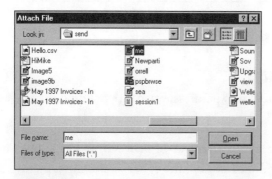

Figure 5.5
The Attach File window does what the Download Manager does, except
in reverse.

located it in the Send folder, I double-click on it to select it. I can highlight it and click on Open to do the same thing.

3. The Reply window appears again, looking much as it did before. There are, however, two minor differences (Figure 5.6). First, the File line (under the subject line) has changed from being blank to having the file name—ME.JPG—next to it, together with the name of the folder in which my PC is storing it. Second, the Attach icon has changed to Detach. If, for any reason, I feel that I don't want to go through with the file-sending operation, or I realise I've selected the wrong file, I can select Detach, and my missive becomes a plain, simple email message once more. But I *do* want to go through with it, so I select Send.

4. A progress bar appears for the duration of the upload. Then Joanna Lumley says "File's finished," which means that it's been sent successfully.

5. The next time my brother signs on, he will see my incoming message in his New Email window (Figure 5.7). It looks like any normal new email except for one crucial difference: There's a little disk icon at the far left, beside the date of the email. This tells him there's a file

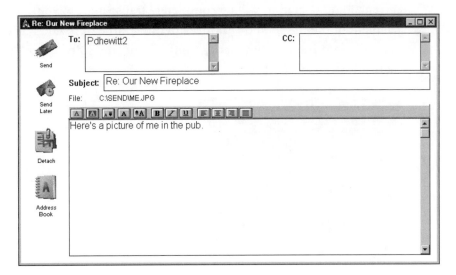

Figure 5.6
The Reply window changes to show me that there's a file attached to my outgoing email.

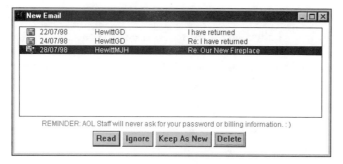

Figure 5.7
The disk icon at the far left (next to the date) indicates that there's a file attached.

attached to that email. And, for the record, when he downloads the file, he sees a picture of me in the pub, pint in hand (Figure 5.8).

Attaching Files To Internet Email

Sending a file to someone with an Internet email account works in exactly the same way as sending a file to an AOL member. The only difference is that AOL will automatically encode the file so that it can be sent over the Internet. This is exactly the same sort of encoding that I talked about in the last chapter when I discussed binary files in newsgroups. However, the encoding operation will be completely transparent to you. The recipient of the file shouldn't notice anything either. Provided he or she has a modern Internet browser and email suite, the software will automatically decode your file.

Figure 5.8
Me, pint in hand, in The Albion.

TIP   *Warning!*

If you receive an attached file from someone you don't know, whether they're a fellow AOL member or from elsewhere on the Internet, *do not* download it, unless you're fairly certain of what it is. It could contain a computer virus or other objectionable material. This is particularly so with files that end in the extensions .EXE or .ZIP. Most files will be quite innocent, but you should always be on your guard.

If you think you've downloaded something you shouldn't have, you'll need to get some advice, and pronto. Use Keyword: **TECHCHAT** for "live" assistance. Or you can use Keyword: **HELPFORUM** and choose the Offline Help category, which contains a list of AOL's Freephone numbers that you can call for help and advice.

Searching For And Downloading Files From AOL

Every morning when I turn on my PC, Bart Simpson's voice greets me with the words, "This is *so* cool!" My Windows wallpaper features the whole Simpson family. Among the programs on my Windows desktop is a paint package called Paint Shop Pro, which I've used to grab the screenshots (computer snapshots) for this book. At the end of the day, when I eventually close down, Bart Simpson's voice says, "I've got to get outta here!"

I know; sad isn't it? Perhaps something traumatic happened to me during my early childhood. But this does at least serve to show how useful AOL is for finding files you want or need; I downloaded all of these files from AOL. They're just a few of the many thousands that are available to you online. You can download pictures, sound effects, video clips, text files, utilities, and even complete computer programs. It's simply a matter of locating the right file and then clicking the mouse button.

So where are they to be found? Many AOL forums and areas have specialised file libraries that contain files whose subject matter is directly related to the forum topic. So from the *Star Trek* forum, for instance, you can download Klingon dictionaries, pictures of the crew of the *Enterprise*, and so forth. In the PC Games forum, you can get hold of such titles as Castle Wolfenstein, Battlechess, and Solitaire. Or on a more practical level, you can go into the Windows forum and download thousands of fonts and utilities. And to make things easier, AOL also stores all the files from every forum in a central repository.

Where do they all come from? Some of the files are put there by the forum management. Some are courtesy of AOL. But a great many are uploaded by AOL members themselves for the benefit of fellow members. Many of the titles are free of charge; for others, you'll be asked to pay a small fee. However, you get to "try before you buy." I'll discuss this concept—*shareware*, as it's called—later in this chapter.

In the meantime, let's cut straight to the chase and download something. As I said, my Windows wallpaper is a Simpson family group "photo." There are several such files available on AOL, so let's find one.

FileSearch

Using FileSearch is similar to using AOL NetFind. This is how it's done:

1. I can either click on the Toolbar's Software Search icon or go to Keyword: **FILESEARCH**. This takes me directly to the Software Search screen (Figure 5.9). Here, I can narrow (and therefore speed up) my search by entering various criteria:

   ▲ *Specify the date the file was uploaded to AOL*—There are three options here: all dates, only those files uploaded in the past week,

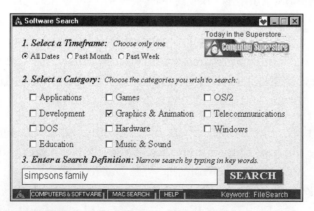

Figure 5.9
You can search for files by date of upload, category, and key words.

and files uploaded in the past month. But unless you've heard through the grapevine that someone has recently uploaded a specific file, you're probably safest clicking on All Dates.

▲ *Specify the category*—So how would you categorise a picture of the Simpsons? Well, it's a graphics file, obviously, so it's worth clicking on Graphics & Animation. If I didn't click on any specific category, AOL would search for the file in such diverse areas as OS/2, Education, and DOS, which would be rather like searching a supermarket's greengrocery section for fishfingers. In other words, I would just slow down the search.

▲ *Search by key words*—To narrow my search even further, I can type in key words. These are terms that are unique to the file in question, and help distinguish it from other, similar files. The more you use, the more precise your result. For example, if I were searching for a file about Mustang cars, my key words would include "car" and "Mustang". If I didn't use the key word "car", but just used "Mustang" alone, my search might produce files about the breed of horse. In this case, I type in "Simpson" and "family" and then click on Search.

2. With this, the search engine buzzes away in the background and, after having checked the file repository against all of my search criteria, presents me with two files that satisfy them (Figure 5.10). The file at the top—Simpson Family Portrait—is an animation,

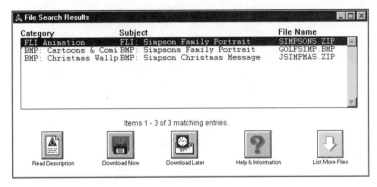

Figure 5.10
Success! I've found a number of Simpson-related files.

not a picture, so it isn't quite suitable. The file names alone aren't telling me much, however. I'd like more information before I download.

3. I therefore highlight a file and click on the Read Description button. This gives me a blow-by-blow account of what the file is, who wrote it, and exactly when it was uploaded (Figure 5.11). It will also tell me the file name, its format, roughly how long AOL reckons it will take to download using my 28,800bps modem, and how many people have already downloaded it. If a lot of people have already downloaded it, then it stands to reason that the thing is worth having. In some cases, the description will also feature a small thumbnail picture of the file if it's a graphic.

4. At this point, as you'll see from the buttons at the bottom, I've got four options:

   ▲ *Download Now*—The Download Now button does exactly that.

   ▲ *Download Later*—This button is used in conjunction with a FlashSession (I'll discuss FlashSessions in more detail in the next chapter).

Figure 5.11
The Read Description button tells you everything you need to know about the file. From this, you can find out whether it's worth downloading.

▲ *Ask The Staff*—If, having read the description, I'm still a bit unsure as to whether or not this is the file I really need, I click on the button and the Ask The Staff screen appears. This lets me send an email message to the manager(s) of this file library who, hopefully, will come back to me in short order.

▲ *Related Files*—Click on this and it will list all similar files on the system.

I'm one of those impulsive types, so I click on Download Now and hang the consequences. The Download Manager screen, which we met earlier, pops up and tells me that it intends to deposit the file GOLFSIMP.BMP in my Receive folder. I've got no particular quibble with that, so I click on OK. Of course, if I wanted it put somewhere else, I would just select another folder.

5. The file transfer begins. Once the thing is done, Joanna says, "File's finished!" and the picture is displayed (Figure 5.12).

Figure 5.12
The file has arrived safely.

Search Tips

Try using so-called Boolean logic when searching for items. This means qualifying your searches with operators such as OR, AND, or NOT to narrow them down. For example, let's suppose you're looking for Simpson references. (What a coincidence!) However, you only want the Springfield-based variety rather than, say, ex-football players who've had serious run-ins with the law. In this case, you would enter the words:

Simpsons NOT OJ

If you were looking for references to places of worship but didn't want to bring up any references to famous child film stars of the 1930s, you would enter:

Temple NOT Shirley

Let's now suppose you're searching out a specific American president. Then the search string

Theodore AND Roosevelt

would return files containing Theodore Roosevelt but *not* FDR. On the other hand, if you don't care which Roosevelt you retrieve, the words

Roosevelt Theodore OR Franklin

should do the job.

 Author, Author

AOL file library managers typically assign key words to uploaded files, which is how Filesearch knows which files to show you when you do your search. One of these key words is the author's name. If you find that a given file is particularly good, keep a lookout for its author's name when you perform subsequent searches. Use it as a key word in your search and you can find other files created by the same author.

Compressed Files

Many large files, especially graphics and program files, are compressed—or, to use the parlance, *zipped*—by a program called WinZip (or similar packages like PKZip and ZipMagic). You can easily identify them because they have a .ZIP extension. The idea behind compressing files is to reduce their size and thereby reduce the time it takes both to upload and download them. For more information about the wonderful world of zipped files, you can go to Keyword: **ZIP**.

By default, AOL will automatically decompress—*unzip*—compressed files when you sign off. If you don't want this to happen, however, you can disable this function in Preferences. I'll discuss downloading and other preferences in greater detail in Chapter 10. If you can't wait, turn to it now.

TIP *Keeping Busy During Downloads*

You can, if you wish, simply sit there while the file downloads and watch its progress over the telephone line. However, I would rate this somewhere alongside pro/celebrity paint-drying observation or the *Times Educational Supplement* in the adrenaline-pumping stakes.

What you can do, especially if it's a long download, is go somewhere else within AOL while AOL downloads the file to your computer—a message board, maybe, or the Internet, or anywhere, for that matter. This won't affect the download. It will still be happening, albeit in the background. And even if you are somewhere else online, when the download is done, a message will still pop up and Joanna Lumley will still make her announcement.

The Software Centre

I can't leave this section without a word about the Software Centre, AOL's guide to finding files of all kinds (Figure 5.13). You'll find it in

Virus Alert

I mentioned computer viruses earlier in the chapter. Basically, they are malicious self-propagating computer programs that surreptitiously attach themselves to other files. If let loose within your computer, they can spread and damage your data, or erase it completely. There are, unfortunately, hundreds of computer viruses in the world; they're manufactured by twisted individuals who write the things for kicks.

So check files for viruses before you upload them, and check the files you download, too. Although AOL does check the files they offer, you don't get any such assurances for stuff you pick up off the Internet or receive as attachments to emails. If you don't have a virus checker, download one from AOL. Keyword: **VIRUS** is a must-see. It contains answers to common questions and links you directly to forums where you can get some of the most effective antivirus software—the digital equivalent of penicillin. And there's the Safety Online area (at Keyword: **SAFETY ONLINE**), which provides pointers to keep you and yours safe from harm.

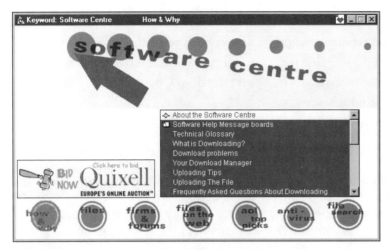

Figure 5.13
AOL's Software Centre—a repository of all the most useful files.

the Computing Channel or by going to Keyword: **SOFTWARE CENTRE**.

There are countless varieties of software and utilities here, grouped according to function. So, for example, you'll find sound files in one location, home-page-building software in another, multimedia applications in yet another, and so on. Just click on the appropriate buttons and menus to view them. There's also a whole section dedicated to files on the Web, which is well worth looking at.

In addition, the Software Centre reviews files based on various Web sites and picks out what AOL techies reckon are the best. They regularly award accolades like Best of the Day, Best of the Week, and Best of the Month. Have a look every so often to see exactly what's getting them excited—it might get you excited, too. In fact, it's worth taking a look at the Software Centre on a regular basis.

File-Name Extensions

As you scour AOL for files (or the Internet, see "Searching For And Downloading Files On The Internet" later in this chapter), you'll see that different ones have different extensions. The extension is the bit that comes after the full-point, so if a file is called HELLO.TXT, its extension is .TXT. In other words, it's in text format. I've listed some of the more common file extensions you'll find on AOL (there's a huge list of them in the Technical Glossary at Keyword: **SOFTWARE CENTRE**, but these will do, for now).

Here are common extensions for text files:

▲ *.TXT*—A standard text file without formatting codes

▲ *.DOC*—Usually a document created in either Word or WordPerfect

▲ *.RTF*—Rich Text Format; an intermediate file format used for transferring word-processed files between different word processors

The following extensions are used with compressed files:

▲ *.ZIP*—A file that has been squashed (or compressed) with a compression program so it doesn't take so long to either upload or download via a modem

▲ *.SEA*—Self Extracting Archive

▲ *.SIT*—A file that has been compressed using StuffIt, the Macintosh equivalent of WinZip

You'll find these extensions on graphics files:

▲ *.BMP*—Windows bitmap (all Windows wallpaper pictures are in .BMP format)

▲ *.EPS*—Encapsulated PostScript

▲ *.GIF*—Graphics Interchange Format

▲ *.JPG*—Joint Photographic Experts Group; denotes a compressed graphics file

▲ *.PCX*—PC Paintbrush/Windows Paintbrush native file format

▲ *.TIF*—Tagged Image File Format

Here are the most common video file extensions:

▲ *.AVI*—Microsoft's video format

▲ *.MPG*—Moving Picture Experts Group video format (an open standard, as opposed to .AVI, which is controlled by Microsoft)

▲ *.MOV*—A QuickTime file (the Macintosh equivalent of .AVI; will also play on Windows PCs if you have the QuickTime plug-in)

Sound files often have the following extensions:

▲ *.AU*—Netscape sound file format

▲ *.WAV*—Windows sound file format

▲ *.WVE*—Psion sound file format

And finally, here are some other file extensions:

▲ *.XLS*—Microsoft Excel worksheets

▲ *.XLC*—Microsoft Excel charts

▲ *.WKS*—Lotus 1-2-3 worksheets

Uploading Files To AOL

Of course, before you can download a file, someone has to first upload it to AOL. It's a straightforward operation. I mentioned earlier on that I sent my brother a picture of myself in The Albion pub. But why should he alone benefit from my largesse? I've decided to share that picture with the rest of AOL. In order to do this, I'm going to upload it to an area called the Gallery. Here, you'll find the mug shots of thousands of AOL members. To get there, go to Keyword: **GALLERY**.

Here's how to upload a file to AOL's Gallery:

1. Figure 5.14 shows Gallery's opening menu. I click on the New Files & Free Uploading button at the bottom of the screen.

2. The Gallery New Files screen appears (Figure 5.15). To upload a file, I click on the Upload button.

3. At this point, Gallery's New Files screen appears (Figure 5.16). Here, I need to add some details that will help other people find the file I'm uploading and distinguish it from all the others:

Figure 5.14
AOL's Gallery, where members can upload and download pictures of each other.

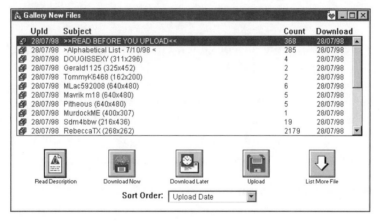

Figure 5.15
Click on the Upload button to initiate an upload to Gallery.

▲ In the Subject box, I enter "Self Portrait".

▲ In Author, I put "Michael Hewitt".

▲ In the Equipment box, you should mention whether or not any special hardware is required to make proper use of the file you're uploading. For example, if I were uploading a WAV sound file, I would say that anyone wanting to listen to it would need a Soundblaster card (or something similar) in his or her PC. In this case, though, I'm just uploading a standard graphics file that can

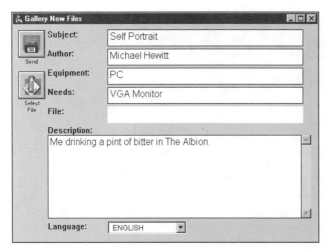

Figure 5.16
You should include as much information about the file as possible in the Upload screen. This helps people decide whether they want to download it.

be displayed on any computer. Hence, I enter "PC" in the Equipment line.

▲ In the Needs box, you should specify the particular software application or ancillary hardware that's needed to access your file. An AVI file, for instance, requires an AVI player. But in this case, my graphics file only needs a VGA monitor.

▲ Finally, a full description of the file—something to make it stand out from the herd if possible—should be entered in the Description box. If fellow AOL members are searching for pictures of people drinking pints of bitter in pubs called The Albion, the information here will enable them to locate this particular file in a trice.

4. I click on the Select File button and the Attach File window appears; we encountered it earlier when we attached a file to an email message. As before, I locate the folder containing the file, double-click on the file name, and then click on OK.

5. The file transfer starts. How long it takes, as always, depends on the speed of the modem, the size of the file, and how busy AOL is when

the file is being uploaded. Note that you'll need to drum your fingers on the desk while you wait for an upload to finish—AOL won't let you lark about and do other things like it will while you're downloading.

6. When it's done, Joanna announces "File's finished!" and an information box appears. "Your file has been submitted and will be reviewed," it says. Before AOL makes my file available to AOL members, they first scrutinise it to make sure it's suitable for public consumption, virus-check it (even though I've already done so myself, of course—I wouldn't want to inadvertently download a program that has a virus in it), make sure it's even approximately what it says it is, and so on.

And that, in a nutshell, is how to upload files to AOL. The upload procedure might differ ever so slightly from area to area, but essentially that's it. And by the way, if your file is really big—over 200K, say—please compress it before you upload it. This is the polite thing to do. If it's a massive thing that takes you 20 minutes to upload, then it's going to take someone else 20 minutes to download—even longer if his or her modem isn't as fast as yours. So save time, phone bills, and tears all round and compress the file.

You can find compression software at Keyword: **ZIP**. The programs take about five minutes to download using a 28,800bps modem and less time if you're possessed of a faster one.

Searching For And Downloading Files On The Internet

It's quite straightforward, isn't it? You just go to a search engine such as AOL NetFind, enter the appropriate search terms, and the WWW sites containing those files are displayed. Then all you need to do is click on Download File. Well, yes, nowadays it *is* that straightforward. However, just for the sake of completeness, I'll tell you about several other ways you can find files on the Net.

AOL NetFind™

Let's go back again to that rather useful search engine, NetFind.

We've already seen that you can use NetFind to specify exactly where to search for a site. In Chapter 3, for example, I restricted the search to sites from the U.K. and Ireland. In the same sort of way, you can restrict not just *where* it looks, but also the *type* of files it searches for.

Let's click on the Pictures & Sound button and enter "Simpsons Family" (Figure 5.17). This tells NetFind that I wish to find sites on the World Wide Web that have downloadable graphics or sound elements— pictures and sound effects, in other words. But to further restrict the search to pictures only, I select Pictures And Graphics and click on Find.

NetFind whirrs away and in a few seconds presents me with 64 hits. All of these sites contain the words "Simpsons" and "Family", as well as related pictures. As if that weren't good enough, at the end NetFind produces a report:

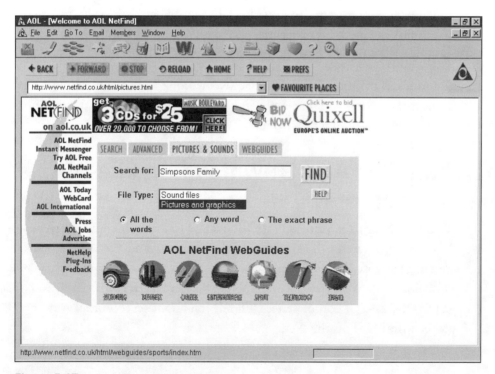

Figure 5.17
Searching for graphics and sound files with NetFind.

"You searched for 'Simpsons Family'. Related topics:

Webpages Worldwide: Simpsons Family

Pages in UK/Ireland: Simpsons Family

Sounds: Simpsons family."

These are all links to sites that, although they may not contain graphics, are (in NetFind's view) close enough to what I'm searching for to warrant a look at least.

You should also check out NetFind's WebGuides. They too group sites according to subject matter. In this case, the subject matters include Entertainment, Careers, Sports, and Travel, among others. Each contains what are, in AOL's view, some of the best sites of their kind on the Internet.

File Transfer Protocol (FTP)

File Transfer Protocol is a blast from the past. Today, if I want to download a plug-in from AOL—AOL NetMail™, say—I'll simply go to AOL's Web site, select the plug-in, and click on Download. This is the way most people do it, but there is an alternative.

The main drawback with the World Wide Web is that it can sometimes be quite slow. So if I want to download a file at a busy time of day, File Transfer Protocol—hereafter referred to as FTP—is a slightly faster alternative because it deals directly with the server on which the files reside. Internet old-timers, incidentally, use the term as a transitive verb. So they will "FTP" a file. Let us FTP one ourselves and see what it feels like.

Go to Keyword: **FTP** and you are delivered unto AOL's main FTP screen (Figure 5.18).

Click on the Go To FTP button. This takes you to the Anonymous FTP screen. It's so called because, when people log on to an FTP site manually, they usually enter their username as "anonymous". Don't worry about it—it's just one of those weird Internet conventions. AOL does it all for you. Here (Figure 5.19), AOL has kindly drawn up a list of what it reckons are interesting FTP sites, one of which, naturally, is its own: **ftp.aol.com**.

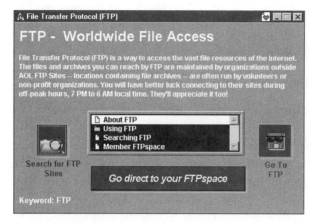

Figure 5.18
AOL's FTP screen.

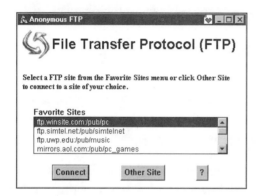

Figure 5.19
AOL's Anonymous FTP screen gathers together several potentially useful
FTP sites.

You'll find, as shown in Figure 5.20, that FTP sites are organised rather
like your PC's hard disk. In other words, files are stored within folders,
and folders can contain subfolders. To get at these subfolders, and the
files within them, simply double-click on the folder in the usual way. In
this instance, I've selected a folder called aol_win95. To download a file,
highlight it and double-click on the Download Now button.

Likely as not, though, you'll want to go to an FTP site that isn't listed
here. For example, when I was writing this book, I delivered files to and
downloaded them from the publisher's own FTP server. Obviously, they

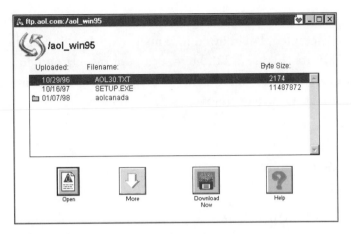

Figure 5.20
The contents of **ftp.aol.com/aol_win95**.

didn't want just *anyone* turning up and arbitrarily uploading and down-loading files, so they gave me a unique username and a password. Many commercial and educational establishments will do the same in order to prevent unauthorised access to their sites.

If you know where you're going and you know that you've been given permission to access the site, go to it by clicking on the Other Site button on the Anonymous FTP screen. This brings up the Other Site screen, into which you enter the name of the FTP site (Figure 5.21). In this case, it's **ftp.coriolis.com**. And because they're expecting a username and a password, I check the Ask For Login Name And Password box before I click on Connect.

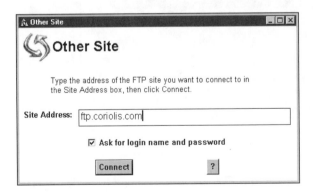

Figure 5.21
Connecting directly to an FTP server.

At this point, I'm prompted for my username and password. Once they've been accepted, I'm allowed into my personal section of the Coriolis FTP site (Figure 5.22). Here, I can upload files and download them. Or I can delete them and rename them. Basically—within reason—I can treat the area as if it were a folder on my own PC.

Gopher

Last, and purely because AOL still features it, there is another option: Use AOL's Gopher search.

Why is it called Gopher? Some people say it's because the mascot of the University of Minnesota, where the thing was conceived, is a gopher. Others maintain that it's a contraction of the phrase "Go for this, go for that." Anyhow, go to Keyword: **GOPHER** and you get the Gopher search engine (Figure 5.23). Click on Search, enter your search criteria, and follow the online instructions.

Originally, Gopher was intended to search out only those sites that contained files. Today, however, it performs much the same as any other search engine. As such, it has become largely redundant. Nevertheless, it's worth mentioning for Internet old-timers. And—who knows?—like Abba and flared trousers, it could undergo a revival.

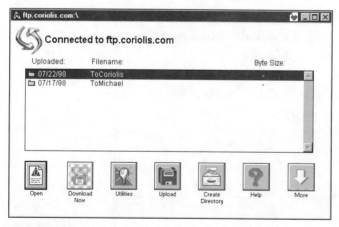

Figure 5.22
I can treat the contents of this FTP site as if it were a folder on my computer.

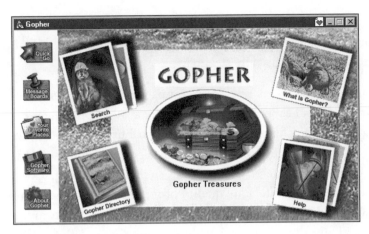

Figure 5.23
AOL's Gopher search engine.

Shareware And Freeware

I've talked a lot about files, but not much about who produces them and, therefore indirectly, who owns them.

Many genuinely altruistic people write computer software and then upload it to AOL or the Internet for the sheer fun of it. They expect no recompense. Their only reward is the thought that someone else is deriving pleasure or benefit from using the software. They're typically rather excellent programmers who believe that programming isn't really all that hard and that the whole process of marketing and packaging software screws it up. This view is hotly contested by the software industry, but while the two corners are slugging it out, we get lots of free software, so that's OK. The free programs and files that they produce are known as *freeware*.

The authors of *shareware*, on the other hand, are just a bit more mercenary. They would like you to pay them for their work, including their ongoing efforts to support and update their software. But before you pay, they allow you to download the program and use it for a while—usually 30 days—in order to assess its worth. If you think it's OK, you're supposed to send the money to the address that's included with the program. Some shareware programs self-destruct after the 30-day period. Others restrict some available features until you register, and still others just keep on displaying a message to the effect that the program hasn't been registered. This is to make you feel guilty for what, if you think hard enough about it, is basically stealing.

Although the cost of shareware programs varies enormously, they do tend to be a lot cheaper than commercially available packages because their authors don't have marketing and distribution overheads to worry about. Whether shareware packages are as good as those bought in the shops is another matter, though. Some, such as the paint package Paint Shop Pro, most definitely are quality programs. Some others, quite frankly, are a waste of space. However, as you get the opportunity to try before you buy, this shouldn't bother you unduly.

And now, from here to the next chapter, in which I'll show you how to *really* get your money's worth out of your AOL account by making the most of your online time.

Chapter 6

Maximising Your Online Time

Doing everything "live" online—writing email, reading message boards, posting to newsgroups, and so on—can be quite fun. It can also cost you some serious money; even if you're on AOL's Unlimited Access pricing plan, there's still your phone bill to think about. Besides, certain things are sometimes better done offline: reading and replying to love letters, for example. Were he around today, I'm sure that Cyrano de Bergerac would work offline. Many canny AOL members do so, regardless of nose dimensions.

How do they do it? In this chapter, I'll tell you exactly how to maximise your online time by doing as much as you can offline and by using a few tricks to speed things up when you *are* signed on.

Setting Up A FlashSession

What, pray, is a FlashSession? I'm glad you asked. A FlashSession is basically where AOL acts like a golden retriever and responds to the command "Go fetch!" In other words, it signs on for you and automatically downloads material from AOL to your PC's hard disk. Unlike a golden retriever, it will send things away, too. Or rather, it will automatically post material from your computer to AOL and even the Internet (at your direction, of course). And when it's done, it signs off again, unless you tell it otherwise.

What can you send and retrieve during FlashSessions?

▲ Email

▲ Message board messages

▲ Newsgroup messages

▲ Files

You can choose to perform any or all of these actions during the course of a FlashSession. You can, for example, set up the FlashSession so that it sends and receives email and files but leaves message board and newsgroup messages where they are. Or you can tell it to ignore all email and attachments and only fetch and send message board messages. It's up to you.

What I'm going to do here, though, is go for a "full house." That's to say, I'm going to tell AOL to fetch and receive all my pending email, send and receive all files attached to those emails, and send and receive all the message board and newsgroup messages in which I'm interested. As you'll see, you can enable each function individually by checking on the corresponding control. Therefore, if you *don't* want a particular action to be performed during a FlashSession—downloading message board messages, say—simply make sure the relevant control remains unchecked.

TIP *A Note Before We Begin*

You cannot perform a FlashSession if you're signed on as Guest. AOL presumes that if you're online as a guest, you're not using your own computer (otherwise, you would be signing on as yourself). A FlashSession downloads email, messages, and so on to the computer's hard drive. You wouldn't want to download your love letters (for example) onto someone else's hard drive, would you? AOL thought not, and that's why you can't do FlashSessions when you're signed on as Guest.

Onward without further ado. By the way, you needn't be online to do the following. Indeed, it would defeat the whole object of the exercise if you *were* online. Here's how to set up a FlashSession:

1. I start up my AOL software (but I don't sign on). I then select Set Up FlashSession, which is under the Email menu. Doing so brings up the FlashSessions screen (Figure 6.1).

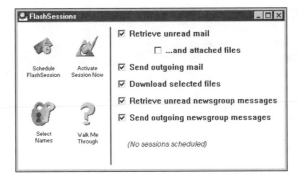

Figure 6.1
AOL's FlashSessions screen, from which you can automate many
common functions.

⚠ A Warning!

Do you entirely trust the people around you?

I pose this question because, whenever you set up a FlashSession, you enter your
password. The AOL software then helpfully saves this information on your PC's hard
disk to use when it performs the FlashSession. This means that someone could possibly
come along and activate a FlashSession on your behalf.

Of course, this person's motives might be completely altruistic. He may, for instance,
simply want to save you the trouble of doing it yourself. How public-spirited of him.
On the other hand, it could be a bit more sinister than that, particularly if he checks the
Stay Online When Finished box. If he does that, he can then do with your account as
he pleases, and for as long as he pleases—all without needing to know your password.

Therefore, if there's the potential for this kind of mischief—if your PC is in a crowded
office, for example, or a home with mischievous computer-literate kids—*I strongly
recommend that you do* not *keep your password stored*. When you've finished a
FlashSession, delete your password until the next time. OK, it involves a little more
hassle, but is that worse than having someone use *your* AOL account at *your* expense?

2. AOL will perform the FlashSession for any or all of the screen names
   on your account. You just need to tell it which one(s) and supply the
   appropriate sign-on password. To do so, choose the Select Names
   button. The corresponding window appears (Figure 6.2). This account has three names. I activate HewittMJH and enter my usual
   password. Then I click on OK.

Figure 6.2
Choosing which screen name is going to perform the FlashSession.

 Have A Care

Don't accidentally check more than one screen name. If you do, AOL will sign on, perform a FlashSession for the first name, sign off, automatically sign on again, and perform another FlashSession for the second name.

3. This done, I'm back to the FlashSession screen in Figure 6.1. Here, I instruct AOL to retrieve and send mail (but *not* to retrieve mail attachments—see the tip, "Have Another Care"), to download selected files, and to retrieve and send newsgroup messages. I could, by the way, have AOL "walk" me through setting up a FlashSession by clicking on the question mark icon. That yields a series of "Do you want to do this? Do you want to do that?" screens. I prefer not to be walked through, though. At this point, with everything selected, I close the FlashSession screen.

Why don't I activate the FlashSession now and be done with it? I don't because I haven't yet told AOL which newsgroups and which message boards I want to automatically download. This I shall do forthwith.

 Have Another Care

I would advise you *not* to set your FlashSession to automatically download email file attachments. Sometimes, junk emailers will attach binary files to their rubbish. You wouldn't want to download that, would you? Or some malicious person could attach an infected file to an email. Or you simply might not be in the mood to receive files. It happens. Essentially, this is another warning against downloading files of whose provenance you are in doubt. Obviously, if they're all downloaded automatically without you first seeing from whom they've come, you're taking their provenance on faith—not necessarily a prudent choice.

Selecting Newsgroups

Here's how to select newsgroups:

1. Sign on to AOL in the usual way. Then go to Keyword: **NEWSGROUPS,** which will take you to the Newsgroups area (Figure 6.3). Click on the Read Offline button. This brings up the Choose Newsgroups screen (Figure 6.4). AOL displays all the

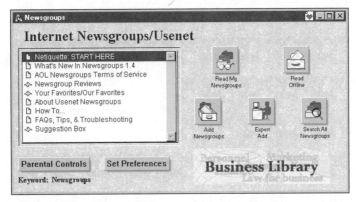

Figure 6.3
The by-now-familiar Newsgroups screen. Select Read Offline.

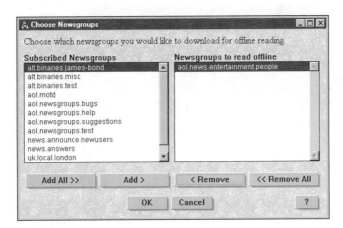

Figure 6.4
Selecting newsgroups for offline reading.

newsgroups to which you're subscribed in the left-hand window. Highlight those you want to read offline and click on the Add button (or don't highlight any and click on Add All if you want all of them). Your selected newsgroups appear in the right-hand window. Should you not be satisfied with some or all of your choices, highlight and employ the Remove button as appropriate.

2. Now return to the main Newsgroups screen and click on the Set Preferences button. Here, if you wish, you can specify exactly how many newsgroup messages you want downloaded in a single FlashSession (Figure 6.5). This is useful if you belong to groups containing lots of encoded binary files because the messages can get very big. Unless someone else is paying your AOL and phone bills and your hard disk is huge, you wouldn't want to download too many messages automatically. Set the maximum number of messages you want to download and click on OK.

And that, ladies and gentlemen, is how you prepare newsgroups for offline reading.

Selecting Message Boards

Next, let's set up a message board for similar treatment. Because there's no central listing of message boards as there is for newsgroups, AOL

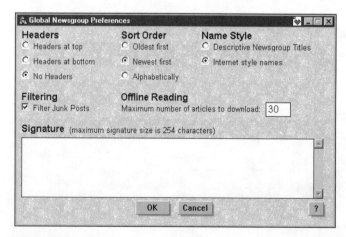

Figure 6.5
Specifying the number of newsgroup messages to be downloaded during a FlashSession.

leaves it to you to select each of your favourite message boards individually for offline reading. Here's how:

1. Click on the Read Offline button you'll see at the bottom of the message board's front screen (Figure 6.6). You'll need to do this for each board you want to be able to read offline.

2. Next, click on the Preferences button on any message board (Figure 6.7). Remember this? We were here in Chapter 4. As with the

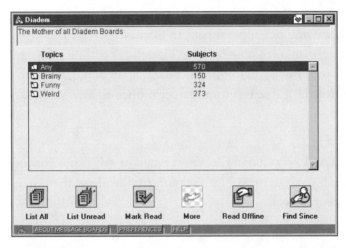

Figure 6.6
By choosing the Read Offline button, you can read and write offline posts to any given message board.

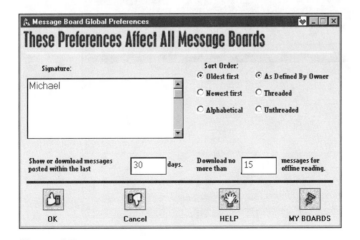

Figure 6.7
Specify the number of message board posts you want to download during each FlashSession.

newsgroups, you can limit the number of messages to be downloaded from a board during any given FlashSession. I choose a modest 15. Until I decide otherwise, my selected message board(s) will be automatically downloaded whenever I fire up a FlashSession.

3. If you want to toggle between online and offline reading for any message boards you've selected, go to Keyword: **MY BOARDS** (Figure 6.8). In the Read My Message Boards screen, highlight the board you want to change and click on the Read Offline button. When you do this, you'll notice that a symbol that looks like a note with a drawing pin appears next to the name of the message board. This means that it's now been deselected for offline reading. If you change your mind, highlight the board again and give another click on the Read Offline button to select it once again.

Selecting Files

You don't have to download files from email or AOL file libraries on the spot. Instead, you can use a FlashSession to download them whenever it's convenient for you.

Recall, if you will, Chapter 5, where I dealt with FileSearch and downloads. At the time, so impulsive was I that I clicked on the Download Now button. Since then, I've mellowed and acquired a taste for delayed

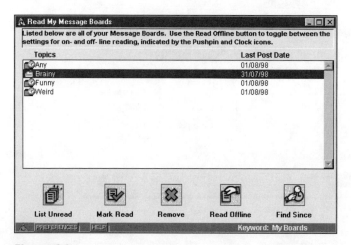

Figure 6.8
At the Read My Message Boards screen, you can choose which boards to read offline.

gratification. So now I click on the Download Later button instead, at which point a message appears telling me that the file has been added to my download list (Figure 6.9). If I click on the Download Manager button, I can see it sitting there, waiting expectantly to join the other files on my hard drive (Figure 6.10). There will be more about the Download Manager in Chapter 10, incidentally.

At this stage, let's sign off and let the file wait. Ignore the "You have added one or more files to your pending queue" message that then appears. You probably wouldn't under normal circumstance, but indulge me for the purpose of this exercise.

Composing Email Offline

As long as you check the Retrieve Unread Mail option in the FlashSession setup screen, AOL will know to grab any waiting email for you. To *send* email during a FlashSession, you simply need to make sure it's in your

Figure 6.9
If you select Download Later, AOL adds the file to your Download Manager.

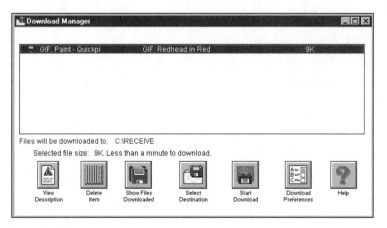

Figure 6.10
The Download Manager is a holding tank for pending files.

Outgoing FlashMail queue and remember to check the Send Outgoing Mail option in your FlashSession setup.

Being able to compose mail offline is a blessing. Using your laptop on an aeroplane with no phone connection? Phone temporarily out of order? Just want to save money on your phone bill while you dot every "i" and cross every "t"? Why, then, writing email offline is for you. To do so, proceed as follows:

1. Just as you would if you were online, select the Toolbar's pencil icon or go to the Email menu and select Compose Email. The Write Email window dutifully appears. When you're offline, however, you'll notice that the Send icon is greyed out. It has to be; you're offline so you can't send anything at the moment. If you move the mouse over it, the cursor won't turn into a hand pointer either.

2. Compose your message exactly as usual. When you're done, click on Send Later. AOL will now store the email on your hard drive in the Outgoing FlashMail queue. It then confirms that the mail is to be processed later and reminds you how to schedule a FlashSession.

Which you'll do. In a minute.

A Mini FlashSession To Send Email

Before we get to the main feature, here's a supporting item.

If all you're doing is sending email, there's little point in setting up a complete FlashSession to do it. Instead, compose each email message offline, as you did in the preceding section. When you click on Send Later, they're saved to the aforementioned Outgoing FlashMail folder. You can see its contents by selecting Read Outgoing FlashMail from the Email menu (Figure 6.11). When you're offline, you'll see two buttons on that window—Edit and Delete—which give you the option of either editing each stored message or zapping it.

To perform this mini FlashSession, sign on as you normally would. Once Joanna has done her stuff, select Read Outgoing FlashMail again. This time, you'll see that the window now features a third button: Send All.

Figure 6.11
Your Outgoing FlashMail folder shows email waiting to be sent.

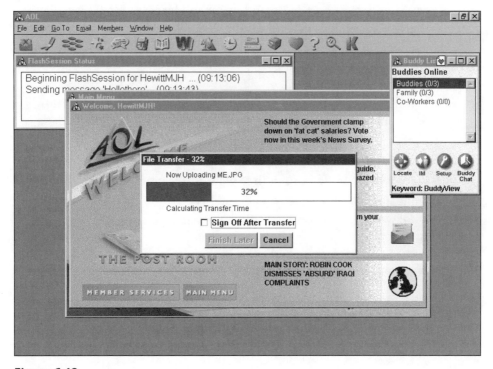

Figure 6.12
If you've attached a file to a message in your Outgoing FlashMail folder, it will be sent
as well.

Clicking on this speeds all the waiting email messages on their way. And,
as you can see in Figure 6.12, if they've got file attachments, they'll be
sent up, too.

Activating A FlashSession

After all of that preamble, this is probably going to be somewhat anticlimactic. Nevertheless, herein is the main feature:

1. I select Activate FlashSession Now from the Email menu. The corresponding screen appears (Figure 6.13).

2. At this point, you can review all your options—exactly what functions you want automated and the screen names you want to use—with the Set Session button. (Keep in mind that your FlashSession settings apply to all screen names on your account.) Or, as I'm about to, you can simply click on the Begin button and let it fly. Note, by the way, that I did not check the Sign Off When Finished box. If, however, you want AOL to sign on, do the business, and then automatically sign off, leave it unchecked.

3. I click on Begin, and the drama unfolds. AOL dials up, signs on, reads email, posts email, downloads pending files, and downloads pending newsgroup and message board messages. And—as we'll see shortly—if there had been any newsgroup and message board messages waiting to be posted, they would have gone up, too. All the while, Joanna says, "Welcome!" and "You've got Post." The status window in the background tells you what's going on (Figure 6.14).

Figure 6.13
The Activate FlashSession Now screen.

Figure 6.14
The FlashSession status window keeps you informed of all the actions that are being performed in the background.

4. That's it. Pat yourself on the back. Everything that needed to be uploaded has been uploaded. Everything that needed to be downloaded has been downloaded.

Great...where has it been downloaded to?

Your Personal Filing Cabinet

Whenever you use a FlashSession to download mail, messages, or files, AOL automatically saves them to your computer's hard disk in an area called the Personal Filing Cabinet. Likewise all messages you send. It's really quite clever because it's able to distinguish, say, a newsgroup message from an email message and deposit each in a separate, dedicated folder where they won't get mixed up.

You'll find your Personal Filing Cabinet under the File menu. (You can also get to it by clicking on the Toolbar's file cabinet icon.) In Figure 6.15, for example, you can see the aftermath of my last FlashSession. The downloaded files are in the Download folder. The incoming mail is in a separate folder from the outgoing, and there are folders for newsgroup and message board messages. Indeed, each individual message board and newsgroup has its own separate folder. In them, there are subfolders, each holding a separate topic.

I'll talk more about how you can configure the Personal Filing Cabinet in Chapter 10. Suffice it to say, at this stage, all you have to do to read your incoming messages or email is double-click on them or highlight them and click on the Open button.

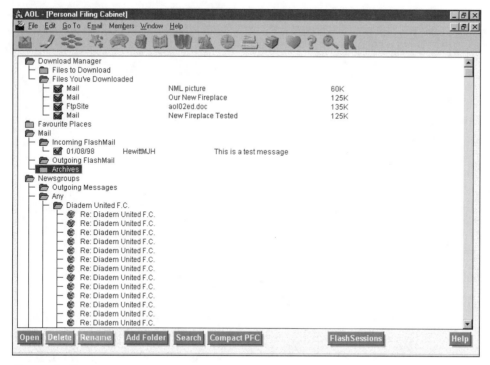

Figure 6.15
A place for everything and everything in its place: the Personal Filing Cabinet.

Reading And Replying To Messages Offline

It's all very well that the downloaded messages are residing in your Personal Filing Cabinet. But how do you then reply to them and post those replies to AOL? No problem.

Reading And Replying To Downloaded Email

Naturally, you'll want to both read and reply to your downloaded email. It would be unforgivably rude, otherwise. There's nothing to it, as you'll see.

Take a look again at Figure 6.15. The incoming email message—"This is a test message"—has been stored to a folder called Incoming FlashMail. Double-click on it to open it and you'll see that it looks like a regular email message (Figure 6.16). The reason for this is quite simple: it *is* a regular email message. To reply, click on the Reply button. The standard Reply screen appears, you type away, and click on Send Later. Presto—

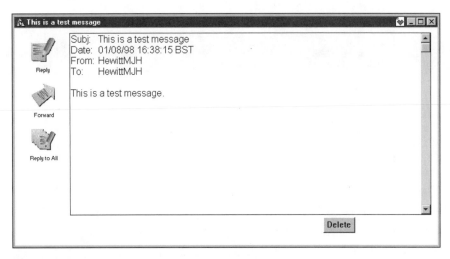

Figure 6.16
A downloaded email is exactly the same as any other email and can be read
and replied to in the same way.

your reply is automatically stored to that now familiar Outgoing FlashMail
folder. There it stays until you activate your next FlashSession.

Reading And Replying To Downloaded Message Board And Newsgroup Messages

When you read them online, message board messages and those in
newsgroups look quite different. But when they're downloaded into your
Personal Filing Cabinet, they look pretty much the same. Indeed, the
Personal Filing Cabinet treats them the same. But don't worry: It won't
accidentally post a newsgroup message into a message board or vice versa.

So, having established that the messages have been downloaded, how do
you reply? Simply double-click on the message to open it in the same
way you double-click on a downloaded email message. As you can see
from Figure 6.17, it looks a bit austere compared to its online counterpart, but it's functional nonetheless.

Note the buttons along the bottom of the screen. You can scroll through
all your downloaded messages, in either direction, by clicking on the
right and left arrow buttons. (Figure 6.17 is the first message on the list,
so there's no left arrow button.) Reply To Group means that your reply

Figure 6.17
Downloaded newsgroup and message board messages lack some of the
aesthetic appeal of their online counterparts but retain the same functionality.

will be posted to the message board or newsgroup itself, where all the
members can read it. Reply To Author creates a private email message
that will only be sent to the person who originally posted the message.
New Message creates a new topic.

When you click on the Reply To Group button, the Reply screen appears.
Having written your reply, you have just one option: Send Later. Clicking on this brings up a message saying that your reply has been stored
and will be sent when you run your next FlashSession.

When you click on the New Message button, a Post New Message
screen appears (Figure 6.18). Here, enter a subject, the text, and then
click on Send Later. Again, you'll receive the standard confirmation that
your message has been saved. Just in case you're curious, all outgoing
messages are saved in your Personal Filing Cabinet in a folder called,
with stunning originality, Outgoing Messages. There they'll stay until
you invoke another FlashSession.

But if all the outgoing messages are stored in the same folder, might they
not get mixed up? Could you, by mistake, end up posting a message on,
say, cold fusion into a country music message board? Nope. AOL knows
exactly what it's doing and where to post what. There is no danger
whatsoever of things going astray.

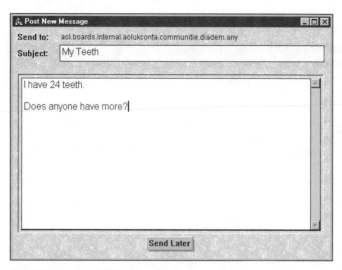

Figure 6.18
The Post New Message screen.

 Don't Forget To Check Your Outbox!

It's entirely possible to compose a book's worth of emails and posts offline, store them for a later FlashSession...and then forget they're there. AOL won't remind you that you've got items in your outbox, so if you *do* work offline, make sure to check your outbox regularly or use scheduled Flash-Sessions (more about that shortly). There's nothing like complaining to someone that they haven't replied to an email you haven't actually sent yet!

Scheduling A FlashSession

As you've seen, one way to initiate a FlashSession is to click on the Activate FlashSession button or select the same from the Email menu. However, there's yet another option. You can *schedule* a FlashSession. This means that you can command AOL to fire up at any given time, sign on, and do the business—in the middle of the night when phone rates are down, while you're out in the garden, or even while you're out of town, if you're so inclined.

Here's how. Simply click on the Schedule FlashSession button on the main FlashSession screen, whereupon the corresponding window appears (Figure 6.19). Having checked the Enable Scheduler box, I have to decide at what time and on what days I want AOL to perform.

Figure 6.19
Scheduling a FlashSession for 4.36 A.M. every weekday.

My weekends are my own, so I select only the working days, Monday through Friday. What time do I want AOL to fire up? Well, 4.36 A.M. is as good a time as any, given that I don't plan to be around at the time. And how often should it fire itself up? AOL gives me a number of options: every half hour, every hour, every two hours, and so forth. But I'm content for it to happen just once a day. So with everything filled in, I click on OK. Henceforth, every Monday through Friday at 4.36 A.M. precisely, AOL will perform a FlashSession—provided, of course, that my computer is turned on, the modem is connected to the phone socket, and the AOL software is open. Scheduled FlashSessions won't happen otherwise.

Those who do schedule FlashSessions in this way wake up (or return home) to find all their email, newsgroup, and message board messages waiting for them in their Download Manager.

Favourite Places

We've seen how you can use Keywords to speed up the way you get around AOL. Just click on the Toolbar's big K (or use Ctrl+K), enter the Keyword you want, and you're taken to your desired area in a second or two. It's much faster than having to plough through a series of menus.

There is, however, an even faster way.

Once you've found your Favourite Places—in AOL or on the Web— returning to visit them again is easy. AOL's Favourite Places feature lets you create a customised list of links to your favourite online areas or Web sites. When you find an area online you know you'll want to see again, click on the heart icon on its title bar. When you do so, AOL will ask "Add this window to your Favourite Places?" Click on Yes and the deed is done. The area will be added to your list.

And where's your list? Click on the big heart icon on the Toolbar to see it (Figure 6.20). Simply double-click on the place you want to visit and you're there. Notice, incidentally, that you can create folders to organise your Favourite Places list. Several of your Favourite Places, for example, might be travel-related. Others could be entertainment links. If so, create a different folder for each. It helps keep your list clutter free and makes finding the place you want to go that much easier. I'll tell you how to do this in Chapter 10.

Here are some final points on Favourite Places. In addition to being useful permanent markers for your preferred areas, they can also be good temporary ones, too. Remember in Chapter 4 when I placed a message in Diadem and wanted to know if it had been read and if anyone had

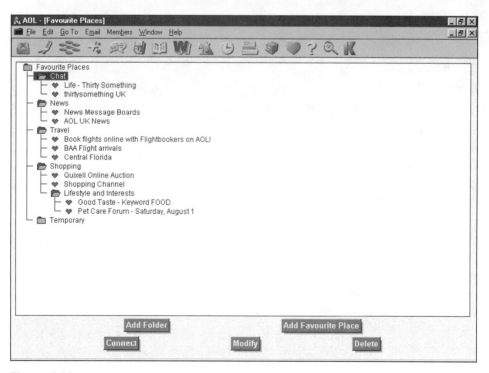

Figure 6.20
Some of my Favourite Places on AOL. Just double-click and you're there.

replied to it? There were two ways to find out. The first was to go to Keyword: **DIADEM**, seek out the Any topic, and scroll down until I located my message.

A long process, I'm sure you'll agree. With a bit of planning, however, I could have avoided all this. How? Simply by clicking on my message's heart icon when I posted it. This would list it in my Favourite Places, thereby making it just a mouse click away (Figure 6.21).

If you *really* prize one of your Favourite Places, why not share your discovery with other AOL members? Email them and tell them about it. In fact, you can do more than that. You can actually insert your selected Favourite Place into your email message simply by highlighting the Favourite Place in your list and then dragging it into the email. Presto— it becomes a hyperlink (Figure 6.22). When your recipient clicks on the highlighted text, provided he's online, he'll be transported there directly. If he isn't signed on, AOL will ask him if he wants to be.

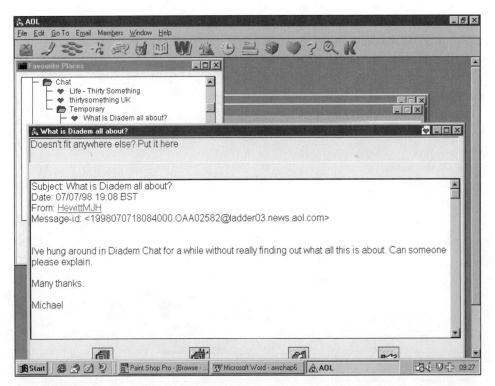

Figure 6.21
Add specific message board messages to your Favourite Places list to speed things up.

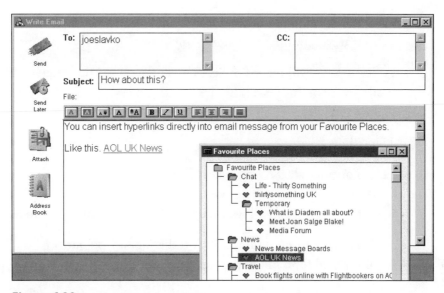

Figure 6.22
Favourite Places can be inserted into email messages. Your recipient simply clicks on the highlighted text to get there.

You can also drag Favourite Places into Instant Messages. And not to wax too rhapsodic on the topic, but a place doesn't have to be one of your Favourite Places to share it via email or Instant Message. You can simply drag the heart straight off the window of the place you want to share and deposit it into the message text.

Logging

Logging is a convenient way to save on phone bills and online time and easily save articles or conversations that interest you. The Log Manager lets you transfer online text to a file you can read or print when you're offline. You can transfer text from:

▲ News or reference articles, or the text (not graphics) of any AOL page you read online

▲ Message board posts

▲ Instant Message conversations

▲ Chat rooms and auditoriums

A Chat log will record the chat text of all rooms you enter in the course of your travels online—including any private rooms you create or enter.

A Session log will record the contents of every AOL screen you read while you're online—whether it's email, a message board, or a page from a news story.

Here's how it's done:

1. To open or start a Log, select Log Manager from the File menu. You're presented with a window that comprises an upper half for Chat logging and a lower half for Session logging (Figure 6.23).

2. To open a Logging file, click on the Open Log button. You'll then be prompted for a file name and a location. The default is Session.

3. Choose the Session log name and click on OK. If you're logging your session and want to log Instant Messages as well (more about Instant Messages in Chapter 8), click the box next to Log Instant Messages. Logging of your online session is now enabled. From now on, the text of every screen you see will be logged, so go ahead and check out all the areas that you want to read later offline.

TIP   *Logging = Speed*

You don't have to read the entire page or message—which is the beauty of logging. As soon as it's onscreen, the log will record all of it, so you can go right on to the next area you want to log.

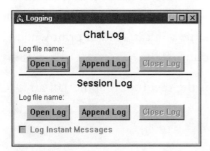

Figure 6.23
The Logging window.

4. Once you're done, go to the File menu again, select Log Manager, and click on the Close Log button. Your log is now saved to your hard disk so you can read it another time. Closing the log before signing off will ensure that you don't lose it.

5. Once you're offline, you can access your log at any time via the Open option in the File menu. If the log file is larger than 32K, AOL won't be able to open it, but you can use your word processor to do so. In Figure 6.24, for example, I've opened my log file using Word for Windows.

By the way, you don't have to record *everything* you open. At any time during a session, you can go to Log Manager and choose Close Log. This disables logging and you can do something else without it. But if you want to resume logging a few minutes later, choose Log Manager again, but this time, click on Append Log. AOL will prompt you for a file name. Choose the one you want to resume using. All subsequent items will be added to the original log.

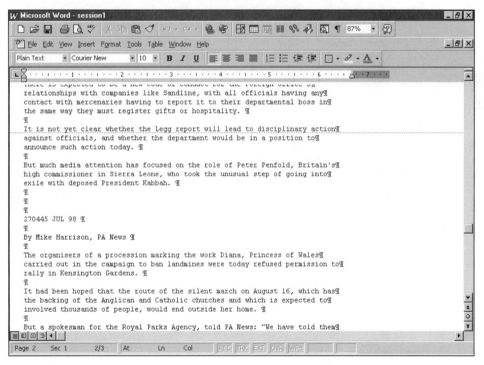

Figure 6.24
Reading my log file in Word for Windows.

News Profiles

Session logging is one way to reduce the time you spend online reading news. News Profiles is another. Here, AOL becomes your own personalised "clipping service." What News Profiles actually does is to deliver news stories directly to you as email. You specify beforehand exactly what subjects you want to read about. AOL then scours the online newsfeeds and newspapers for stories containing those subjects and emails them to you as they come in off the wire.

As this book was being written, the U.K. version of News Profiles was still under development, so I'll look briefly at the U.S. version. Although our homegrown one *should* work in much the same way, don't take what follows as being necessarily written in stone:

1. I go to Keyword: **NEWS PROFILES** and the News Profiles Step 1 screen appears (Figure 6.25). By default, it will be called News Profile 1, and the number of stories that will be delivered to me each day is set at 10. The maximum number is 50. For the sake of this experiment, I decide I can live with the default, and so I click on Next.

2. I tell AOL to seek out articles containing either the words "Steve" or "Ballmer" (Figure 6.26). Some chap called Ballmer is a big cheese at Microsoft. I'm not entirely sure of his first name, however, hence the either/or. And I click on Next again.

3. Next, I say I want AOL to source articles that *must* contain the term "Windows 98" (Figure 6.27). This is because Ballmer was, I believe, instrumental in its development.

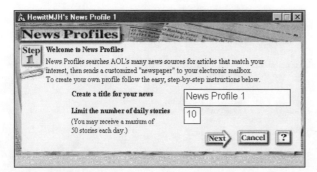

Figure 6.25
News Profiles allow you to create a customised online clipping service.

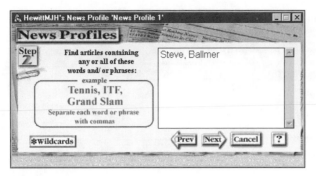

Figure 6.26
The article should contain either "Steve" or "Ballmer."

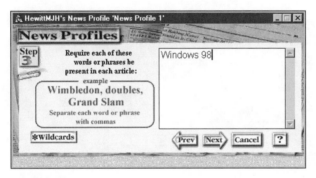

Figure 6.27
The article *must* contain the term "Windows 98."

4. Next step: I don't want any articles that contain "Bill Gates". So I'll accept articles containing "Steve" or "Ballmer" and "Windows 98," but reject those containing "Bill Gates."

5. Which news wires do I want AOL to search in order to find these articles? (Figure 6.28) I highlight the desired news wires in the left-hand window and click on Add to transfer them to the window on the right.

6. Finally, AOL summarises the choices I've made, the search terms I've input, and so on (Figure 6.29). To have the system go away and start collecting features, I click on Done. Thereafter, AOL will scan the news for my preferred stories and deliver them to me.

The more search terms you use, the more accurate your "hits" are. You can also use a form of Boolean logic, which is detailed in the step-by-step

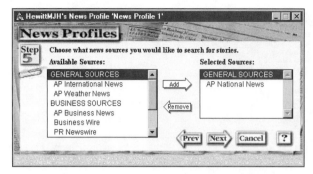

Figure 6.28
Specifying the news wires that AOL should search in order to find my articles.

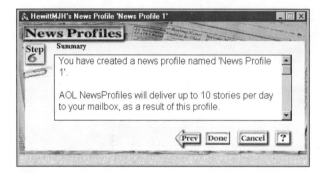

Figure 6.29
Now News Profiles is set to automatically create a personalised news-delivery service for me.

instructions if you click on *Wildcards. However, as this product is still very much in beta, I don't at this stage propose going into any detail, just in case—as it quite probably will—the whole thing turns out very differently when it eventually goes live.

The Go To Menu

An oft-overlooked feature of AOL, Go To, lets you whiz around the service by assigning navigation commands to Ctrl+key combinations. You'll find them under the Go To menu (Figure 6.30). Selections 1 through 8 come preset by AOL so you can start using them straightaway. For instance, Ctrl+4 will take you to Chat and Ctrl+6 will take you to Weather. However, you can customise the keys yourself and change them to go to any AOL Keyword you like. Just remember to click on Save Changes if you do so.

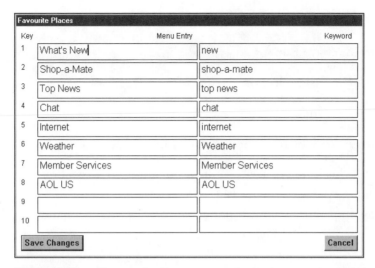

Figure 6.30
The Go To menu allows you to assign navigation functions to your keyboard.

"Hot Key" Combinations

Hot keys give you yet another way to turbo-charge AOL. The following Ctrl+key combinations bypass the menus and allow you to perform common functions with just a couple of keystrokes:

▲ *Ctrl+A*—Select All

▲ *Ctrl+C*—Copy Selection

▲ *Ctrl+E*—Write Email

▲ *Ctrl+F*—Find

▲ *Ctrl+G*—Get A Member's Profile

▲ *Ctrl+I*—Instant Message

▲ *Ctrl+K*—Keyword

▲ *Ctrl+L*—Locate A Member Online

▲ *Ctrl+N*—New File

▲ *Ctrl+O*—Open File

▲ *Ctrl+P*—Print

▲ *Ctrl+R*—Read Email

▲ *Ctrl+S*—Save File

▲ *Ctrl+V*—Paste selection

▲ *Ctrl+Z*—Undo

▲ *Ctrl+Enter*—Send Current Email/Instant Message

With all this time I'm saving online, I'm going to take a breather. Next up is an overview of AOL's 14 Channels. Likely as not, you'll have already dipped in by now. If not, what follows will be a handy preview.

Chapter 7

AOL's Channels

We've now reached the halfway stage. This is the point at which we pause awhile and maybe grab an ice cream and an interval drink. And while doing so, let's take a brief look at AOL's Channels. Each is devoted to specific activities or areas of interest. We've already perused a few of them *en passant*, but here's an opportunity to sit back and review, in a bit more detail, what each of them does. Of course, if you want to find out properly what they all do and what's in each, sign on to AOL. That's what it's there for. This is just a taster.

News & Weather

AOL's online News Channel combines the up-to-the-minute immediacy of television and radio news with the read-it-whenever-you-please convenience of a newspaper (Figure 7.1). There's a whole newsagent's worth out there, and more.

The sheer volume of material available is quite impressive. Articles from leading news providers—such as the Press Association, Reuters, and (exclusively to AOL) Out There News (Keyword: **OUT THERE NEWS**)—are combined with carefully researched Web resources and remarkable pictures. You can also use News Profiles to have the news *you* want delivered direct to you as email. (For more on this, refer back to Chapter 6.)

The Seven Days area offers detailed analyses of the week's major stories, rather like the weekend supplement of a Sunday newspaper. AOL also offers specialised sections on Finance (business news and updates from

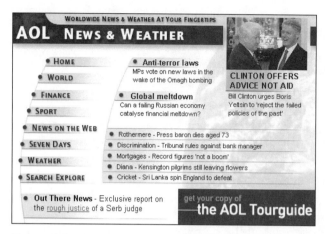

Figure 7.1
AOL's News Channel.

the City) and Sport (everything from athletics to windsurfing, with a live football scoreboard) that add depth as well as breadth to the coverage.

AOL members themselves can become part of the News Channel by joining twice-weekly online debates, responding to surveys, and voicing their views on the News message boards. Use Keyword: **NEWS TICKER** and all the late-breaking stories will automatically scroll across the top of your screen wherever you happen to be in AOL or the Internet—a must for news junkies.

And on to Weather. Is it a day for T-shirts or raincoats? Find out from the Met men at AOL's Weather service. The first thing you'll see when you click on the Weather button is a map of the U.K. with gently scudding clouds and, depending on the season, dazzling little suns. If you want forecasts for this evening, tomorrow, and tomorrow evening click on the appropriate buttons. You can also get forecasts for wind speed and direction, and sea conditions. And if you want the weather closer to home? No problem; just click on the weather symbol that's floating over (or is nearest to) your area and a local forecast will appear.

But maybe you're travelling and would like to know how things are faring further afield. If so, select the Europe button and a map of Europe appears with the major cities listed. If you require more detail still, try out the various Web links. From here, you can get U.S. and world weather, hurricane reports, satellite photographs, travel weather, and snow conditions in the major ski resorts. In fact, if you hunt around for long enough and in the right places, you can probably get every weird and wonderful meteorological fact known to man. Good hunting!

Travel

The AOL Travel Channel gives you all the information you need to plan a trip, whether it's a holiday in the Far East or simply a local train journey (Figure 7.2). Most important, AOL's Travel team works tirelessly to bring you the best deals—many of them exclusive to AOL members. Make sure you check the Travel Channel's Bargains page before you go anywhere. You can even book flights and hotels online, just to make certain you catch that hot deal.

If you're undecided as to where to go, Travel can supply you with plenty of ideas. Browse through UK Guide and World Guide, for example, for extensive destination information. There's also a Special Interests section for those of you with exacting requirements. AOL's partners, Lonely Planet (Keyword: **LP**) and Thomas Cook (Keyword: **THOMAS COOK**), keep you up-to-date on the top places to visit.

The Timetables section gives you all the practical travel information you might need and has a link to the Travel Channel's handy Resource

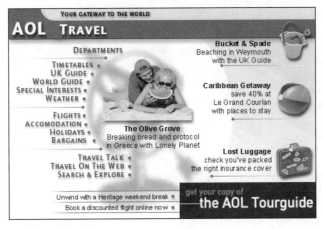

Figure 7.2
AOL's Travel Channel can help make your mind up about where to go.

Centre. If it's quick access to direct information you need, AOL makes it easy for you by providing separate sections called Accommodation, Flights, and Holidays. However, if you just want to sit at home and share your travel experiences with others, make sure you visit AOL Traveller. Here, you'll find plenty of like-minded people to chat with and swap messages with. It's also the place to find the best travel writing and even to contribute your own.

Computing

On the Computing Channel, you'll find hundreds of computer- and software-related areas (Figure 7.3). Whether you're a computing tyro who doesn't know a mouse from a rat or a PC guru who likes nothing better than to tinker with his CONFIG.SYS and WIN.INI files, there's something to suit you.

Do you know how to make the most of your computer? The Computing Forums bring you in-depth knowledge about your computer and its software. AOL also has a section aimed at beginners, featuring advice on everything from how a mouse works to using word processors and other software. If you want to upgrade your system, you'll find advice and step-by-step instructions in the Upgrading Forum (Keyword: **UPPC**). If your PC is too clapped out to be upgraded, check out AOL's buying advice

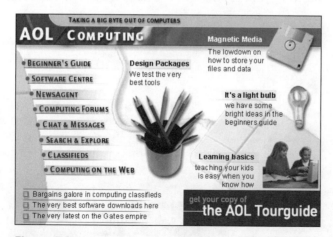

Figure 7.3
For all you wanted to know about computers, and things you didn't dare ask, check out AOL's Computing Channel.

areas: the Buying Forum (Keyword: **BUYING COMPUTERS**), PC Finder (Keyword: **PCFINDER**), and AOL's own classified ads.

Should you be looking for a particular company, go to Keyword: **COMPANY FORUMS** to see if they run an area on AOL to help you. If they don't, find their address in the Computing Directory (Keyword: **COMPUTING DIRECTORY**) or find their Web site in Computing Web (Keyword: **COMPUTING WEB**), which also selects the best sites on everything from the history of computing to online comics and the best Computing Web sites every week.

AOL's Computing Channel also brings you the latest computing news every day, along with reviews of the latest hardware, software, and gadgets, and a host of competitions. Computing Diary (Keyword: **COMPUTING DIARY**) lists computer shows, exhibitions, and fairs and reports back on the best. Each week, AOL's Software Centre offers a selection of what AOL and its members reckon to be the pick of the best files, both on AOL and the Web, ready for downloading. Also check out *Practical PC*, *MacFormat*, and the ZD magazines for more news, reviews, and software.

Finance

The Finance Channel is where you can find out all about money matters—yours and everyone else's (Figure 7.4). It's a bit like having an independent financial adviser in your home, except you don't have to make it a cup of coffee or feel pressured into signing on for a pension scheme.

So if you've got a little nest egg tucked away somewhere and would like to know whether a Building Society or PEP would be the best place for it, here's where to get the lowdown. AOL's Finance Channel has been designed to answer many of the questions that personal-finance issues raise. It offers in-depth analysis and editorial information on investments, mortgages, and pensions, including the latest calculators, rates, and glossaries of terms. Members can even ask the experts for advice through the message boards and Chat areas.

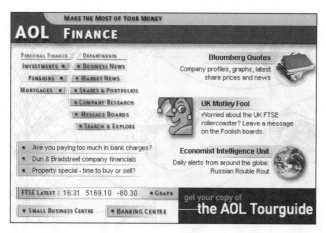

Figure 7.4
Whether you have an offshore account or just a piggy bank, Finance is the place to come for advice on what to do with it.

It could be that your plans are a bit more ambitious—maybe you're thinking of making a hostile takeover bid for Glaxo. No problem. The Finance Channel also carries the latest in market and business news from companies such as *The Economist* (Keyword: **EIU**) and Reuters. Company research tools, such as those from Dun & Bradstreet (Keyword: **D AND B**) and Bloomberg (Keyword: **BLOOMBERG**), provide the very best in company information. There's also a U.K. company database that can be searched by business type, turnover, and number of employees. And for those thinking of investing further afield, Dun & Bradstreet offers country profiles with company statistics and business education information.

Members can check the latest company share values, track their own selected stocks using the portfolio service, and see the lighter side of investing through the Motley Fool (Keyword: **FOOL UK**). In addition, there is a small business area and special links to online banking, as well as links to stock exchanges worldwide and a permanent FTSE update on the main Finance screen.

Learning

AOL's Learning Channel has something to teach everyone, whether school-based or just for general interest. For the younger audience, you'll find interactive tasks and puzzles that enable children to become more familiar and confident with the Web. For primary and secondary school children, Homework Help (Keyword: **HOMEWORK HELP**) provides online teachers to help with schoolwork and questions. They don't simply provide the answers; they offer guidance and pointers, too (Figure 7.5).

AOL's National Curriculum content and downloadable worksheets are provided for both teachers and pupils, building a mutually beneficial education area. Message boards complete the community, allowing visitors to post their own queries and respond to others. The U.K. Schools (Keyword: **UK SCHOOLS**) area houses school Web sites, allowing you to see what projects other schools are setting up online.

For more in-depth research and general interest, visit *Hutchinson's Encyclopaedia and Almanac* (Keyword: **HUTCHINSON**) for information on a range of subjects, from anatomy to botany and from English literature to famous historical figures and inventions. Another great partner on the Channel is the *New Oxford Dictionary of English* (Keyword: **OXFORD DICTIONARY**). Not only will this improve your spelling, it will also broaden your vocabulary (watch for the Word of the Day) *and* your mind (read Quote of the Day)!

The Careers area (Keyword: **CAREERS**) provides advice on employment as well as tips for further education. Here, too, you'll find the latest career news and lots of jobs on offer.

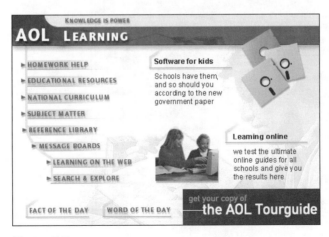

Figure 7.5
Expand your mind in AOL's Learning Channel.

Shopping

Now you can shop till you drop, and beyond, with AOL's Shopping Channel (Figure 7.6). Gifts, food, books, music? Whip out your credit card and buy. I'll be devoting all of Chapter 9 to Shopping, so if you can't wait, turn to that chapter now.

Internet

Surfing the Internet has become an integral part of the AOL members' online experience, so the Internet Channel is here to act as "your guide to the hottest destination in the world." The whole purpose of the Channel, as I mentioned in Chapter 3, is to streamline and improve your time on the Web (Figure 7.7).

The Channel is broken down into five sections:

▲ *What Is It*—A guide for people new to the Web

▲ *Where To Go*—Recommended Web destinations

▲ *Who To Talk To*—Where you can locate others on the Internet who share your interests

▲ *How To Build*—Learn how to build your own Web content

Figure 7.6
Purchase from the comfort of your armchair with AOL's new Shopping Channel.

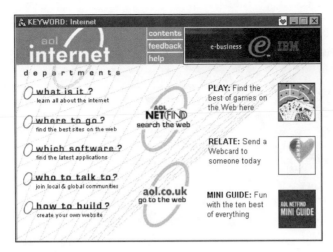

Figure 7.7
AOL's Internet Channel.

▲ *Which Software*—Download programs to improve your surfing and
   Web building

The Channel also provides direct access to AOL U.K.'s home on the
Internet, **http://www.aol.co.uk**, and to AOL NetFind™, a powerful
Internet searching tool. Put it all together and you have a launching pad
that will take you anywhere you want to go on the Web.

Local Life

As the name suggests, the Local Life Channel deals with what's going
on in your area, whether your area is John O'Groats or Land's End or
Belfast. To access your own particular piece of real estate, click on the
schematic map (Figure 7.8). If you're not sure where you are—and it's
something that can occasionally happen to the best of us—there's a link
at the bottom of the screen for you to click. Thereupon, AOL will
attempt to solve your conundrum.

Essentially, Local Life is AOL's equivalent of a tour guide, restaurant and
pub guide, A to Z, hotel guide, events listings, film guide, gazetteer,
personal columns, classified ad section, and general talking-shop, all
rolled into one. It's what a Baedeker's would probably aspire to be if it
could become interactive and offer Web access, Chat, and message boards.

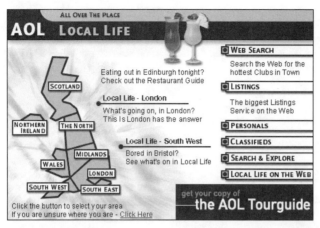

Figure 7.8
AOL's Local Life Channel. Click on your area to find out what's happening.

Aptly, then, Local Life's slogan is "All over the place." This is the Channel for resources and information spanning the length and breadth of the country. Whether you're looking for a local business, wanting ideas for days out, searching for a romance or friendship in your area, or just want to talk with people from a particular part of the U.K., Local Life strives to deliver. To help you, Local Life is structured into regions and cities, each with its own supportive and knowledgeable host and dedicated information. Themes such as Leisure and News and Media within each Local Life area organise resources into accessible sections. These themes are also echoed in the Web Search facility, which enables you to search quickly and effectively for services and businesses. Local Life also offers entertainment listings for Glasgow and Edinburgh provided by The List. The *Evening Standard*'s This Is London guide gives you news, reviews, guides, and entertainment listings in the capital.

As part of the Channel's strategy to "go local," Local Life will present AOL's very own classifieds section where the members will be able to buy or sell anything from a car to a new motherboard. The Channel will also present comprehensive entertainment listings from around the country, enabling members to find out what's on anywhere in the U.K., be it the *Eastenders* omnibus or an Oasis gig.

Entertainment

Fancy a night out at the cinema or theatre? A visit to an art gallery, perchance? Perhaps you would rather have a night in with a few cans of lager while watching television or listening to the latest Oasis or Blur album. Whatever your entertainment predilections, AOL's Entertainment Channel is here to help you get the most out of them (Figure 7.9). Here, you'll find the Music, Film, Arts, Television, Hype, and Cult sections and the Blah Blah Blah community forum.

In the Music section, you can do an Alan Freeman and run through the official chart listings, albums, and singles (Keyword: **CHARTS**). You'll also find music sites, NME News, a classical guide, jazz, world music, and more. And should you want to talk to fellow pop-pickers about what's cool, there's Music Chat. In the Competition area, you can win the latest album from the latest group of the moment. And for those who want to try before they buy, music tracks can be downloaded and played on your PC. You should also check out Music Boulevard if you *are* intending to buy. Many CDs can be purchased here for substantially less than you would pay in the shops.

Entertainment also contains links to theatre and film areas. Try the massive Internet Movie Database, for example (Keyword: **IMDB**). Enter the name of a film, or its star, and within a few seconds you can read

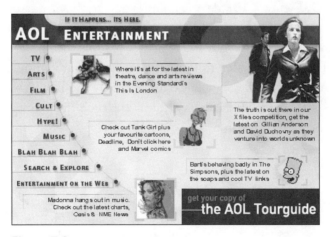

Figure 7.9
The whole world of entertainment in AOL's Entertainment Channel.

reviews, download pictures, and get background information. This Is London and the Yellow Pages provide theatre and film listings. For the lowdown on the background behind the making of upcoming films, and for insider gossip, try the infamous Ain't It Cool site.

In Hype, you'll find AOL shooting from the hip with the latest gossip and entertainment stories, featuring message board threads on what's hot, what's not, and who's around. Cult will have you dallying with a concoction of weird and wonderful from The Strip, featuring Marvel and DC Comics, the infamous *Deadline*, featuring Tank Girl, and even the legendary *2000AD*, the 451 Sci Fi forum, and more. Last, but not least, there's Blah Blah Blah, AOL's entertainment community area, which picks out themes from various chat rooms and message boards.

If your idea of entertainment is a sofa, a six-pack, and a television, On The Box contains listings for all television and satellite channels (Keyword: **ON THE BOX**). It's a sort of interactive *Radio Times*, except with downloads, more features, and links to hundreds of other television-related areas for the latest news on what's happening in the televisual world. Talk about TV events and programmes with fellow AOL members in the dedicated Chat sections or on the message boards. Inside Soap (Keyword: **INSIDE SOAP**) delivers all the latest soap gossip.

And here's one final word on an exciting new area: AOL Radio (Keyword: **RADIO**, Figure 7.10). As the name suggests, this is a radio station. But instead of being broadcast over the airwaves, it comes over the phone line directly into your PC courtesy of sophisticated *streaming* technology. That's right: listen to the radio through your computer. At press time, the service is being beta-tested and only the BBC World Service and sports news are available. But by the time this book appears, there should be a lot more on offer.

AOL Today

When this book was being written, AOL Today wasn't quite up and running. However, I'm told that when it is, this Channel will provide "a friendly, authoritative daily digest of the best AOL content in a way that appeals to a broad range of AOL members and has relevance to their daily lives."

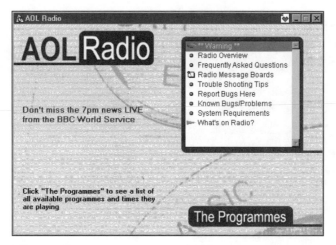

Figure 7.10
Listen to the radio through your PC with AOL Radio.

To this end, the AOL Today team will choose the best of what's happening on any one day on AOL to offer a stepping stone to the best content available. The Channel will also contain daily essentials, including stock quotes, stars, weather, and so forth, much as you would find in your daily newspaper.

Sport

AOL's Sport Channel combines the comprehensive, detailed sort of sports coverage you'll find in a newspaper but with the immediacy of television (Figure 7.11). The UK Sport Channel covers everything from the major sports to the esoteric. So you'll find golf, tennis, rugby, athletics, bowls—more or less everything. Indeed, for those constantly having sand kicked in their face, there's even bodybuilding.

For those whose bodies are already built, the Rugby Club (Keyword: **RUGBY CLUB**) might be worth a look. It contains the latest Rugby Union news, both from the U.K. and worldwide. In the Results Service, you'll find league tables, a guide to forthcoming fixtures, and of course, up-to-the-minute results. If you prefer your balls round, AOL Football (Keyword: **FOOTBALL**) will be more your scene. It's AOL's premier soccer service, providing in-depth news and information on every league, club, and player in the English and Scottish Leagues. It, too, contains

Figure 7.11
AOL's Sport Channel covers every sport you've ever heard of, and more besides.

guides to forthcoming fixtures, together with results and league tables. The service also features a Live section for coverage of all the top matches and the latest score updates, so you can sit by your PC with your Pools coupon to see if your luck is in.

With strawberries and cream at the ready, we move on to tennis (Keyword: **TENNIS**). This area serves as the home of all tennis news, such as Wimbledon, the Davis Cup, and the U.S. Open. The AOL Golf area (Keyword: **GOLF**) has all the latest golfing news from the U.K. and around the world. There's information and results on current tournaments, and you can find profiles of leading players, together with advice from them on how to improve your game. For an even slower-paced sport, take a look at AOL's online version of the *Cricketer*, the world's best-selling cricket magazine (Keyword: **CRICKETER**). Here you'll find a regularly updated news area, superbly written features, and a scoreboard service.

And now to high-octane sport. Autosport (Keyword: **AUTOSPORT**) is the site for all petrolheads. This is the online version of the world's leading motorsport magazine, and it covers news and information on all aspects of motorsport, including Formula 1, Rally, Indy, and British Touring Car racing. In addition to guides to all the tracks in the world, you'll find detailed profiles of teams and their drivers, the usual Web links, and race reports and results. The Autosport Photo Gallery contains hundreds of racing-related graphics files featuring all the leading drivers and their cars, past and present. And for the very latest on what's happening, check out Autosport News.

Elsewhere in the Sport Channel is Re:Play, which houses trivia quizzes on a range of sports. Also in this area is a section called The Week In Pictures, featuring the previous week's very best sports pictures and stories, courtesy of Allsport. And check out the Talk Time Chat schedule to find out about hosted sport Chats, a daily results and fixtures service, and the chance to win great prizes.

Games

For many people, games are their PC's raison d'être. If you're one of them, or someone in your family is, then you'll appreciate AOL's Games Channel (Figure 7.12). If you're into games of any description—they don't have to be computer games; chess and card players, amongst others, are welcome, too—then there'll be something here for you. The Games Channel keeps you up-to-date on everything that's going on in the games world. Its five sub-Channels deal with online games and with games on the PC, PlayStation, Nintendo 64, and Mac.

To get up-to-the-minute details (or up-to-the-day, anyway) of what's going on in the world of games in general, you should check out Game-Spot News (Keyword: **GAMESPOT**). In addition, take a look at *Play*

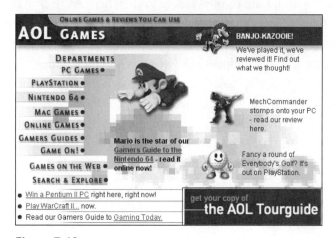

Figure 7.12
AOL's Games Channel. If you can't find what you want in here, it probably doesn't exist.

Magazine, Powerstation, 64 Solutions, and *64 Magazine*. It might also be a good idea to subscribe to The Wire. This is the Games Channel weekly newsletter, which is delivered to you as email (and archived on the Channel itself). It contains all the latest news, reviews, previews, gossip, hints and tips, and cheats.

The Game On! section (Keyword: **GAME ON**) gives you access to some very lively message boards. Swap strategies with other players. Share your discomfiture with them over having been slain by a dwarf in the Enchanted Forest. Have a good gripe (or gloat) about the latest *Star Trek* video game. Experienced game-players and novices alike will get a lot out of the discussions and the cheats and tips here. For those who need to talk games on an even broader scale, click on the Game On! newsgroups icon. Out of the thousands of newsgroups that are out there, AOL has managed to collect together in one place all of those that deal with games.

For realtime discussion of games, check out the UK Games Chat room. Here you can exchange ratings with other game-players and vouch for the latest offerings from the makers—occasionally you'll drop in and find quite a stimulating discussion going on when, for example, someone discovers a good cheat or a source of bargain software. And there are regularly hosted chats based around set themes, such as strategy games, Quake night, PSX hints, and so forth.

And you can go from here to the Games Web, where AOL brings together games sites from all over the Internet and puts them into separate genres. In this way, AOL members can get what they want straight away, and very easily. The sections include 3D Action, Console Games, Games Companies, Web Games, Role-Playing Games, Cheats and Tips, and Downloads. Finally, don't miss Gamers' Guides. Published twice monthly, they carry features on every subject, from the very basic to the advanced theories of gaming. Each Guide will have plenty of Web links to let you explore for yourself. Reviews, genre guides, walk-throughs, speculative articles—you name it, it will be there.

Chat

The Chat Channel welcomes people of all interests, ages, and beliefs to join one of the Chat rooms (Figure 7.13). You can choose from amongst a

Figure 7.13
AOL Chat allows you to have realtime conversations with fellow AOL members.

wide range of topics, and they all offer simple and easy access through easy-to-navigate screens. The Chat Rooms button opens the door to all the Chat rooms you could possibly use, including U.S., Canadian, Australian, French, and German. The Chat rooms are listed by name or by interest.

Chat also offers a timetable of hosted chats and events for the coming week. *Hosted* means that AOL's online volunteers (or in some cases, a representative from the content provider) is there to moderate the conversation and help any newcomers along. There will be a lot more about Chat in the next chapter.

Lifestyles

Look upon Lifestyles as a bit like the equivalent of the "lifestyle" section in W.H. Smith, except you don't have to elbow your way through dozens of people dawdling in front of the computer and games magazines to get to it. The Lifestyles Channel offers like-minded AOL members the chance to interact with each other and gain easy access to relevant and useful information (Figure 7.14). Long-standing members used to individual community areas such as The Outer Edge, Utopia, The Love Shack, Mystic Gardens, and professional forums will now find those areas contained within five generalised categories: Teenagers, Gay & Lesbian, Love & Romance, Spirituality & Beliefs, and Work. AOL plans

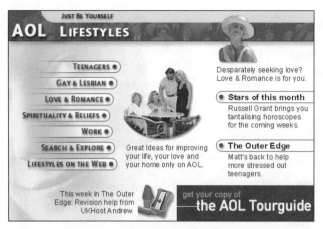

Figure 7.14
AOL's Lifestyles Channel, for yours and everyone else's lifestyle.

to continually develop community areas to widen the scope of the Channel. Although it's not quite ready yet, the key content for the five new categories should, I'm informed, be as follows:

▲ *Teenagers*—In addition to housing the magazine-style Outer Edge and Stressed Out (Keyword: **OUTER EDGE** and **STRESSED OUT**, respectively), Teenagers will be divided into three topics: People, Looks & Life, and Fun.

▲ *Gay & Lesbian*—Welcomes everyone, be they gay, bi, straight, or just curious (as long as they're courteous). Its features include the magazine-style Utopia area, Youth, the Transgender Forum, and Resources.

▲ *Love & Romance*—Includes the ever-popular Love Shack (for Personals, Messages, and Chat), AOL Cards (to send an electronic greeting to those you love), and for a more tangible expression of your devotion, Send A Gift.

▲ *Spirituality & Beliefs*—Expands from the traditionally strong Astrology & Esoterica areas (Mystic Gardens and Russell Grant, to name but two). Spirituality & Beliefs will include several religious forums. Christianity, Judaism, Islam, Hinduism, and a number of other religions will have their own space for discussion together with both AOL and Web resources.

▲ *Work*—Still very much at the "acorn" stage at the time of this writing. However, with time it should grow into an indispensable set of information and resources for all professionals. The Channel will be divided into the following categories: Business, Medical, Legal, Media, and Education. Each will contain a Chat room, message boards, and both AOL and Web resources.

Interests

What's yours? Camping? White-water canoeing? Photography? Whatever it is, you're sure to find it here, either on AOL itself or via the extensive Web links (Figure 7.15). Interests is about what people choose to do in their spare time, away from the pressures of work. As such, it's concerned with people's passions and obsessions, the things that people do to give their life meaning. It's also a place to meet like-minded people. Although many of the Interests covered are solitary activities, they have strong community aspects because people want to share their interests with others.

Here are a few of the areas in Interests:

▲ *Drive*—For the motoring enthusiast, this area covers both cars and motorbikes. Car combines content, news from the Car Showroom, a guide to all the manufacturers and their Web sites, and car classifieds.

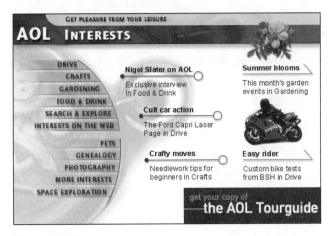

Figure 7.15
AOL's Interests Channel should provide you with much of interest.

Check out the thriving Classic Car community and the soon-to-be-launched car maintenance forum. You can even read online versions of *What Car* and *Autosport*. For those more comfortable on two wheels, Bike contains information on everything from good buys to AOL members' own bikes. *Back Street Heroes* is aimed at the true biker community, and well-known bike journalist Kevin Ash runs Complete Bike. You can ask the experts for advice or dish it out yourself in the message boards and chat rooms. Get all the latest industry news and read the monthly road tests to see which bike you should be spending your time drooling over. If mechanical failure rather than drooling is your problem, ask AOL's bike experts in the forums and they'll help you get that bike back on the road.

▲ *Food & Drink*—If this is what you hunger for, check out Good Taste. Here you'll find everything to delight the food fan, whether it be DIY or someone else's handiwork. Food & Drink includes a recipe archive, regional British foods, wine columns, restaurant guides, and coverage of the main food shows in the U.K. It also gives you the chance to ask the experts or send in your own recipes. And, of course, there are the usual message boards and Chat rooms. The hugely successful This Is London site provides a great restaurant guide and recipe of the day.

▲ *Gardening*—This popular community is presided over by two experienced landscape gardeners who manage Chats, write monthly columns, and answer queries on the message boards. There are plans afoot to use a gardening columnist and to develop partnerships.

▲ *Crafts*—Covers everything from needlework to quilting. The community area is managed by AOL's very own Crafty Owl (which comes from an interest in owl collecting) and has a dedicated following. With links to Hobbies Central, just about all your crafting needs are covered.

Also included in the Interests Channel are extensive links to U.S. areas, which include Genealogy, Pets, Photography, and Space Exploration. A Health & Fitness area is currently under development, containing sections for men and women.

Kids

The Kids Channel provides youngsters with an excellent introduction to computers and the online world (Figure 7.16). It offers educational material, games, entertainment, Kids' Chat, Kids' Internet, Kids' Message Boards, and a lot more—all aimed at a 6-to-13 age group and carefully vetted to make sure it's appropriate for them. Kids' Games is your starting point, with links to all games for kids. If you or your child wants reviews, hints and tips, and all the latest cheats, then it's all here. In addition to the links, there's a monthly competition here too, run by the Kids' Games people.

From here you can go to Nickelodeon (Keyword: **GAK**)—a central entertainment repository. Click on the various buttons and you reach, amongst other things, the MegaQuiz, Daily Diaries, information on top children's shows, and previews of forthcoming U- and PG-rated films. There are also links to kids' horoscopes, information on celebrity birthdays, and a whole lot more.

Move on to Kids' Internet, which is a somewhat sanitised version of the adult counterpart (Figure 7.17). In other words, adults can happily let their offspring surf the Net in complete safety. It simply will not allow access to dubious sites. Those that it does allow have been thoroughly vetted.

Figure 7.16
AOL Kids—a junior version of the real thing.

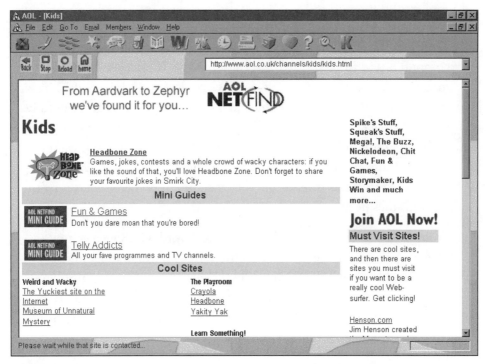

Figure 7.17
Kids' Internet has been specially vetted to guarantee that everything is suitable
for children.

Likewise Kids' Chat, which is a somewhat more regimented version of
adults' AOL Chat—partly, of course, to prevent youngsters from doing
too much damage to their parents' credit cards. As such, Chat sessions
are usually scheduled for specific times and don't last more than a couple
of hours each. Chat is monitored by an adult at all times. And naturally,
participants are asked to adhere to a few common-sense rules to protect
their security. Of course, AOL always recommends that parents supervise
their offspring's time online, much as they would supervise their television viewing. "Let this become a fun electronic clubhouse but not a
financial burden," says AOL, which "cannot be held responsible for
charges you deem excessive." *Caveat parens*, therefore. For more on
Parental Controls, refer to Chapter 10.

Finally, take a look at the new Kids Only feature. This allows parents to
let their children stay online with their own screen name and password,
without the fear of them running into anything undesirable, either on
AOL or the Internet.

International

International is your one-stop gateway to AOL's other online services (Figure 7.18). With the click of a mouse, you can easily jump to the American, Canadian, French, German, Australian, and other international services. However, they *do* recommend that you check out their local Conditions of Service before hopping across their borders because AOL operates under a "when in Rome" policy regarding infractions when visiting the other services.

Just to prove how truly international AOL actually is, the International Channel also shows you how to access AOL when you're travelling across the globe (see Chapter 14 for more on this). Here, too, you'll find international content such as International News, International Finance, and Worldwide Guides.

Well, after that little interlude, we're off to the next chapter—Chat.

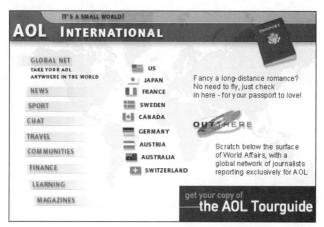

Figure 7.18
Travel the world from your armchair with AOL's International Channel.

Chapter 8

Chat

Chat is where you can have realtime "conversations" with fellow AOL members, except, of course, you type rather than speak. These conversations can take place in a public forum where everyone babbles together. If you want a bit of privacy, you can create your own private Chat room or hold a one-on-one conversation using an Instant Message. You can even chat with celebrities who appear in the AOL Live auditorium. If even *that* fails to impress, you can chat with non-AOL members on the Internet with a program called AOL Instant Messenger™.

But before I get to all that, here's a word about your Member Profile and Buddy List; they can be very useful in Chat and elsewhere on the service.

Member Profiles

In true *Blue Peter* tradition, here's a Member Profile I made earlier (Figure 8.1)—mine, in fact. So what is the function of a Member Profile?

The more you use AOL, the more you'll want to know about fellow members. In the Love Shack, for instance—an area devoted to romance—it can be rather useful to determine the gender of the person you're trying to chat up. (Or maybe you're into surprises, in which case it doesn't matter—to each his/her own.) You might also want to know where the object of your affections lives so you can assess the practicality or otherwise of a romance. This is where the Member Profile comes in handy.

To check a Member Profile, select Get A Member's Profile from the Members Menu (or type Ctrl+G) and enter the screen name of the member whose Profile you wish to view. Click on OK and the Profile

Figure 8.1
My Member Profile.

appears, unless one hasn't been created. In fact, by default, no one has a Member Profile. To create yours, go to Keyword: **MY PROFILE** and click on the My Profile button. A blank form appears (Figure 8.2). Enter whatever you choose (it's all optional), bearing in mind that you can go back and change it whenever you like. When you're satisfied, click on Update. Your Profile will then be included in the Member Directory for all to see and search.

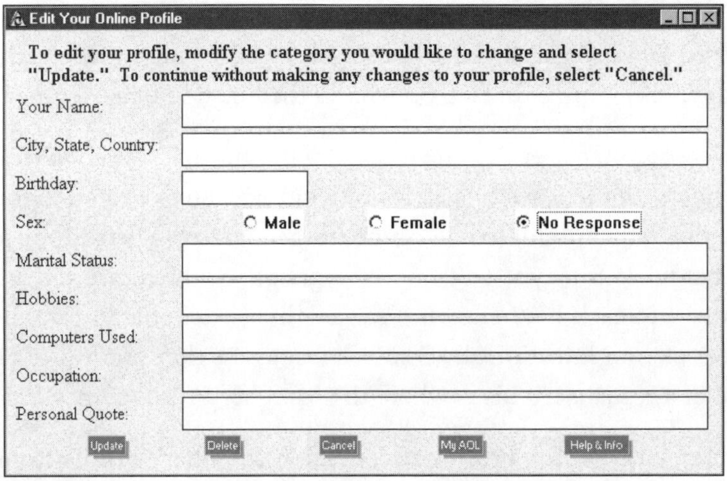

Figure 8.2
A blank Member Profile waiting to be completed.

If you want to make it easy for people to find your Profile (I'll talk about searching Member Profiles in Chapter 10), it's best to be as detailed as possible. In my Profile, I've included my name, whereabouts in the U.K., date of birth, marital status, occupation, hobbies, type of computer I use, and the maxim by which I live my life. Not all Profiles need be as detailed, though. You can include as much or as little information as you like. Indeed, you can make sure that your profile is a complete blank if you desire total anonymity.

Buddy List™ Groups

The more you use AOL, the more people you're going to meet online. Likely as not, some of them will become firm friends. If you use Chat rooms regularly, it can be fun to have online discussions with your new-found mates. But how will you know whether they're online when you are?

The Buddy List automates the process of finding out whether or not selected people are online. Every time you sign on, you can have AOL automatically tell you who, from each of your Buddy List Groups, is currently online and available for Instant Messages or Chat. You can also get AOL to ping at you when a Buddy signs on or off, as well as prevent other AOL members from adding you to their Buddy List.

To set up a Buddy List, select Buddy List from the Members menu or go to Keyword: **BUDDY**. The Buddy List screen appears (Figure 8.3). By default, of course, you have no Buddies selected. By default, too, AOL creates three Buddy List Groups for you to populate: Buddies, Family, and Co-Workers. If you don't like these Group names, fine. Just employ the Delete button and use the Create button to create your own categories.

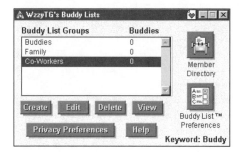

Figure 8.3
The Buddy List screen.

At this stage, let's assume that you're happy to insert the names of some of your online friends into one of the categories that AOL has thoughtfully provided. Simply highlight a category—in this example we'll use Buddies—and click on Edit. This brings up the Edit List Buddies screen (Figure 8.4). Enter your friend's screen name into the designated window and click on Add Buddy. Your friend's name then appears in the window to the right. Then click on Save. Should you have a falling-out, return to this screen and zap him with the Remove Buddy button.

Thereafter, whenever you're online, AOL will display the names of your Buddies who happen to be online at the same time. They're listed in a little window that, traditionally, resides in the upper-right corner of your screen. In Figure 8.5, you can see that someone by the name of IrishDan98 is on at the same time as WzzyTG. The asterisk by the side of the name indicates that he's only just this minute signed on. Should brackets appear—(IrishDan98)—that means he's just this minute signed off. Shortly after, the name will disappear from the list until he's next online.

You can also set your Buddy List Preferences so that, amongst other things, a sound file will play whenever your Buddies sign on or off AOL. But more about that in Chapter 10. Now it's time to deal with Chat.

Chat

Just as most AOL areas have message boards, they also have Chat rooms. But what is a Chat room?

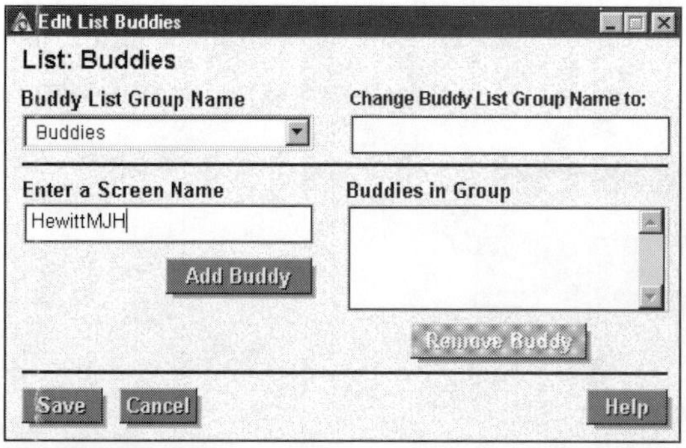

Figure 8.4
Adding a screen name to a Buddy List.

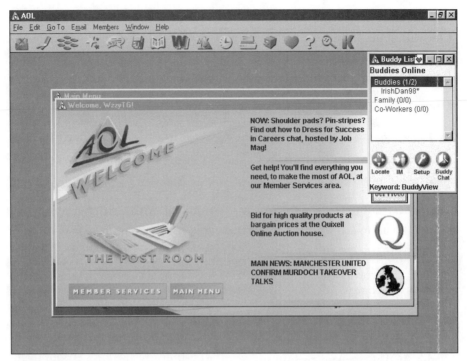

Figure 8.5
Buddies who are online with you are displayed in a window in the upper-right corner of the screen.

Let us turn back to the 17th century. Lloyd's of London was a chat room. It was a coffee shop where gentlemen hung out wearing huge wigs, drinking coffee, and smoking huge pipes of fashionable tobacco. They swigged, they puffed, they exchanged ineffective cures for the pox, and they founded the organisation that insures the world.

The Lloyd's story is not, in a general sense, unusual. When people get together to chat, they gas on, they share their ideas, and maybe something comes of it. Even if nothing does, it can be fun to banter.

Chat rooms on AOL are not, of course, physical chambers full of mad Princes Regent and nervous French aristocracy. They are purely software constructs, but the effects are very much the same (and because you can do AOL Chat from home, the coffee's cheaper).

To converse in an AOL Chat room, you type a comment and it gets displayed on a scrolling window along with everyone else's comments.

The result is rather like TV subtitles or a running sports commentary. One difference, however, is that it's very democratic. Anyone who joins in a Chat room can speak. This can lead to unruliness, but more often it leads to a lot of ideas and personalities to bounce off.

Why chat on AOL? Here are a few reasons:

▲ *Fellowship*—Chat rooms provide a good way to meet fellow AOL members and learn more about them. Online friendships are often struck up this way.

▲ *Problem-solving*—Say you're having problems with a software package. Head to Computing Chat and explain your dilemma. If it's exams that have you stymied, try the friendly faces in Revision Chat. You'll often get an instant diagnosis and it's even faster than the message boards.

▲ *Meet the famous...and the infamous*—AOL members conduct live discussions with celebrities, politicians, athletes, and professionals in the AOL Live Auditorium.

▲ *Business meetings*—Private Chat rooms provide a cost-effective alternative to the time-honoured conference call, and you don't even have to wear a tie.

So how can you get started? Let's look at Chat and how it works.

The Chat Channel

I should point out that, at the time this book was written, Chat was undergoing considerable revamping and will probably look somewhat different than the screenshots here. However, that won't affect the way it works. To go to Chat, click on the Chat icon on the Toolbar or the Main menu, or go to Keyword: **CHAT**. This takes you to the main Chat Channel (Figure 8.6).

Here's a brief rundown of what all the buttons do:

▲ *Chat Rooms*—These are the public Chat areas, listed by name and by interests. You can also access international Chat areas from this menu.

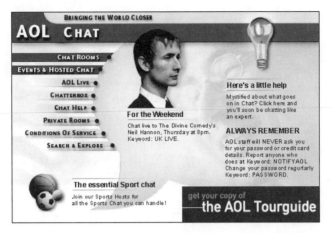

Figure 8.6
The Chat Channel main screen and its choices.

▲ *Events & Hosted Chat*—A daily guide to specialist Chat sessions. For example, the Computing Channel might have a resident expert presiding over a highly technical Chat session, or a sports guru could have some interesting things to say about football.

▲ *AOL Live*—Where members get to meet celebrities online and ask them questions. This, as you'll see later in the chapter, is AOL's version of Question Time.

▲ *Chatterbox*—A community area, with links to message boards, Jonathan's Letter, and the Chat Editor's letter of the week.

▲ *Chat Help*—All you need to know about Chat.

▲ *Private Rooms*—Click here to create your own private Chat area.

▲ *Conditions Of Service*—AOL's Member Agreement and Community Guidelines. A guide to etiquette and online behaviour.

▲ *Search & Explore*—Find the type of Chat that specifically interests you.

Let's plunge in at the deep end and click on the Chat Rooms button. This reveals AOL's public Chat rooms, which you can list by name or interest (Figure 8.7).

Being thirtysomething myself (for a few more months, anyway), I decide to go into the Thirtysomething Chat room. There, I make my presence

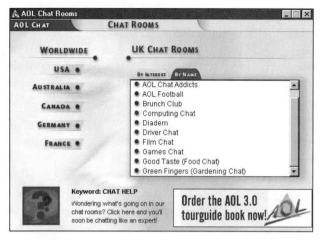

Figure 8.7
All of the UK-flavoured Chat rooms, listed by name and interest.

known (Figure 8.8). I explained how Chat works very briefly back in Chapter 2. You just type your message in the box, click on Send, and it appears in the window. It's as simple as that.

Note: Just because a chat room is called, say, Film Chat or Thirtysomething Chat, it doesn't necessarily follow that people are going to chat about films or thirtysomethings when they're in there. In fact, in the nontechnical Chat rooms, especially, you'll find that the subjects are often completely off-topic.

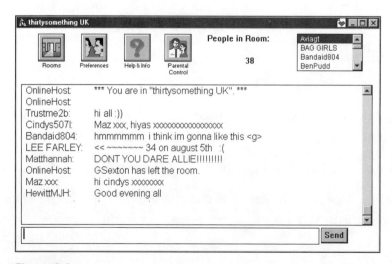

Figure 8.8
Introducing myself to other Chat room participants.

As you can see from Figure 8.8, a program called OnlineHost automatically detects my presence and tells me where I am. If they've set this option in their Chat Preferences, it also informs everyone else in there that I've arrived. When I depart, it will tell them that, too. Essentially, it's the software equivalent of one of those liveried servants who take your visiting card when you arrive at a posh do and announce to the gathering, "Sir Frederick and Lady Chomeley Masterson-Smythe."

Incidentally, if it's a very busy Chat room, you might want to preface your messages with the name of the person with whom you're attempting to converse. Then he knows that what you've said is meant for him and not anyone else. Alternatively, you can configure the Chat room so that the screen only displays messages from the participants that you specify and filters out everyone else. I'll come to this shortly.

At this stage, let's customise the way the Chat room works.

Preferences

Click on the Preferences button at the top of the screen and you can configure the Chat area. You'll see that there are five options:

▲ Notify Me When Members Arrive (that is, tell OnlineHost to inform you whenever someone enters the chat room)

▲ Notify Me When Members Leave (as above, except you'll be notified when they leave)

▲ Double-Space Incoming Messages (self-explanatory)

▲ Alphabetise The Member List (self-explanatory)

▲ Enable Chat Room Sounds (see later in this chapter)

Filtering The Undesirables

If someone's Chat is bothering you, or if you want to focus on the conversation of just a few people in a busy room, you can "ignore" anyone you wish so that you don't even see what they're saying. How, you ask? Easy. I'm still in Thirtysomething. I go to the top-right window and double-click on each screen name that I don't want to "hear." In this case, I click on SaphNPearl (Figure 8.9). Not that I've got anything against

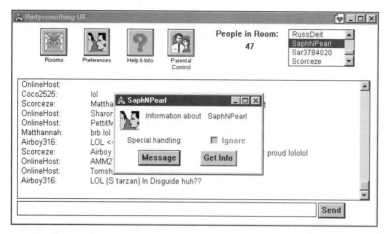

Figure 8.9
You can exclude certain members from Chat to make the room less "noisy."

this member, mind you; this is just an example. To make sure contributions from SaphNPearl are excluded, I click on the Ignore box. And I repeat the procedure for everyone else I don't want to hear. Thereafter, it will be as if they're not in the Chat room for as long as they're there—unless and until I unignore them.

You'll also notice the Get Info button in Figure 8.9. Clicking on this brings up that screen name's Member Profile, assuming, of course, one has been set up. If you're going to use Chat a lot, it's regarded as courtesy to have a Profile.

Notice, too, the Message button. Clicking on this allows you to send a private Instant Message to that member. I'll discuss this later on in the chapter.

Sounds

AOL Chat allows you to invoke sound effects, too, provided your PC has a sound card or its internal speaker is enabled (and these days, very few PCs *don't* come equipped as standard with a sound card and speakers). When you first go into a Chat area—especially a newcomers' or teen Chat area—likely as not you'll frequently hear Joanna piping up for no apparent reason and completely out of context. "Why," you ask yourself, "does she keep saying, 'File's finished' and 'Welcome' when I haven't done anything?"

What's happening is that the participants are sending them—not the sound effects themselves, but codes that fire up the sound files already on your hard disk. The sound files, which you'll find in your main AOL directory (usually called AOL30i), will have a little loudspeaker icon attached. Go into My Computer on your Windows 95 or 98 desktop, select the AOL folder, and take a look (Figure 8.10). There you'll see Goodbye, Gotpost, and so forth. Just to be sure, if you double-click on them, they'll play their sounds.

Of course Welcome and Goodbye, as well as a few others, are part of AOL's standard repertoire. However, if someone sends the code for a sound effect that you haven't got, nothing will happen.

Here's how to enable sound effects within Chat:

1. First, make sure that you have a sound card and that your PC's speaker is working.

2. In your Chat Preferences, select Enable Chat Room Sounds.

3. Note the names of the necessary sound files and make sure they're in your main AOL directory. Note that they must have the .WAV extension (the Microsoft Waveform format). The little speaker icon on the file tells you it's a WAV.

Figure 8.10
AOL's sound files.

4. OK, now you're in the Chat room and you want Joanna to say "Welcome." You know that the file of her saying this is called Welcome. So go to the chat text field, type "{S Welcome}", and click on Send. (The format is {S <name of sound file>}.) Immediately, you'll hear her say "Welcome." If you want her to say "Goodbye," type "{S Goodbye}", and click on Send.

As I said, you will hear Joanna Lumley say "Welcome." So too will everyone else in that Chat room who has that sound file in their AOL directory. However, any American members in the room will hear "Welcome" spoken in an American accent. That's because you're invoking *their* AOL sound files, which were recorded by a U.S. AOL executive.

If, on the other hand, a U.K. member enters "{S Gotpost}", which gets Joanna to say, "You've got Post," U.S. members won't hear anything at all. That's because their sound file is called Gotmail. Likewise, European members have their own sound files, which correspond to their native tongues.

5. You can combine sound effects and normal text messages. What you have to do is put the sound effect in the squiggly brackets, append the text to it, and then click on Send, as you would with any normal text message; for example "{S Welcome} to the Chat room".

If you don't have a sound file that someone else plays in a Chat room, you won't be able to hear it. So if you see the name of a sound you think you would like but don't have—Arnold Schwarzenegger saying "I'll be back" for example—you can ask that member to email the file to you (bearing in mind my previous caution about taking candy files from strangers). You can also find thousands of sound files in the Software Library in the PC Music and Sound Forum, at Keyword: **SOUND**. If Joanna Lumley really gets on your nerves, check out the WAV Event Sounds category for alternatives to the AOL default sound effects.

One last word on sounds: Please go easy on them. Most members find them very, very irritating when used to excess. Do so and you risk a rebuke from the Conditions of Service team, not to mention the wrath of your Chat roommates.

Private Chat Rooms

Why would you want a private room? They come in handy when you want to chat with friends, family, or colleagues online; you can keep your conversation amongst yourselves and not be joined by other AOL members you might encounter in one of the "public" Chat areas.

Private rooms are different because they're yours and yours alone while you're in them. Their names don't show up on any list of rooms anywhere, and the only way to enter one is to know its exact name (hence the term "private room"). This means that only certain people—you and your invited guests—will have access to the room. You can also enter someone else's private room if they tell you the name of the room. Private rooms only exist for the time that you're in them—once everyone leaves your private room, it's gone until the next time you create it.

How do you create, or enter, a private Chat room? Proceed as follows:

1. Simply go to Keyword: **PRIVATE ROOM**. Having done so, you're prompted for the name of the Chat room you want to either create or enter (Figure 8.11). Being stunningly original, I call it HEWITTMJH and click on Go.

2. That takes me into my private Chat room. I could, I suppose, stay there and talk to myself. But I would like to invite other people to join me. There are a few ways I can do this. I can email them, of course. Or I could send them an Instant Message (more in a couple of paragraphs). If they're in my Buddy List, I can page them and invite them to join me whenever they sign on. More about that in Chapter 10.

Figure 8.11
Creating or entering a private Chat room.

3. Entering a private Chat room is exactly the same as creating one. You can go to Keyword: **PRIVATE ROOM**, enter the name of the room, and click on Go. Of course, if someone has sent you a hyperlink to a private room, you can enter simply by clicking on the link.

A private room, as you can see from Figure 8.12, looks and behaves exactly like a public room, and holds a maximum of 23 members.

A few caveats here: Be original when you name your private Chat room. If you choose a name that already exists, you could find yourself blundering into the middle of someone else's private conversation by mistake. On the other hand, it's possible that someone might blunder into yours. Also, AOL's Guides can't be summoned to private rooms should you have any problems.

Etiquette

The rules that apply to message board etiquette apply equally to Chat—so keep it courteous. It has to be said, however, that the U.S.-run Chat areas—the public ones, anyway—tend to be somewhat stricter than their U.K. counterparts when it comes to what they'll tolerate. Although some salty ripostes might go unremarked in late-night Sports Chat, try it in an American Chat room and officialdom could rear its ugly head. In fact, all

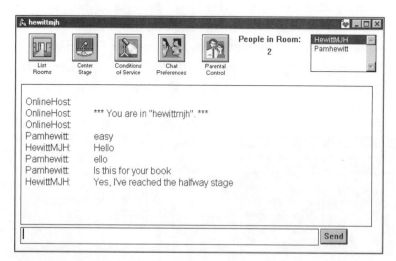

Figure 8.12
Chatting with my sister-in-law in private room HEWITTMJH.

the different AOLs have their own rules, so make sure to watch carefully for what's acceptable in each part of the service. Remember, "When in Rome, do as the Romans do!"

Instant Messages

I mentioned these briefly in Chapter 2. Instant Messages are private, one-to-one conversations between AOL members. You might want to tell someone you've got a file for him, for example, or perhaps you simply want to say hello, in which case, use an Instant Message.

Instant Messages In Chat

Instant Messages aren't actually limited to Chat rooms. They work wherever you may be in AOL (except free areas, for those of you on the Light Access plan). I'll talk about their application outside Chat a few lines down, though. For the moment, I'm concentrating on how it's done within Chat.

During normal Chat, the online exchanges between the various participants are displayed on the screen for all to see. But it could be that you want to have a private word with someone. For instance, you may be in a Chat area with a business colleague and you want to remind him that he's late for a meeting with the boss. You could, of course, send him an email to that effect. An alternative, where both parties happen to be online simultaneously, is to send an Instant Message.

To do so, double-click on the People In Room list. This brings up the dialogue box that you already saw in Figure 8.9. Click on the Message button, which produces the Send Instant Message screen (Figure 8.13).

Figure 8.13
The Send Instant Message screen

Entering Ctrl+I brings up the same window. Compose your message and click on Send. Off it goes. The recipient will hear a little jingle (assuming he's got a sound card) and the message window will appear toward the left of his screen (Figure 8.14). To reply, click on Respond.

Instant Messages Outside Chat

As I said earlier, you don't have to be in Chat to use Instant Messages. So long as your intended recipient is online, you can contact him. To find out if he is around, either press Ctrl+I and then click on the Available? button when the Instant Message window appears, or go to the Members menu and select the Locate A Member Online command. If, on the other hand, you've got a Buddy List set up and he is included in it, it will tell you whether or not he's signed on, as in Figure 8.5. If he is, highlight his screen name and click on the IM button.

As you can see from Figure 8.15, Instant Messages outside Chat look and behave exactly as they do when you're in a Chat room.

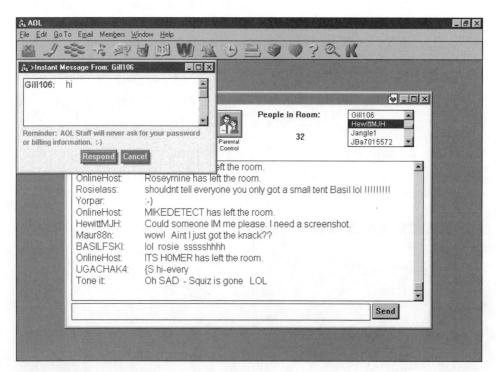

Figure 8.14
Instant Messages appear, accompanied by a jingle, in the upper-left corner of your screen.

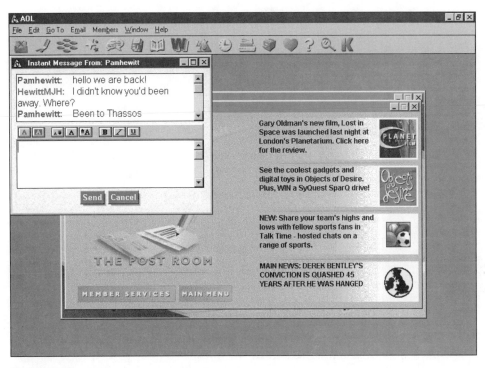

Figure 8.15
Instant Messages can also be used, as here, outside Chat.

Turning Off Instant Messages

Unfortunately, ever since your latest blockbuster film opened and your album reached number 1 in the charts, you have become Mr. Popularity. Every time you sign on to AOL, you're bombarded with hundreds of Instant Messages from adoring fans. But you would rather just do a Greta Garbo. So is there a way to turn off Instant Messages so you can be left alone? There is. Go to Keyword: **IM**, and you'll bring up a toggle switch (Figure 8.16). Click on the Off button, and Instant Messages to you will be automatically rejected until you go to Keyword: **IM** again and click the On button.

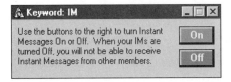

Figure 8.16
Turning off Instant Messages.

To find out how to block selected AOL members only, turn to Chapter 10. And to find out about an exciting new program, Instant Messenger, turn to the end of this chapter.

AOL Live

AOL Live (Keyword: **AOL LIVE**) is the area on AOL where members can interact with the stars and personalities. It's a bit like one of those "An Audience with..." shows that ITV is always televising. Except, in this case, the invited audience of celebrities is you (Figure 8.17).

People who have appeared on AOL Live have included top sportsmen, statesmen, TV and film stars, writers, musicians, and other notables too numerous to mention. AOL Live is your chance to ask them questions as part of an audience in a virtual auditorium.

On AOL Live's main screen, you'll see a picture of the celebrity who's going to be on stage, together with details of the day and time of the event. Click on the picture and in you go.

Tonight, our celebrity is Joe McAlinden, lead singer of the band Superstar. Clicking on his picture takes me into the auditorium (Figure 8.18). You'll see that the auditorium is somewhat like a conventional Chat room, except an auditorium can hold hundreds of members simultaneously. However, the whole thing is emceed by an AOL equivalent of Robin Day—here, UKMC 3—to ensure that it doesn't descend into anarchy.

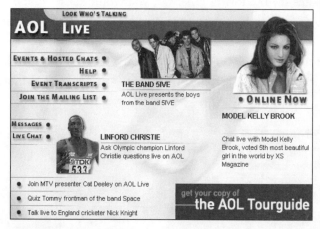

Figure 8.17
AOL Live, where you can meet the stars and ask them questions.

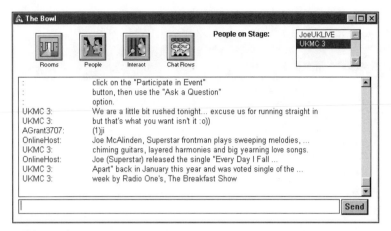

Figure 8.18
The AOL Live auditorium looks a lot like a conventional Chat room.

To take the theatre analogy further, click on the Chat Rows button and you'll observe that the auditorium is divided up into virtual rows, like rows of theatre or cinema seats (Figure 8.19). There are currently four rows: three containing eight participants, the other, six. You can jump seats from one row to the next by highlighting the row and clicking on the Go button. To find out who's in each, double-click on the row or highlight it and click on List People (Figure 8.20). Or if you want to be unsociable and sit by yourself, click on Create Row.

Not let's look at Figure 8.18 again. What happens here is that people in a row can exchange messages with others in the same row. To send a message, just type it into the window at the bottom and click on Send.

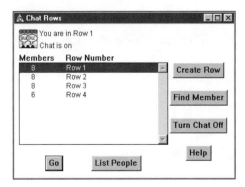

Figure 8.19
The auditorium has virtual rows of seats.

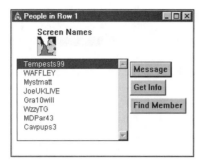

Figure 8.20
Listing the people in your row.

Then it appears in the main window, along with the messages from the speaker and the Host. However, these messages can be seen only by the people in your row, not by any other row and not by the speaker on the "stage." So you can make derogatory comments about him if you like, and he won't know.

If you want to address the speaker on the stage, click on the Interact button and the Interact With Host screen appears (Figure 8.21). Type your question or comment, and it's then passed through to the Auditorium Host, who, if he sees fit, relays it to the speaker. The buttons Vote and Bid are used very occasionally, in online debates and auctions.

The questions and answers, together with comments from the stage, scroll up the main screen as they do in Chat. But be patient. Although the MC will get your message at once, there may be many questions ahead of yours, so he won't necessarily get to it at once, or perhaps at all.

"But," you're asking, "if audience heckling is being mixed in with questions and answers, how can you tell which is which?" Easy: All messages

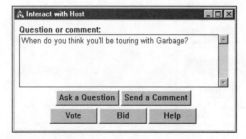

Figure 8.21
Click on Interact to ask your questions.

from people in your row are flagged with a row number. If you are in row 12, a message from a neighbour would look like this:

Benzig: (12) Wrong! We MUST finance the new royal yacht!

Whereas a message from the stage would have no row number, like this:

UKMC: Has anyone here ever actually been to a hunt?

If you detest the people in your row or just find them tiresome, you can, as I said, change rows. Or if you're intensely interested in what the speaker is saying and don't want to be distracted by your neighbours' gabble, you don't have to see what your row-mates are saying. Click on the Chat Rows button and then Turn Chat Off. You won't hear another word from them, and there's not a thing they can do about it.

If there's a megastar appearing on AOL Live, the event will usually be posted on the Welcome screen when you sign on. But it's a good idea to check out AOL Live itself on a regular basis. Here, too, you'll find information on future events and full transcripts of previous chats and events, which you can download. You'll also find details of AOL's daily hosted chats (Figure 8.22), which you can also reach at Keyword: **HOSTEDCHATS**. These take place in the various AOL channels and are usually presided over by experts in the relevant fields. For instance,

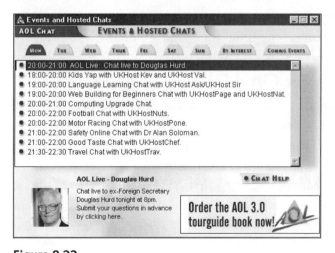

Figure 8.22
Check out the wide range of moderated discussions in AOL's Chat rooms and in AOL Live.

Computing will host a chat where a major techie takes part; Good Food will have an online gourmet taking Q&As; and so on.

AOL Instant Messenger™

AOL Instant Messenger (AIM) is a rather clever program that allows AOL-style Instant Messages to be exchanged, not just with AOL members, but with *any* Internet user. AOL members using AOL software don't need to use AIM. AIM is intended for non-AOL members, and for AOL members who don't have access to AOL software (say, at work). All you have to do is download your copy of Instant Messenger and register it, and then you're off.

At the time of writing, the U.K. version of Instant Messenger is still in "coming shortly" mode, so the description that follows is of the U.S. model. However, I'm sure the differences—if, indeed, there are any— won't be too significant. To download AIM, simply go to **http://www. aol.co.uk/aim** and follow the instructions.

So how does it work?

When you register, you're prompted for a username and a password. If you're an AOL member, you can use the same screen name and password you use on AOL. Internet users, however, must use their imaginations and come up with something memorable. Having come up with that memorable name, they should then inform their friends of it.

Instant Messenger On AOL

Let's see one in action—first, from the AOL member's perspective. In fact, we already have. If you look back at Figure 8.5, you'll see the name IrishDan98 in the Buddy List. AIM names can be added to your Buddy List in exactly the same way AOL screen names can be added. And, just like AOL screen names, when that AIM user is online at the same time you are, provided you've added him to your Buddy List, his name will appear there for the duration.

Let's have AIM user baratus99 send me an Instant Message. When he does so, his message is first held in a "pending" queue and I'm asked if I

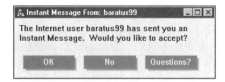

Figure 8.23
When an Instant Messenger message first appears, AOL members are asked if they want to accept it.

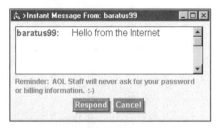

Figure 8.24
To an AOL member, communication with an Instant Messenger user looks exactly like an Instant Message.

want to accept it (Figure 8.23). If I say No, then all such communications from baratus99 will be blocked. However, if I click on OK, the "pending" screen turns into a conventional Instant Message screen (Figure 8.24). Thereafter, I can converse with him as if he were an AOL member. Indeed, as far as I'm concerned, it *will* simply be a bog-standard exchange of Instant Messages.

Instant Messenger On The Internet

Over on the Internet, though, things are slightly different. Instant Messenger simply sits there as a window in the corner of your screen while you surf the Net, go into newsgroups, download FTP files, or whatever. As you can see from Figure 8.25, it looks—and indeed, works—rather like a Buddy List.

Instant Messenger has two modes: List Setup and Online. In the first, you add additional Buddy Groups or Buddy names, or delete them as desired. The major difference between Instant Messenger and AOL, of course, is that those Buddy names don't have to be AOL members; they can be anyone else on the Internet who has registered with Instant Messenger. Online mode is just that (Figure 8.26). It displays which, if

Figure 8.25
Instant Messenger looks not
unlike a Buddy List.

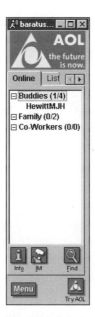

Figure 8.26
Online mode displays which of your
Buddies are online and lets you
contact them.

any, of your Buddies are currently online. At the moment, there's just
one: HewittMJH. In Online mode, you'll eventually be able to get a
user's profile by clicking on the Info button. And, of course, it's in Online
mode that you send your messages. So let's do so.

Either double-click on the Buddy name or highlight it and click on the
IM button. When the Instant Message screen appears, type out your
missive (Figure 8.27). Note that you can prettify the text, exactly as you
can in an AOL Instant Message. Also as in an AOL Instant Message—
the version 3.0i software, anyhow—you can add a hypertext link. In
other words, you can insert a URL that your recipient can then click
upon in order to be transported hither and yon throughout the Internet.

Anyway, assuming the person at the other end accepts your message,
discourse then continues in something resembling the AOL manner.

Other Instant Messenger Features
Here's a run-through (necessarily brief, because I don't know which of the
following are going to make it to the U.K. version of Instant Messenger) of
a few other AIM features:

▲ If an Instant Messenger user appears to be "coming on strong" or is generally abusive, you can send him a warning. If he accrues too many warnings, his messages will then be automatically blocked. Other Internet users can view his Warning Level and thus his online shame (as shown in Figure 8.27).

▲ Search out other registered Instant Messenger users by entering their Internet email address.

▲ Display automatic "I am away from my computer" type messages. Anyone who tries to contact you when this facility is enabled will obtain either a default or a user-defined absence message.

▲ Go to NetFind directly from Instant Messenger.

▲ You can time-stamp your messages (this can be particularly useful for messages that arrive when you're away from the keyboard).

▲ If you have more than one copy of AIM installed (say, one on your laptop and one on your work PC), you can export your Buddy List from one to the other so you don't have to re-create it from scratch.

So much for Chat. In the next chapter, credit cards to the ready, we're going shopping.

Figure 8.27
Instant Messenger offers the same text-enhancement features Instant Messages offer.

Chapter 9

Shopping

As its name suggests, AOL's recently launched Shopping Channel allows you to go shopping from your PC (Figure 9.1). Here in the U.K., this is a fairly innovative concept, so the number of online shops and services is somewhat modest (although growing steadily as more and more retailers take the plunge). Over in the U.S., where they've been doing it for years, you can now buy any number of goods and services via your computer. For example, people routinely purchase groceries from online supermarkets, computers from online PC showrooms, and even mortgages from online banks.

Why would you want to shop via your computer?

Figure 9.1
AOL's Shopping Channel.

Well, your right leg might be encased in a plaster cast, thereby limiting your ability to negotiate the aisles and escalators of a typical city department store. Maybe you live in a remote country area and the nearest shop is in the next village, which is some 20 miles away and down a narrow dirt track. Or, like many people today, it could be that you have a very busy lifestyle and your time is precious, in which case, being able to choose and buy goods online, without having to leave your home, is a positive boon.

But there are other advantages to buying online. Online shops generally cost much less for the retailer to maintain than do the 3D variety (computer pixels work for nothing and don't demand union rights), which means they can pass those savings on to you, the customer. They stay open around the clock, so you can shop when it suits you best. And they make it awfully easy to research your purchases, as well as to comparison shop.

So much for the theory. Let's see it in practice. Just click on the Shopping Channel from the Main Menu or go to Keyword: **SHOPPING**.

Buying A Compact Disc

I don't know about you, but I like to get in and out of my local music store as quickly as possible. There are two things about it that bother me. The first is the background music. Invariably, they have the latest teen-idol album blaring away in the background—not to my taste at all. The second thing that bothers me is the cost. Unless you're a fan of, say, Manuel and the Music of the Mountains (in which case, you'll be well served by the contents of the bargain bucket), you're normally obliged to pay upward of £15 for a typical CD.

Thankfully, AOL members now have an alternative source of supply.

Music Boulevard

I'm a big fan of musicals, particularly the Rodgers and Hammerstein classics from the '40s and '50s. One of my favourites is *Carousel*. I have it on tape, but the cassette is now about 25 years old and probably won't see out the century. I would therefore like to buy the musical on CD. Unfortunately, my local high-street music emporium has it in mind to charge me £15.99 for the privilege. I think, however, I can do a little better than that.

Click on the Music button, and you're delivered unto Music Boulevard, one of the largest and most popular online music stores in the world. Whatever your taste—from Beethoven to the Beastie Boys—likely as not, you'll find it here, along with special offers, the latest music news, and assorted sound clips that allow you to "try before you buy."

Here, I enter "Carousel" and click on the Go Get It button. This produces 11 "hits," among them unrelated albums by various artists. What I'm after is the soundtrack album from the 1956 film starring Shirley Jones and Gordon MacRae. So I scroll down the 11 results and find what looks to be the right one (Figure 9.2). And at a mere $11.49 (just over £7 at the current rate of exchange), it's less than half what I would pay in the U.K. I will, however, have to add shipping to that cost. I'll come to that shortly.

Anyhow, just to make sure this really is the album I want, I select Listen To Samples. This presents me with a list of short extracts—in MPEG (a

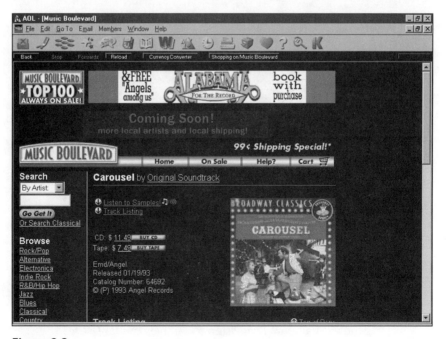

Figure 9.2
Searching for *Carousel* in Music Boulevard.

file compression standard for sound and video) and RealAudio formats—from tracks on the CD. These samples download in a few seconds and can be played while you're online (Figure 9.3). Alternatively, you can save them to your PC's disk and play them later when you're offline.

It turns out this *is* the version of *Carousel* I'm after, so I click on Top Of Page, which delivers me back to where I was in Figure 9.2. Here, I click on Buy CD and I'm given a summary of my choice, or choices, and the cost so far. (Figure 9.4).

Now notice the icon of the shopping trolley at the top and the accompanying legend, "Your Shopping Cart," below. If you're shopping in a conventional supermarket or department store, you'll normally browse the various shelves or aisles, load what you want into a trolley or a shopping basket, and pay for everything at the end. The majority of online stores, whatever they're selling, let you follow a similar modus operandi and assign you a *virtual* shopping trolley (or sometimes a virtual shopping basket) into which you can load your—thus far—virtual goods.

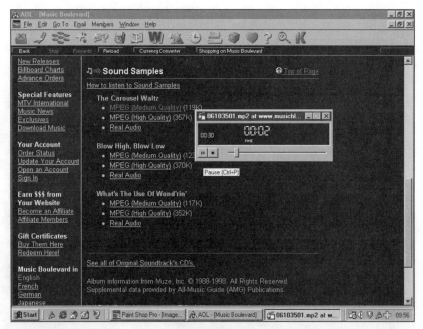

Figure 9.3
Is this the right album? I can listen to samples to make sure.

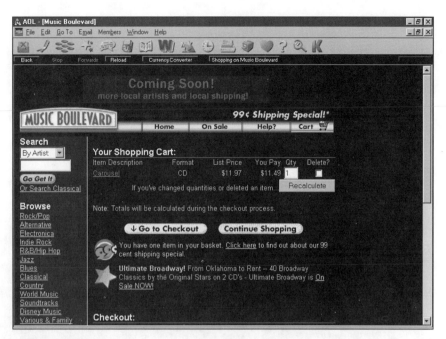

Figure 9.4
Carousel sells for the very reasonable sum of $11.49.

That's how it works in Music Boulevard. You search out a particular CD or tape, load it into your trolley, and then move on to the next selection (if you want more). And, as in any normal store, if you change your mind halfway through, you can put items back. At this point, I have *Carousel* safely on board. I could click on Continue Shopping and choose a few more CDs, but for the purposes of this exercise, I'm content to click on Go To Checkout, which takes me to the payment stage.

The first thing you'll always see at this point—unless you choose to disable it—is a message from your browser that says the connection is absolutely secure (Figure 9.5). In other words, no one will be able to eavesdrop and pick up your credit card details to go on their own little spending spree at your expense. I'll talk a little more about security later in this chapter. Thus reassured, you're prompted for your address (Figure 9.6).

I don't intend to go through every verification stage that follows because they vary from store to store. Suffice it to say, all of them include requests for credit card information and your email address. In the case of Music Boulevard, if you're a first-time visitor, you're also prompted to open an

Figure 9.5
The browser reassures you about credit card security.

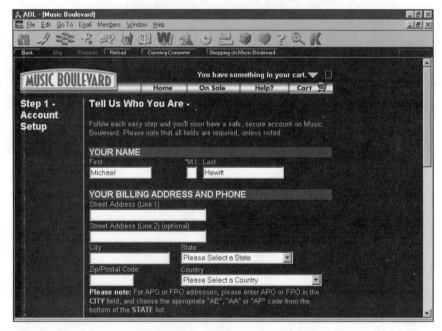

Figure 9.6
Entering address details for delivery.

account. This is common for most online stores. To open an account, you'll enter a user ID (typically your AOL address) and an easily remembered password. This account business is simply to speed things up next time you visit. When you make subsequent purchases, you won't have to fill in your address details again because they'll have been saved and assigned to your account name. Your credit card information generally won't, however, for the sake of security.

Finally, we come to shipping information. How do you want the goods delivered? Different stores have different shipping policies. Some will only dispatch by registered courier. Others only use surface mail. It depends. Currently, Music Boulevard, by default, sends goods by airmail, which takes about a week to reach the U.K. They charge a fee of $5.49 for airmail, plus $1.50 for each item. So my total bill is $18.48—just over £11. When I confirm the order, they automatically email confirmation (Figure 9.7). If you want goods sent overnight by courier, they'll do this, too, but of course, it's far more expensive.

Can Someone Steal My Credit Card Details?

Many people are unduly worried about giving credit card information online. They needn't be. It's actually far more risky to give your credit card details by telephone to a theatre agency or a catalogue store, or even to pay by credit card in a restaurant, yet no one ever seems to express any concern there.

The credit card information is protected so that only the online shop can read it. When the information is encrypted, it would take someone several thousand years to go through all the possible permutations and extract the data. Of course, Hollywood films—*Mission Impossible*, for example—make out that there are teams of super-hackers who can just plug in and, by dint of hi-tech, "crack" encrypted data in an instant. There aren't. And even if there were, they wouldn't be interested in ripping off *your* credit card, which, if it's anything like mine, probably has an upper limit that wouldn't get them very far. They would rather hack a bank and get away with several million.

Buy in confidence, therefore.

Figure 9.7
Confirmation of my online order.

So, as you see, even with packaging and shipping, I've saved about £5 over the U.K. price. It would, of course, have been even more cost-effective had I chosen more than one CD. This is true for the majority of online purchases, whether you buy CDs, books, clothes, or whatever. Buying in bulk largely negates the shipping charge. And talking of shipping, the majority of online stores usually give you the option of checking exactly where your purchase is at any given time. In the case of Music Boulevard, you can click on an Order Status button and input your account number and password, and the details are displayed (Figure 9.8).

A Roundup Of The Rest

Here are some of the other online stores accessible via AOL's Shopping Channel. As I said, the actual mechanics of purchasing, although they may vary slightly from store to store (as, of course, will the different interfaces), are fundamentally the same as described earlier. You'll see, too, that there are certain overlaps. For instance, Fine Food is listed under both Gifts and Food for the very simple reason that, say, a side of smoked salmon is (or at least, can be) both. Anyhow, onward.

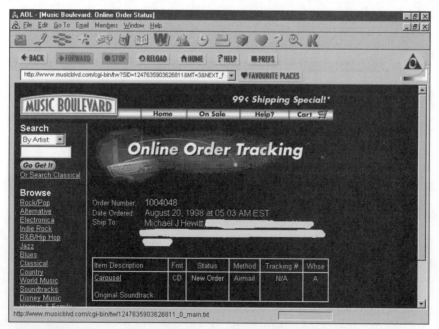

Figure 9.8
Checking the status of my order. Where is it?

Gifts

Perhaps you've forgotten that it's someone's anniversary in a day or two, but the shops have now closed. No problem. Go to Gifts and select something suitable (Figure 9.9). Here, amongst other things, you'll find flowers, Thorntons chocolates, exotic foodstuffs, and CDs. In the case of Interflora, your selection will usually be sent out the same day (Figure 9.10). Don't, however, depend on this round about Valentine's Day. At

Figure 9.9
Last-minute gift-giving made easy with AOL Shopping's Gifts section.

Figure 9.10
Sending flowers online, courtesy of Interflora.

peak times, the service can be booked up several days ahead, but there will be plenty of warning on the site about holiday order deadlines.

Food

Perhaps it would be better to call this section Exotic Food because if you expect to buy a can of beans online, you'll be disappointed—for the time being, anyhow. You can, however, buy a number of specialty foodstuffs, including cured meats, smoked salmon, sausages, pies, and all sorts of organic produce (Figure 9.11). It's ideal for ensuring that you and your friends and family eat well, and in style, all the year round. If it's the chocoholic in your household who needs feeding, you can reach the Thorntons shop through the Gift area or at Keyword: **THORNTONS** (Figure 9.12).

Books

Just as buying CDs in the U.K. can be a wallet-punishing exercise, so too is buying a book, especially a hardback. Unless, that is, you buy them online. So try one of AOL's online bookstores (Figure 9.13). They have

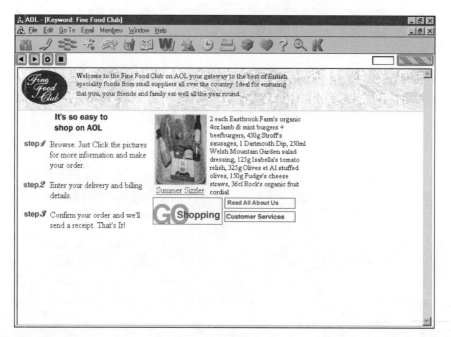

Figure 9.11
Organic sausages anyone? Buy a whole variety of specialty foodstuffs online.

Figure 9.12
Thorntons offers Choc Heaven with an occasional special deal just for AOL members.

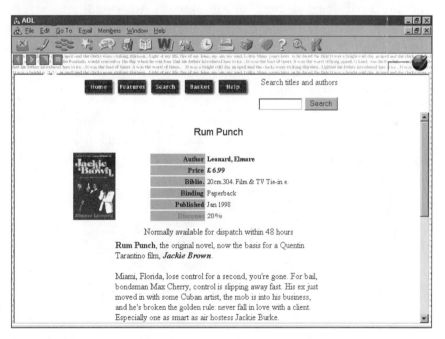

Figure 9.13
A library's worth of books, and more, is available from AOL's online bookstores.

hundreds of thousands of titles in stock. You can search by author, title, key words, genre, ISBN number, and so forth. Then the purchase procedure is much the same as it is for buying CDs. In most cases, expect to pay about two-thirds of what you would in your high-street book store. And look out for all sorts of special offers that can mean ever more reductions.

The AOL Shop

Tell the world that you're an AOL member by buying AOL-branded goods at the AOL online shop, usually at significant discounts. You can even buy this book if you feel so inclined (Figure 9.14), if not for yourself, then for a friend.

The Online Auction

Here's an area where you can snap up some incredible bargains on big-name computer and hi-tech equipment. At the Quixell Online Auction, you can usually buy goods for half of what you would pay in the high street, and usually well below even mail order (Figure 9.15). The items are listed alongside their "opening" prices. You decide what the item's worth to you and make a bid for it. This you do either by email or by bidding "live" on the Web site. If you're successful, Quixell will email you and then dispatch the goods. So enjoy the thrill of an auction, and get yourself a bargain into the bargain.

For even better value, Quixell regularly holds auctions exclusively for AOL members, with bids starting at just £1. You'll find the special auctions advertised on the Deal Of The Day spot. As they say, "Auctions

Figure 9.14
This very book is among the products available at the AOL Shop.

Figure 9.15
Snap up bargains at the Quixell Online Auction.

are entertaining—our customers keep coming back because they enjoy the thrill of the hunt and the competitive spirit. You don't just bid at Quixell—you win!"

AOL Webcards

Although they are in the Shopping Channel, AOL Webcards are actually free. If you've forgotten someone's birthday or anniversary, all is no longer lost. Send them an online card (Figure 9.16). Simply choose the appropriate template from a list and then add your comments and terms of endearment. Finally, send the card on its way, and seconds later, its victim will receive it as an email attachment.

Shopping: The AOL Guarantee

To ensure that the Shopping Channel delivers the goods, both literally and figuratively, AOL promises the following:

▲ To process all orders within 24 hours of receipt (Monday through Friday)

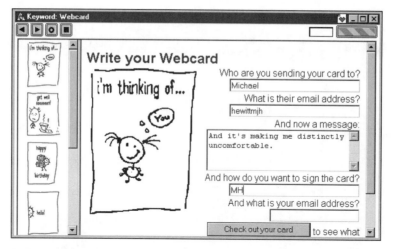

Figure 9.16
Forgotten to send someone a birthday card? No matter, send them a Webcard instead.

▲ To provide professional packaging for all items

▲ To provide dedicated online customer service personnel

▲ To receive and respond to emails within 24 hours (Monday through Friday)

▲ To send a confirmation of any order within 24 hours (Monday through Friday)

▲ To regularly monitor the online shop to minimise/eliminate the promotion of out-of-stock items

▲ To deliver the product as displayed in the online area without substitutions

▲ To offer a comprehensive refund policy should the goods fail to satisfy

So there you have it. As I said at the beginning of this chapter, the AOL Shopping Channel has only recently gone live. By the time this book appears, its range of stores and services should be significantly increased. As with all areas of AOL, check it out regularly to find out what's new.

But now, it's on to Chapter 10, where I'll talk about Preferences and Parental Controls.

Chapter 10

Preferences

So here we are at last. Looking back, I can see that I've made many "more in Chapter 10" references throughout the book. That's because AOL's Preferences give you so many ways to let AOL work the way *you* want it to. If you're happy with the status quo, fine. But if you would like to do some fine-tuning—altering how AOL looks, how it stores files, adding security options such as Parental Controls, and so forth—read on. By configuring AOL to your own personal specifications, you can get a lot more out of the service.

Preference Settings: Offline

Most areas of AOL have a Preferences button that allows you to tailor that area's settings. In Chat, for example, we saw how you can disable Chat sounds, double-space incoming text, and so on. In message boards, you can add a signature and specify the display order, among other things. Indeed, some people prefer to work this way: only setting preferences when they get to a particular area, and then, only for that area. If, on the other hand, you want to do it all in one go, globally, you can. There are two ways: offline, using Preferences, which you'll find in the Members menu, or online, via My AOL. There are slight differences between the two.

First, let's try the offline method. Click on Preferences and the screen appears, with the relevant buttons ready and waiting (Figure 10.1). Let's go through them all.

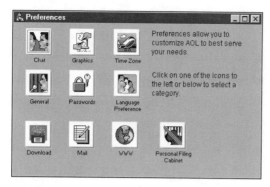

Figure 10.1
The Preferences screen.

Chat

Clicking on the Chat button brings up the Chat Preferences screen, which I dealt with in some detail in Chapter 8. Best to review that section if you want to brush up.

Graphics

In this case, graphics refers to the graphics used by AOL to illustrate its menus and various Channels. When you click on the icon, the Graphics Viewing Preferences screen appears (Figure 10.2). There are four options:

▲ *Maximum Disk Space To Use For Online Art*—When you first go into a new area on AOL, it takes a few seconds for all the graphics to appear. However, if you subsequently revisit, those graphics appear instantly.

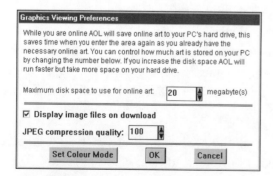

Figure 10.2
Control the way your graphics are displayed via the Graphics Viewing Preferences screen.

On the initial pass, AOL saved them to your PC's hard disk so they don't need to be downloaded again. The maximum disk space option tells your PC exactly how much disk space to allocate to these AOL graphics. By default, it's set at 20MB. If you set it higher, AOL can store more graphics on your computer and will run faster. If you're low on disk space, you might want to reduce the default; the trade-off is that AOL will then run more slowly. As your file reaches the maximum size you've set, the oldest artwork will be discarded when you sign off to make room for the new artwork.

▲ *Display Images On Download*—By default, whenever you download an image file such as a GIF or JPEG, it will be gradually displayed on screen as it arrives. With this option enabled, you can abort the download if you don't like what you see. If you're not bothered, however, or if you like surprises, disable this option.

▲ *JPEG Compression Quality*—This setting is used when you open up a GIF or BMP within AOL and then choose to save it as a JPEG, which is a compressed graphic format. The percentage here is of quality, not compression. The maximum is 100% (the default); reducing it results in more compression—which means a smaller file—but less quality. It's up to you.

▲ *Set Colour Mode*—By clicking on this option, you can decide the number of colours your PC monitor displays. Normally, AOL can detect your colour mode automatically, and so Detect Automatically is, as you'll see, the default. Unfortunately, a few monitors refuse to play ball and produce problems. If so, select either 256 Colours or More Than 256 Colours.

Time Zone

If you're running AOL on a laptop and are engaged in a spot of globe-trotting, this option lets you set the local time to correspond to that of the part of the globe into which you've trotted, or you can switch between Greenwich Mean Time and British Summer Time. You'll notice that whenever you send email or post messages, the mail and messages are time-stamped. Keeping your time zone current ensures that the correct time is displayed. If you're ever in doubt about what to do, a trip to Keyword: **TIME ZONE** will remind you.

General

In General Preferences (Figure 10.3), you have the following options:

▲ *Display Main Menu At Sign On*—In other words, display AOL's 14 Channels.

▲ *Notify Me Immediately Of Network News*—Network News is made up of those announcements that occasionally scroll across your screen informing you of such inconveniences as mail maintenance or impending downtime. But if you prefer not to view them, disable this option.

▲ *Where Possible, Display Text Small, Medium, Large*—It's up to you. How good is your eyesight? How big (and what resolution) is your monitor?

▲ *Save Text With Line Breaks*—When you use the Save command under the File menu to save a news story, a message board or newsgroup message, or an email message, this option inserts a "hard" carriage return at the end of each line of text. This is historical, dating back to the days when some word processors—WordStar was one—couldn't

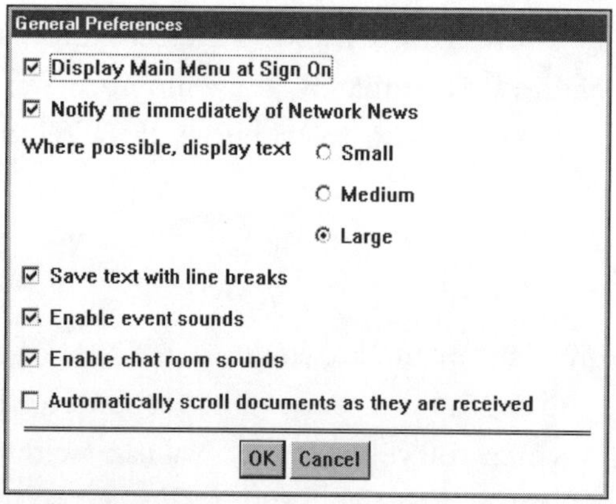

Figure 10.3
The General Preferences screen.

handle text without regular line breaks. Today, however, they all can. So unless you've got some really antique piece of software on your PC, it's safe to disable this option.

▲ *Enable Event Sounds*—In other words, activate Joanna Lumley. If, however, your inclination is more toward the "silence is golden" persuasion, disable her and you *won't* hear "Welcome!", "You've got Post," and so on. (Of course, keeping your speakers off achieves the same goal.)

▲ *Enable Chat Room Sounds*—We discussed this in Chapter 8.

▲ *Automatically Scroll Documents As They Are Received*—If this option is enabled, all incoming text rolls down the screen like the captions at the end of a television programme. By default, however, it is disabled; if your modem is faster than 2400bps—and I hope and pray that it *is* for the sake of both your phone bill and your AOL bill—then the text will scroll by too quickly for you to read, anyhow.

Passwords

Be very, very careful with this option (Figure 10.4). It allows you to store your password to your PC's hard disk, which means that you can sign on to AOL without first having to enter it. And so can anyone else who happens to be around. As you'll see in Figure 10.5, the usual Password window disappears from the Sign On screen. It then simply becomes a

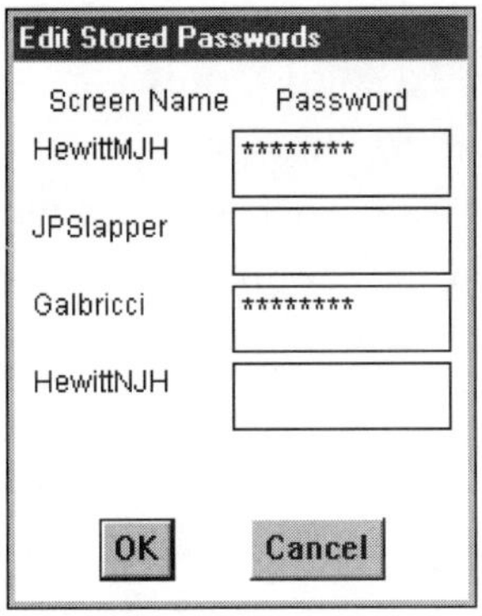

Edit Stored Passwords	
Screen Name	Password
HewittMJH	********
JPSlapper	
Galbricci	********
HewittNJH	

OK   Cancel

Figure 10.4
Passwords can be saved to your PC's hard disk.

Figure 10.5
With your password stored, you can sign on to AOL without having to enter it, as can anyone else with access to your PC!

matter of clicking on Sign On to start the meter ticking. If other people have access to your computer—whether they are colleagues, roommates, or your children—*beware*.

Furthermore, because folks who use this option never need to use their password, they tend to forget it. This can be quite frustrating when they try to sign on as a guest or install a new version of AOL and, to their chagrin, find they can't remember their own password.

Language Preference

Many of the non-English-speaking areas of AOL—AOL Germany and France, to take but two examples—are coded so they only appear to those AOL members who have German and French languages selected. Those members who *don't* have German and French selected won't be able to see them. This isn't an example of xenophobia in action. Instead, it's specifically designed this way so people who don't speak German and French won't get frustrated by following links that might take them to foreign-language AOL pages they won't understand. To enable the languages, select them from the list that appears once you've clicked on Language Preferences (Figure 10.6) and add as per your linguistic ability.

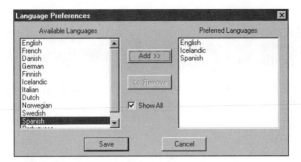

Figure 10.6
Selecting the languages to be displayed.

Download Preferences

Download Preferences modifies the actions of the Download Manager (Figure 10.7). It includes the following options:

▲ *Display Image Files On Download*—We encountered this earlier in General Preferences. Do you want to see graphics as they arrive? If so, enable this option.

▲ *Automatically Decompress Files At Sign-Off*—When you download compressed files (those with a .ZIP extension or StuffIt files if you're using a Macintosh), they're automatically decompressed when you sign off AOL. If you would rather they're not—for example, you might be downloading to a floppy disk that doesn't have the capacity to accommodate a large graphics or program file—then disable this option.

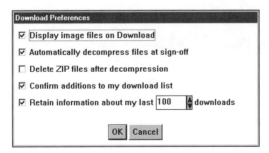

Figure 10.7
Download Preferences modifies the actions of the Download Manager.

▲ *Delete ZIP Files After Compression*—This option removes the ZIP file from your disk once it's been decompressed. By default, it is disabled because many people like to use downloaded ZIP files as a backup.

▲ *Confirm Additions To My Download List*—With this option enabled, the message "This file has been added to your download list" will always appear when you select a file for downloading.

▲ *Retain Information About My Last XXX Downloads*—The Download Manager has a Show Files Downloaded button. This option allows you to determine exactly how many files are listed. By default, it's set to 100.

Mail

I discussed Mail in detail in Chapter 2. Selecting the Mail icon brings up its Preferences screen (Figure 10.8). The options are as follows:

▲ *Confirm Mail After It Has Been Sent*—This option is enabled by default. It produces the "Your e-mail has been sent" message.

▲ *Close Mail After It Has Been Sent*—This closes the email window after you've sent the message (again, it is enabled by default). But if you want to keep it open—perhaps to edit the message slightly before sending it on to someone else—disable it.

▲ *Retain All Mail I Send In My Personal Filing Cabinet*—This option saves a copy of each outgoing email message to your hard disk in your Personal Filing Cabinet.

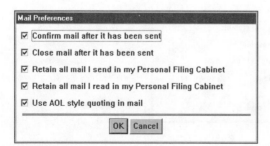

Figure 10.8
Email options.

▲ *Retain All Mail I Read In My Personal Filing Cabinet*—This option is the same as the preceding option except it saves incoming messages.

Note: *AOL 3.0i software comes with the Personal Filing Cabinet options enabled by default because it deletes items from your online Sent and Received lists after a few days. If you don't want to keep permanent copies of the email messages you've sent and received, or if you want to keep them yourself (by saving them as text or by printing them, for example), you can disable these options.*

▲ *Use AOL Style Quoting In Mail*—When you quote a portion of an email message (simply highlight the section you wish to quote and it will automatically be copied to your Reply window), this option configures the style in which the quoted text will appear. If it's enabled—the default—you have AOL-style quoting <<like this>> around the text. Disabled, you get Internet quoting >like this in front of each line.

WWW

The WWW control modifies the way your integrated Web browser, Internet Explorer, functions (Figure 10.9). Because Internet Explorer is actually third-party software (courtesy of Microsoft) rather than AOL software and currently subject to significant change both in appearance and functionality, I don't devote too much space to it here. Besides, your Windows 95 or 98 manual will give you a much more detailed and up-to-date explanation of exactly how it works and how to configure it than I ever could. In general, however, here are some of the things you can do:

▲ Enable or disable the display of pictures, sounds, and videos. With this option disabled, your connections will be faster but you won't see all the snazzy special effects.

▲ Configure the colours and font settings used in Web pages.

▲ Configure the size of the browser's Web cache. The cache is a folder on your PC's hard disk that holds most of the more recent pages and graphics that you've accessed on the Internet. It performs much the

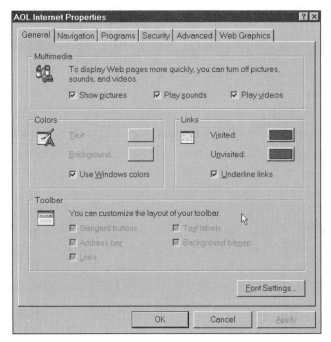

Figure 10.9
Configuring your Web browser. Do so only if you feel you must.

same function as AOL's Maximum Disk Space To Use For Online Art setting you encountered in the Graphics Viewing Preferences screen. In other words, the more graphics you store to your hard disk, the faster your Internet access, especially to pages you visit regularly.

▲ Set security functions. I'll be discussing these later in this chapter when I talk about Parental Controls.

Anyhow, tinker if you must; the WWW defaults are perfectly satisfactory for the way most people work.

Personal Filing Cabinet

As we saw in Chapter 6, your Personal Filing Cabinet (PFC) organises incoming and outgoing files—email messages, downloaded files, newsgroup and message board messages—for the sake of posterity and to guard against accidental deletion. Over time, particularly if you're an energetic correspondent, it will do an Orson Welles and expand dramatically,

which is where the Personal Filing Cabinet Preferences come in
(Figure 10.10):

▲ *Issue Warning About The PFC If File Size Reaches XX Megabytes*—
Excessively large Personal Filing Cabinets can s-l-o-w down your
AOL software. But what constitutes excessive? By default, this option
is set to 10MB. If your Personal Filing Cabinet becomes larger than
this, you'll get a warning message.

▲ *Issue Warning About The PFC If Free Space Reaches XX Percent*—When
you delete a file in your Personal Filing Cabinet, it leaves a certain
amount of free space, like a brick that's been knocked out from the
middle of a wall. This is wasted hard disk space. If this wasted space
reaches a certain percentage—by default, 35—you'll get an error
message. You should then compact your Personal Filing Cabinet. I'll
cover this toward the end of this chapter.

▲ *Confirm Before Deleting Single Items*—When you try to delete something in your Personal Filing Cabinet, by default, you're asked for
confirmation. Disable this option if you are resolute and devoid
of doubt.

▲ *Confirm Before Deleting Multiple Items*—This option is the same as
the preceding option, but it is intended for multiple zapping. And, as
with the preceding option, the default is On.

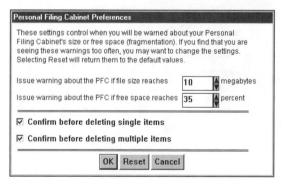

Figure 10.10
Personal Filing Cabinet Preferences.

Preference Settings: Online

All of the settings that can be configured offline can also be configured online via My AOL; frankly, though, there isn't much point running up an AOL bill to do so. Do it offline. A few preferences, however, can *only* be set online because they're functions of the AOL system itself and not the AOL software on your PC. To reach them, select My AOL from the Members menu, go to Keyword: **MY AOL,** or click the Toolbar's My AOL button and select Fine Tuning. The corresponding screen appears in a trice (Figure 10.11).

There are only two preferences here that need concern us. The others can be controlled offline, as described earlier in this chapter. First is Marketing Preferences. Select it and the corresponding screen appears (Figure 10.12). It informs you that AOL may occasionally make its membership list available to reputable companies (interpret that as you will) whose products or services may be of interest to you. If, on the other hand, you *don't* want mail from such companies landing on your doormat, click on Remove. From here, you can find out how to contact the Direct Mailing Association and have them remove you from all other mailing lists, too.

The second button of interest here is Multimedia Preferences. It controls graphic elements such as banners that flit across your screen or photographs that appear in sequence in windows. To be perfectly honest, unless you're

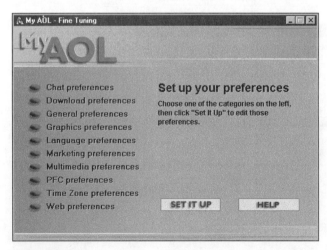

Figure 10.11
The Fine Tuning screen.

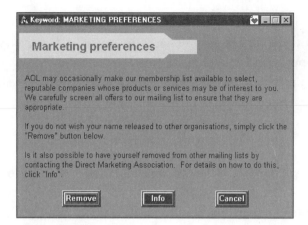

Figure 10.12
Marketing Preferences allows you to determine exactly how much or how little promotional mail you receive.

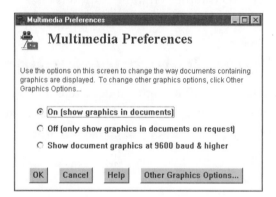

Figure 10.13
Settings for multimedia graphics.

modem is slower than 28,800bps, none of what follows is going to really have an impact on your life in any way. I merely include it for the sake of completeness. Anyhow, in the accompanying screen (Figure 10.13), you'll see three options:

▲ *On (Show Graphics In Documents)*—With this option enabled, you'll always see the full multimedia presentation of a document, including pictures, no matter the speed of your connection. If your modem speed is less than 9600bps, however, you might want to disable this option.

▲ *Off*—With this option enabled, you'll get a text-only version of the document. If there are any graphics accompanying it, however, a button will appear and you'll be prompted to view the full version. This way, you pick and choose which graphics you want to see. Again, this is recommended for people with very slow modems. But if you *don't* want lots of colourful graphics, why are you using AOL in the first place?

▲ *Show Document Graphics At 9600 Baud And Higher*—Set this option and AOL will automatically switch your display depending on how fast your connection with the service is. At 9600bps plus, you'll always get to see the graphics. But if you connect with a slower modem, you'll get text only with the option to view the graphics.

Clicking on the button labelled Other Graphics Options takes you back to the main Preferences screen.

A Roundup Of Other Preference Options

Strictly speaking, these functions don't come under Preferences as such, but they do demonstrate different ways to use AOL in order to get *preferred* results. Accordingly, I think they can be happily inserted here.

Download Manager—Where To?

I mentioned in Chapter 5 that, by default, the Download Manager deposits downloaded files in the AOL30i\DOWNLOAD folder. But suppose you want it in another folder? Or in another disk, even? Sheer simplicity.

In the Download Manager window—remember, you reach this by selecting Download Manager from the File menu—go for the Select Destination button. This causes the Select Path window to appear (Figure 10.14). Here, select a different folder, create a new folder, or select a different disk. When you've made your choice, click on Save.

That's it. Thereafter, the Download Manager will treat that location as its new default until you press the Select Destination button again and choose a new location, at which point, *that* will be the new default.

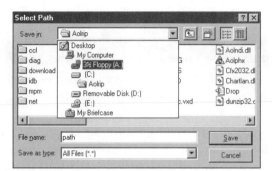

Figure 10.14
Telling the Download Manager where to put its files.

Personal Filing Cabinet Tinkering

The folders and files in the Personal Filing Cabinet behave just like the folders and files stored under your My Computer icon. This is hardly surprising; they *are* the same as the folders and files in My Computer. It's a Windows 95/98 hierarchical filing structure.

Pardon? I'm sorry. Like those Russian babushka dolls, main folders contain subfolders, which themselves contain subfolders, which themselves may contain subfolders, and on and on and so on until, eventually, you find files. Double-clicking on an individual folder makes all its subfolders and files fold inward. Another double-click opens them out again.

Remember what a sprawling mess the Personal Filing Cabinet was in Chapter 6? Well take a look at Figure 10.15. It's the same PFC; all I've

Figure 10.15
A "tidied-up" Personal Filing Cabinet.

done is double-click on the primary folders. The subs and sub-subs are all now nested inside until I double-click again. And just as in My Computer, if you want to create a new folder, click on the Add Folder button. If you find you don't want or need a given folder, highlight it and click on Delete. Finally, if you want to add individual files to a particular folder or move one folder inside another, just drag and drop accordingly.

There are two more things to mention. You'll have noticed the Search button. Double-clicking on it brings up a Search window (Figure 10.16). Input your search term at the top and specify the scope of your search:

▲ *All Folders*—AOL will search them all, open or not.

▲ *Open Folders Only*—AOL will only search those that are open; in other words, that haven't been folded shut as in Figure 10.15.

▲ *Full Text*—AOL will search all the text of all the stored messages.

▲ *Titles Only*—If you normally give your messages a readily identifiable title, this option will speed up your search.

Finally, onward to the Compact PFC button. I mentioned this earlier: Deleted items, although they *have* been deleted, nevertheless leave spaces, like missing bricks in a wall. To close up those voids and thereby reclaim wasted hard disk space, you can compact your Personal Filing Cabinet. Selecting the aforementioned button yields the screen in Figure 10.17.

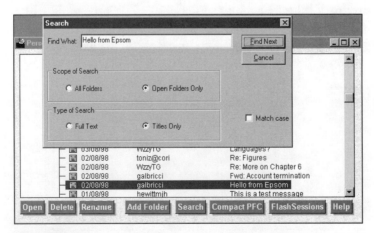

Figure 10.16
Searching the Personal Filing Cabinet.

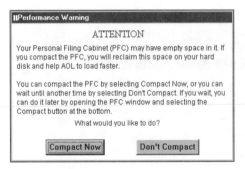

Figure 10.17
Compacting your Personal Filing Cabinet frees hard disk space and can make
AOL run faster.

Searching Profiles

I mentioned in Chapter 8 how Personal Profiles could be useful for
informing other AOL members about yourself. But in addition to acting
as convenient online curricula vitae, together, they act like entries in a
Thomson Local directory. With its millions of members, AOL is one
massive, table-squashing directory. Nevertheless, I'm now going to show
you how easily and quickly you can extract the information you're after
from among those millions of entries.

Why would you want to do this? For a start, it could be that you know
that a particular person is on AOL, but you don't know his exact screen
name. If so, you can enter such search terms as the forename, surname,
and place of residence and, hopefully, extract his Profile. It's possible,
however—likely, even—that several people will share the same name, so
your search might bring up a long list, particularly of Smiths. Nevertheless, if he has filled in his Member Profile properly, you should eventually
locate him.

But we must go on to more mundane matters. Let's assume my house
has suddenly suffered an electrical crisis. I need an electrician. But I need
a local electrician; an electrician based in, say, Aberdeen or Nova Scotia
wouldn't be much use to me. I'd be electrocuted by the time he arrived.

So I go to Keyword: **MY PROFILE,** which brings up the Member
Directory screen. Then I choose Advanced Search to give me the widest
range of search options (Figure 10.18). My search terms are the occupation

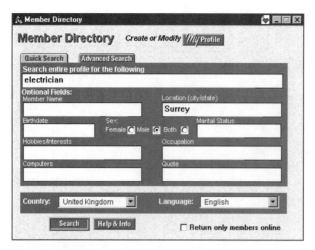

Figure 10.18
Entering search terms into the Member Directory.

"electrician" and the location "Surrey". I also ensure that "United Kingdom" is selected in the Country list, just in case there's a Surrey somewhere else in the world—one with a fringe on top, for instance. Finally, I click on Search. In a flash, I find five electricians, all local (Figure 10.19).

Of course, given that there are so many search criteria options, I could have been a lot more detailed. For example, I might have specified a female electrician by the name of June whose hobbies include philately and who uses a Sinclair ZX-80. It's unlikely that I would have found one, mind you, but the option is there nonetheless.

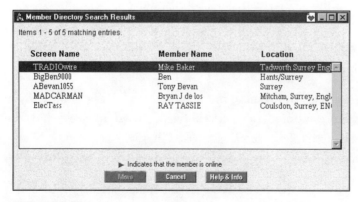

Figure 10.19
Success! Five electricians, all nearby.

Actually, searching the Member Profiles in this way can bring up quite a few startling revelations. Use the search terms "Hollywood" and "actor", for instance, and you'll be amazed at how many AOL accounts such luminaries as Arnold Schwarzenegger and Meryl Streep *apparently* have. And "apparently" is the operative word. Never assume that just because you read it in a Member Profile, it's bound to be true.

I only hope those electricians are what they claim to be....

Creating Additional Screen Names

You can have up to five screen names on your account: the Master screen name, which you can't change, plus four others (which you *can* change). They can be your alter egos, or your family, friends, or colleagues can use them. Here's how to add them:

1. Go to Keyword: **NAMES**. This brings you to the Screen Names window where, among other things, you can create a screen name, delete a screen name, or restore a screen name that you've previously deleted but now want to use again (Figure 10.20).

2. Double-click on the Create A Screen Name button and the familiar dialogue boxes appear, just as they did when you originally joined AOL. And, just as when you originally signed on to AOL, when you enter your first choice, AOL may tell you that the screen name you want to add is already in use (Figure 10.21). Carry on until you create a name no AOL member is already using or until AOL suggests a variation you can live with.

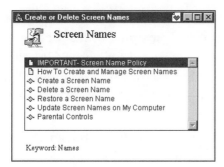

Figure 10.20
Create, delete, or restore screen names from the Screen Names window.

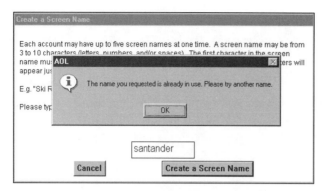

Figure 10.21
Your first choice of screen name may already be taken.

3. Once you've arrived at a screen name that both you and AOL are comfortable with, you're prompted for a password. *Don't* use the same password you use for any other screen name on the account. When the password has been entered and verified, AOL tells you that the new screen name has been created, but it can only be used once you've signed off and then signed back on again.

TIP   *Note Well*

If your children will be using your account, AOL recommends that you allocate one of your additional screen names to them rather than allowing them to use your Master screen name. This way, you can assign AOL's Parental Control to their screen name to help manage their online experience. More about that later in this chapter.

Deleting A Screen Name
To delete a screen name, choose the Delete a Screen Name option from the Screen Names window and you're presented with a list of potential targets (Figure 10.22). When you've selected a victim, AOL asks you if you're sure. When you say yes, it then asks if you're really, *really* sure. If you are, zap it. If you change your mind later, use the Restore A Screen Name button. But bear in mind that AOL will only store deleted names on its system for six months and doesn't absolutely guarantee that you'll get the name back, even within that time. After six months, a deleted name can't be used again for up to a year—by anyone.

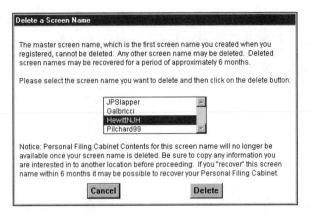

Figure 10.22
Selecting a screen name for deletion.

Buddy List™ Settings

I explained how to set up a Buddy List in Chapter 8. Here, I'll show you how to configure Buddy Preferences. You can also globally enable or disable the receipt of Instant Messages in the Buddy List Preferences screen.

Select Buddy Lists from the Members menu, go to Keyword: **BUDDY,** or click on the button marked Setup at the bottom of your Buddy List. Click on the Preferences button in the lower-right corner of the Buddy Lists window and the corresponding screen appears (Figure 10.23).

As you can see, there are three options:

▲ *Show Me My Buddy List(s) Immediately After I Sign On To AOL—* With this option enabled, whenever you sign on to AOL, your Buddy List window appears in the upper-right corner.

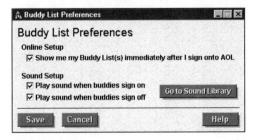

Figure 10.23
The Buddy List Preferences screen.

▲ *Play Sound When Buddies Sign On*—This option is self-explanatory. Or at least it will be in a couple of paragraphs.

▲ *Play Sound When Buddies Sign Off*—This option is also self-explanatory.

Sounds

For the last two options in the preceding list to work, they must be enabled, and you must have the requisite sounds in your main AOL folder. To get them, click on Go To Sound Library and you're presented with the Buddy List Sounds window (Figure 10.24). The preamble tells you that the default sounds are a doorbell ringing when a Buddy signs on and a door slamming when he signs off.

The Download Buddy Sound Installer "Door Theme" button does exactly that and deposits a compressed file called BUDDOOR.EXE to whichever folder you've designated as the default in your Download Manager. Once you've downloaded BUDDOOR.EXE, sign off. To decompress and automatically install the sounds, choose Start and then Run from your Windows 95 or 98 Start menu. Choose Browse to locate and highlight the file and click on OK. When you next sign on, your Buddy Sounds will be enabled.

The doorbell and door slam sounds are the default, but you can use others if you want. Try the Buddy List Sound Library button (Figure 10.25). From here you can choose from among dozens of alternate sounds such as Peekaboo!, Hello Darling!, and goodness knows how

Figure 10.24
Want sounds to accompany your Buddy List? Go to Buddy List Sounds.

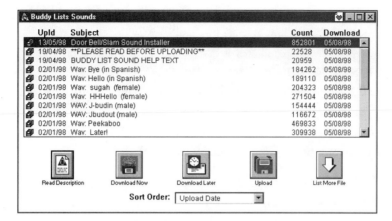

Figure 10.25
You can configure your Buddy List to play dozens of different types of sound effects.

many foreign variations. To get them to play (after downloading them, of course, and copying them to your main AOL directory), you'll first have to go to the Sounds section of your Windows Control Panel and assign them to the Buddy In and Buddy Out events (Figure 10.26). Please refer to your Windows manual or Help files for more information on exactly how to do this.

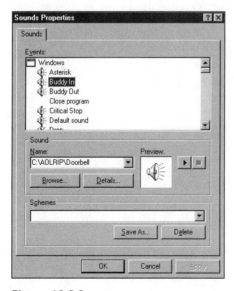

Figure 10.26
Using the Windows Control Panel to assign Buddy List sounds.

I caution you, though: If you have a full Buddy List, your online sessions are going to sound quite cacophonous.

Automatic Invitations

Instead of sending an Instant Message that says, "Come into such-and-such private room," or "Join me in the such-and-such area of AOL," you can take care of it in one swoop with a Buddy Chat Invitation (you can even invite a whole group of people at once):

1. Select a Buddy List Group or AOL member screen name from your Buddy List and click on the Buddy Chat button. The Buddy Chat Invitation window appears (Figure 10.27).

2. Add additional AOL member screen names to the Screen Names To Invite field by selecting additional names from the Buddy List window and clicking on Buddy Chat. Repeat this step for each screen name you want to add. Or type in the exact screen name of a friend you want to invite. (This person must be online and an AOL member to receive your invitation. AOL Instant Messenger™ subscribers cannot be sent a Buddy Chat Invitation and cannot send one to you.)

3. Tab to the Message To Send field. You can send the recipients of your Buddy Chat Invitation a customised message up to 100 characters long. If you don't type a message, AOL uses the default message "You are invited to."

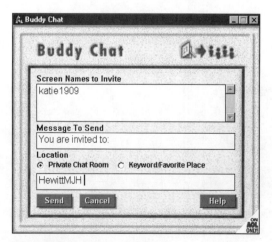

Figure 10.27
Send an automatic invitation via Buddy Chat.

4. Tab to the Location field, where you'll have the following choices:

▲ To talk privately with your friends, select the Private Chat Room radio button. You can type your own Buddy Chat Room name. If you leave the Buddy Chat Private Chat Room box blank, a Buddy Chat Room name will be created for you. Your friends will receive an invitation to join you in that chat room.

▲ To share those places you like best on AOL, select the Keyword/Favourite Place radio button. Enter a Keyword in the text field or drag and drop a Favourite Places heart. You can also drag and drop the Favourite Places heart for Web sites from the AOL browser. Your friend(s) will receive an invitation to join you at that online site.

5. Click on the Send button to speed your invite on its way. You'll also receive a copy of the Buddy Chat Invitation (Figure 10.28) so you can join your friends in your chosen destination. Your invitees can select either Go or Cancel, or they can send you an Instant Message to ask what on earth it is they're being invited to. If they click on Go, they'll be there in a couple of seconds.

Privacy

We saw in Chapter 8 how you can turn Instant Messages on or off. That method, however, was something of a carpet-bombing approach and blocked *all* Instant Messages (or turned them off one at a time). AOL gives you another option, which lets you fine-tune things even further.

Figure 10.28
Having received an invitation, you can go, send an Instant Message, or decline by selecting Cancel.

Select Buddy Lists from the Members menu, or go to Keyword: **BUDDY** and choose Privacy Preferences. You'll see in Figure 10.29 that you have a range of options:

▲ *Allow All AOL Members And AOL Instant Messenger*—You'll get every Instant Message and Instant Messenger message that's sent to you (although you have the option to refuse Instant Messenger messages when they first arrive).

▲ *Block AOL Instant Messenger Users Only*—You'll receive Instant Messages from AOL members but not messages sent from the Internet via Instant Messenger.

▲ *Block Only Those People Whose Screen Names I List*—If someone's bothering you—or you don't want to get an Instant Message from, say, your boss or mother at night—enter the name into the window, click on the Add button, and then click on Save. Thereafter, everyone *except* the person or persons you've specified will be able to send you Instant Messages or messages via Instant Messenger.

▲ *Allow Only Those People Whose Screen Names I List*—Just as in the preceding option, except only those people you add to your list will be able to send you an Instant Message.

▲ *Block All AOL Members And AOL Instant Messenger Users*—A blanket ban. You are now deaf to the world.

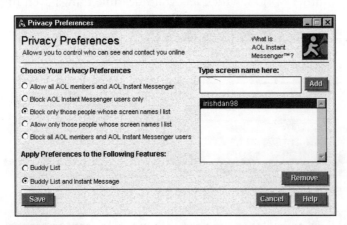

Figure 10.29
Instant Message and Instant Messenger privacy options.

Additionally, you'll see Apply Preferences To The Following Features. If you've already chosen the Allow All AOL Members And AOL Instant Messenger option, this area will be greyed out because you aren't blocking access to any feature.

▲ *Buddy List*—Enabled, this option prevents your screen name from showing in the Buddy List of the name(s) you've indicated. They can still send you an Instant Message, however. If the option is disabled, they *can* add you to their Buddy List.

▲ *Buddy List And Instant Message*—Enabled, this option prevents your screen name from showing in the Buddy List of the name(s) you've indicated, *and* it prevents them from sending you an Instant Message. Disabled, it of course doesn't.

Parental Control

Most responsible parents are concerned about the online material to which their offspring are likely to be exposed. This is where AOL's Parental Control option comes in. If children use one or more screen names on your account, you can attach certain restrictions on AOL access and features to those screen names to prevent possible misuse or exposure to inappropriate material.

Only the Master screen name, the permanent name that you created when you first joined AOL, can assign Parental Control to a name on your account. To do so, select Parental Control from the Members menu or go to Keyword: **PARENTAL CONTROL** (Figure 10.30). Among other things, Parental Control can be set up to do the following:

▲ Block all incoming Instant Messages.

▲ Block access to all Chat areas.

▲ Allow access to Chat, but block access to member-created rooms.

▲ Block access to the special-interest areas and forums within AOL.

▲ Block access to Internet newsgroups, either globally or selectively.

Figure 10.30
The Parental Control screen.

Let's go through the various buttons and their control options. In all of the following cases, click on the appropriate screen name, and when you've made your choice, click on OK.

Chat

In the screen shown in Figure 10.31, I can specify the screen names to which I want the controls to apply. In this case, it's my namesake, HewittNJH. I have three blocking options here:

▲ *Block All Chat Rooms*—He can't participate in Chat, full stop.

▲ *Block Member Rooms*—He can participate in Chat, but only in the public areas. He can't go into a private room.

▲ *Block Conference Rooms*—Note that all of the U.K. Chat rooms are Conference Rooms, so this option will block access to U.K. Chat rooms but not to the international People Connection rooms.

Click on OK and it takes effect.

Instant Messages

As you can see from Figure 10.32, there are just two choices: Either he's allowed to receive Instant Messages or he isn't.

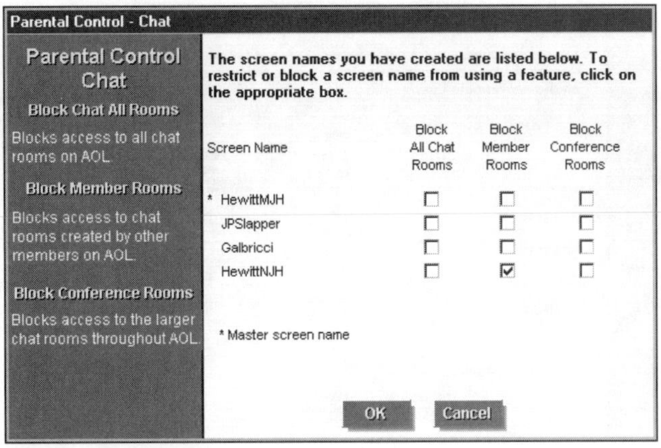

Figure 10.31
Making life difficult in Chat for HewittNJH.

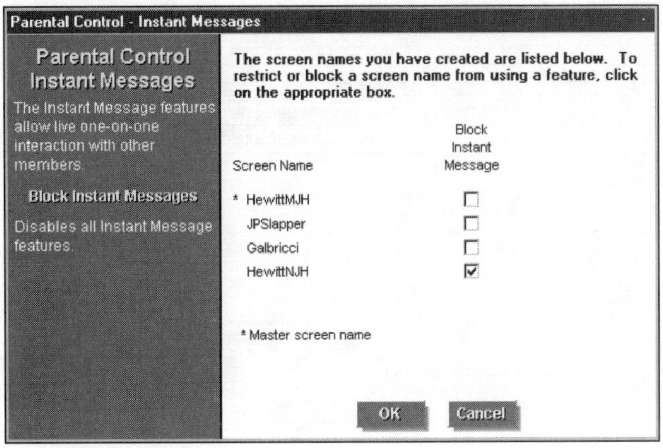

Figure 10.32
Instant Messages—yes or no?

File Downloading

The restrictions, as you can see in Figure 10.33, are as follows:

▲ *Block AOL Software Library Downloads*—He can't download any files from any area of AOL except files attached to email (which, in turn, you can restrict in Mail Controls).

▲ *Block FTP Downloads*—This option prevents him from downloading any files from an FTP site.

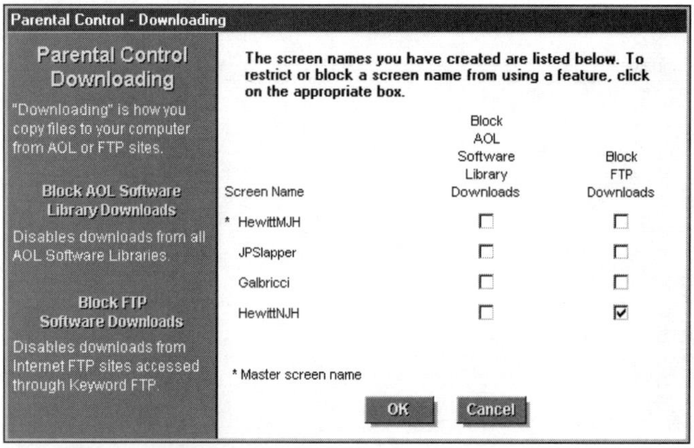

Figure 10.33
Restricting file downloads.

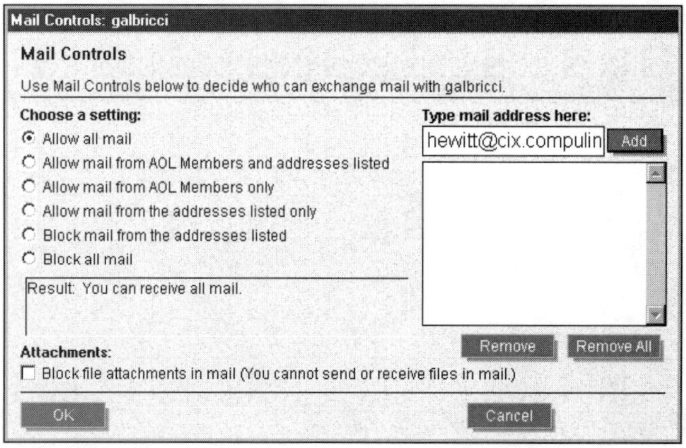

Figure 10.34
Mail Controls.

Mail

As you can see from Figure 10.34, we've been here before. These are the same controls we looked at in Chapter 2 when we were trying to restrict junk mail. I therefore refer you back to that chapter.

Newsgroups

The blocking options in newsgroups (Figure 10.35) are as follows:

▲ *Block Expert Add Of Newsgroups*—AOL doesn't list all of the available newsgroups, especially the more salacious ones. However, as long as

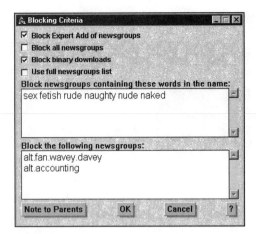

Figure 10.35
Blocking options for newsgroups.

you know their name, you can subscribe to them by using Expert
Add. But with this option checked, you can't.

▲ *Block All Newsgroups*—The ultimate weapon.

▲ *Block Binary Downloads*—Prevents Junior (or your employees, if yours
is a business account) from downloading graphics or other such files
from newsgroups.

▲ *Use Full Newsgroups List*—By default, the Search Newsgroups button
searches only AOL's browsable database of newsgroups. As I said
earlier, this list does *not* contain groups with sexually explicit names.
Nor does it contain newsgroups for which AOL doesn't yet have a
descriptive title. When the Use Full Newsgroups List option is
checked, other screen names using the account are able to search and
browse the complete list of newsgroups AOL carries. Which is why,
initially, this option is disabled. Parents may care to review the full list
before granting access.

You also have the option to block newsgroups whose names include user-
specified words. Here, for example, I don't want junior accessing anything
with "sex," "fetish," "nude," "rude," "naughty," or "naked" in its title. And
you can block specific newsgroups. By way of illustration I've entered
alt.fan.wavey.davey, and, horror of horrors, alt.accounting.

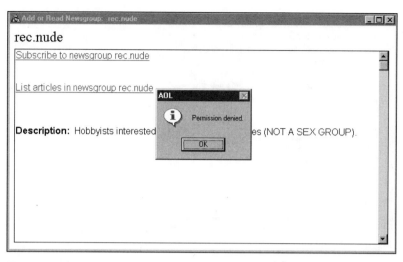

Figure 10.36
If you try to access forbidden territory, AOL demonstrates to you the error of
your ways in no uncertain terms.

Suppose he tries? Then, as you can see in Figure 10.36, he receives an
immediate and sharp rebuff.

I'll end this section with a warning. Parents should, of course, ensure that
they don't let their offspring get to know what the Master account
holder's password is or Junior is liable to do some censorship of his own.

 Caution

> AOL's Parental Control suite provides a range of options to help you manage
> your child's online experience. *There is no replacement, however, for direct
> parental supervision of your child while he or she is online.* Would you let
> your child wander the streets of your neighbourhood alone? Children
> shouldn't be left alone in the online community, either. In fact, AOL's Condi-
> tions of Service *require* that you supervise anyone else using your account,
> and that *you* accept responsibility for their usage of AOL and the Internet
> (see the following section, "Restricting Access To The Internet").

Restricting Access To The Internet

One hears all sorts of horror stories about what's lurking on the Internet
these days. Although there's a certain amount of truth in them, it has to
be said that a lot of it is just newspaper hype. However, there's no smoke

without fire. With this in mind, some of the more responsible Web sites are now giving themselves a rating, similar to the PG, 15, and 18 certificates that operate in the cinema. AOL's Web browser can be configured to read those ratings and filter objectionable material.

To configure the Web browser to restrict access to the Internet, click on the WWW button in Preferences to bring up the AOL Internet Properties screen, which we encountered in Figure 10.9. On this occasion, select the Security tab and proceed as follows.

First, create a Supervisor password for yourself (Figure 10.37). This allows you to change the browser's settings in respect to the material that can be accessed. These settings can only be altered if the Supervisor password is entered (so remember your password!). Click on OK and you reach the Content Advisor screen (Figure 10.38). It has four main controls relating to the levels of language, nudity, sex, and violence the browser will tolerate.

Highlight one of the four—either language, nudity, sex, or violence—and then use the slider bar below to change its rating. Repeat as necessary. It works a bit like the volume control on a hi-fi. It can be set from zero tolerance to, basically, accept all. Nudity, for instance, goes from Accept None to Partially Unclothed right through to Explicit Full-Frontal. Click on Apply when you're done. Thereafter, until those settings are changed, the browser will refuse access to a site that it deems inappropriate according to the settings you've selected. For more detailed information on how to apply these settings, please consult your Windows manual.

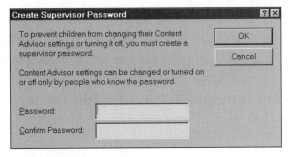

Figure 10.37
Create a Supervisor password before altering the settings.

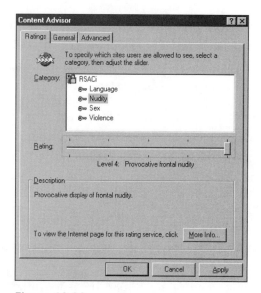

Figure 10.38
How much smut are you prepared to tolerate? None at all, or as much as you can get?

Bear in mind that the system of self-regulation is entirely voluntary. Therefore, potentially undesirable sites that don't regulate themselves can still be accessed. You have three options: Don't allow your children any Internet access at all, restrict them to AOL's own Kids' Internet, or closely supervise their online activities. As I cautioned earlier, the latter is always preferable, regardless of the security settings you've applied to your browser.

AOL Web Controls

The Internet Explorer Content Advisor feature described in the preceding section is only available to Internet Explorer 3.0 users. That means members using the Mac and AOL 2.5i software won't be able to use it, nor will members using the AOL 3.0i 16-bit software who haven't updated their browser to Internet Explorer. (If you're not sure whether you can or should update your browser, go to Keyword: **BROWSER UPGRADE**.)

At press time, AOL was putting the finishing touches on a new set of Web Controls to add to the other Parental Control features (Figure 10.39).

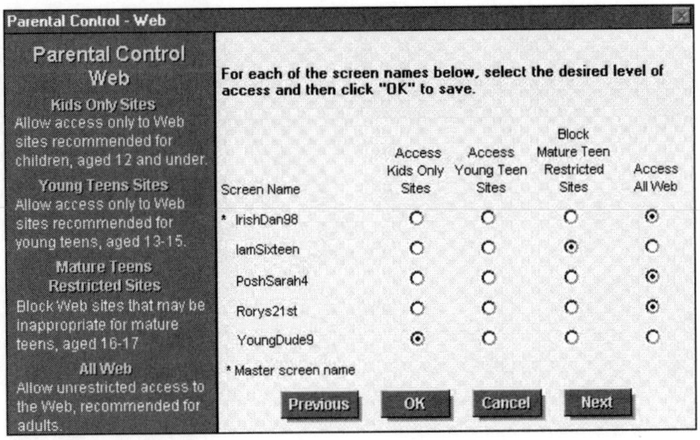

Figure 10.39
Web Controls are the most recent addition to AOL's Parental Control suite.

These Web Controls will complement the Internet Explorer Content Advisor. You'll be able to assign each screen name on your account to one of these four categories: Access All Web, Access Kids Only Sites, Access Young Teen Sites, or Block Mature Teen Restricted Sites.

So much for Preferences and accessing other people's Internet sites. Let's go create some of our own. In the next chapter, I'll show you how to start making a home page.

Chapter 11

Building An Internet Home Page

At one time—not so long ago, in fact—having an Internet home page was regarded by many as a somewhat nerdy hobby, like collecting beer mats or trainspotting. You wouldn't get up in the middle of a crowded bar or restaurant and go public with the fact that you had one. Today, not only is it safe to do that, it's respectable. Almost de rigueur, even. Some of the least nerdy people and organisations in the world now boast home pages—Buckingham Palace, for example, the Vatican, the British Library, and, very shortly, you.

What is a home page? It used to refer simply to the primary menu section of an Internet site; the bit you go to before clicking on submenus and hypertext links to get at underlying information. Indeed, it still does when we're talking about commercial sites. So you get the Microsoft home page, the Polycel home page, and so forth. Increasingly, however, private individuals are setting up their own home pages. Most of them are potted biographies with hypertext links to other Web sites. Sometimes they're just plain text. But in other instances, they can be very elaborately designed and full of fancy graphics, sound effects, and animation.

On AOL, the business of creating a home page is less a business than a pleasure. Within minutes, rather than hours, you too can join the august company of the Pope and the Queen with your own home page.

How? There's the cheap and cheerful approach of using a program called Personal Publisher. This results in a fairly basic page, though nonetheless quite pleasing, very quickly. The second, slightly more difficult method is using a program called AOLPress. When I say "difficult," though, I mean it's difficult in the same sense that using a word processor is difficult at first. In other words, once you've got the hang of it, it isn't.

I'll cover both Personal Publisher and AOLPress in this chapter. However, I'm not going to teach you the finer points of home-page creation, discuss HTML, or anything like that. There are many printed and online resources that go into the matter in far greater detail than I can here (see Keyword: **WEB BUILDING FORUM**). Instead, I'll fill you in on the essentials to get you started, and you can take it from there yourself.

Personal Publisher

Personal Publisher can be found in the Internet Channel or at Keyword: **PERSONAL PUBLISHER** (Figure 11.1). You'll need to download it first, but this doesn't take long and happens automatically, so there's nothing to it. Once done, click on the Create A Page button.

Do you remember when I discussed News Profiles in Chapter 6? In News Profiles, AOL walks you through the whole process. It's exactly the same with Personal Publisher. Step 1 prompts you to select a template for your page (Figure 11.2). Maybe you've used templates before with your word processor. Different types of documents—a business letter, a fax, or a press release, say—require different types of page layout. Word processors take care of this for you by supplying a specific template

Figure 11.1
Personal Publisher is AOL's fast and furious home-page creation program.

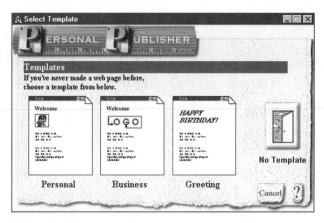

Figure 11.2
Personal Publisher comes supplied with three preformatted page designs, or you can go your own way with no template.

for each. All you then need to worry about is entering the text. It's exactly the same with Personal Publisher. Here, you have four choices: Personal, Business, Greeting, or No Template. In this case, I'm going to choose Personal.

Having chosen my page's layout, I can start to enter text, graphics, and other elements. Upon clicking on Next, I'm prompted to enter a title for my home page and a headline to welcome people to it (Figure 11.3). So, with a stunning lack of originality on my part, I call it Michael Hewitt's Homepage, and for the headline, I type "My home in Epsom", which I

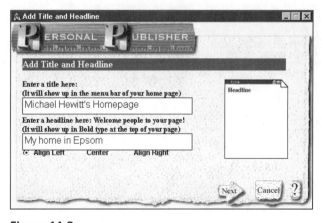

Figure 11.3
Personal Publisher prompts you to enter a title and a headline.

align left. Notice the window on the right. This gives you a visual indication of the order in which the page elements are going to appear. This will become important when you come to edit the page, which I'll talk about shortly. Once you've entered the title and headline, click on Next again.

Do you want a background for your page (Figure 11.4)? You can have patterns, solid colour, or an image of your own choosing. If you want one of your own, click on the Browse My Images button and seek out a suitable graphic from your hard disk. I decide to go for one of the graphics supplied by AOL: a Smiley Tile. I can see what it looks like in the preview screen in the middle. Should that fail to satisfy, I can choose another and view that, too. Or, I can decide not to have a background at all. I can now also determine the colour of the page's body text via the Text Color button. As things stand, my page has a title, a headline, and a background. It needs a bit more than that, doesn't it? So I choose Next once more.

Note: Internet pages will only display two graphics formats: GIF and JPEG. So you can't, for instance, use a bitmap graphic (one with a .BMP extension) as an illustration. What you can do, however, if you're particularly enamoured of a certain graphic and don't want to see it go to waste, is use AOL to convert that file into a JPEG (remember, we discussed this in "Graphics" in Chapter 10). Open up the file in AOL and select Save As from the File menu. Rename the file with a .JPG extension, click on Save, and you're all set. These days,

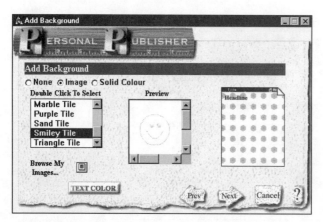

Figure 11.4
Choosing a background for my home page.

most people use the JPEG format in their Internet pages because they can be highly compressed (and therefore don't take as long to load as the larger GIF files) without exhibiting too much image degradation.

An image of its creator is what this page needs. So in the next screen (Figure 11.5), I bypass the collection of images thoughtfully supplied by AOL, click on Browse My Files and choose one called HEWITT. In this instance, HEWITT resides in my Upload folder. Double-clicking on the file name (or selecting it and clicking on Open) inserts the file into the page. Then, I choose Next and move on.

At this point, I'm prompted for personal information (Figure 11.6), so I enter my name, location, and some of my interests and hobbies. You can leave this blank if you want to remain mysterious and enigmatic. I'm an open book, however, and I want to add something to liven that book up: some text and maybe a few links to other pages. So I click on Next.

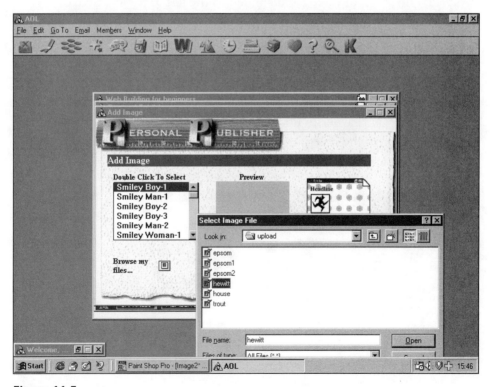

Figure 11.5
Inserting one of my own graphics into the home page.

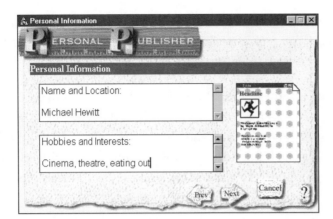

Figure 11.6
Entering personal information.

The Body Text screen appears, and I type in a few sentences (Figure 11.7). You can make portions of the text in larger or smaller fonts; in bold, underline, or italics; and aligned to the left, right, centred, or justified. Highlight a word or phrase and click on any of the font style mini-icons located just above the text box. You can create hyperlinks to Internet and AOL resources by highlighting a word or phrase and dragging an item from the list of Favourite Places over the text. If you would like to make a link to an Internet or AOL resource that isn't already in your Favourite Places list, click on the Add New Location button, type in the description and the Internet address, and click on OK. Here, for instance, I've dragged and dropped BAA flight arrival

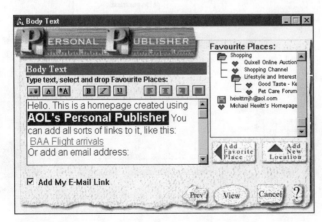

Figure 11.7
Entering text and URLs into the home page.

information. Do you want people to be able to email you simply by clicking on a link in your home page? If so, check the Add My E-Mail Link box. After all that, I think it's time to see what progress we've made. Choose View.

You're shown a preview of how the page will eventually appear once it's been "published" on the Internet (Figure 11.8). As you can see, I've included a graphic of me having a beer on Derby Day at Epsom Race-course. Anyway, the personal information is there, too, as is the text and the URL I inserted earlier. And at the bottom, I've added "Let me know what you think about my page. Send mail by clicking here." If I had left the Add My E-Mail Link box in Figure 11.6 unchecked, this wouldn't have appeared.

So, what do *I* think about my page? If I were satisfied, I could click on the Publish button. But actually, I think I need to improve it a bit. So I choose Edit Page so I can do exactly that.

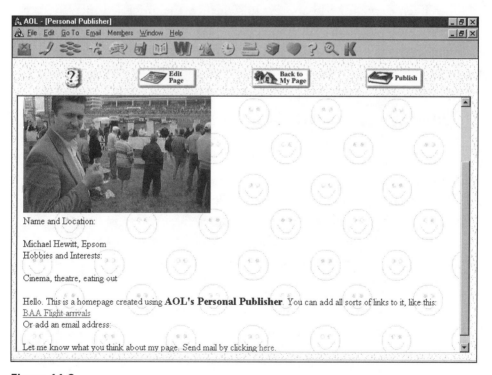

Figure 11.8
The page as it will appear once it is published on the Internet.

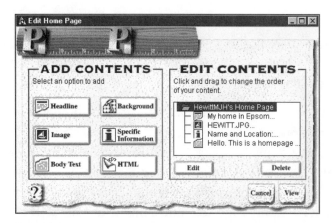

Figure 11.9
If I don't get my page right the first time, I can edit it.

The Edit Page button takes me to the Edit Home Page screen (Figure 11.9). Here I can add, delete, or edit the various elements as the fancy takes me—another headline, another graphic, or some more text, possibly. Each element I add appears in sequence; the order is displayed in the Edit Contents window. If I don't like that order—maybe I want three graphics to appear, one after the other, rather than text, graphic, text, graphic—then I can simply rearrange the sequence by dragging the elements accordingly until they end up in the right order.

When everything has been added that needs to be added (or deleted, or edited), I select View, which takes me back to the image (albeit slightly modified, now) shown in Figure 11.8. Next, I select Publish and I'm immediately prompted for a file name for my page. hewitt.html will do, I decide. I click on OK. And that's it. A few seconds later, a message appears telling me that the Internet address of my page is: **http://members.aol.com/hewittmjh/hewitt.html**. To prove it, I can go to Keyword: **http://members.aol.com/hewittmjh/hewitt.html** and I'm taken straight there (Figure 11.10).

Easy or what? Now, you may not be particularly pleased by your first effort. Many folks aren't. But it doesn't matter; you can keep tweaking and tweaking until you *do* get it right. Don't worry about making a hash of things. Until you actually publish your page on the Web and tell everyone its URL, no one except you will know it's there.

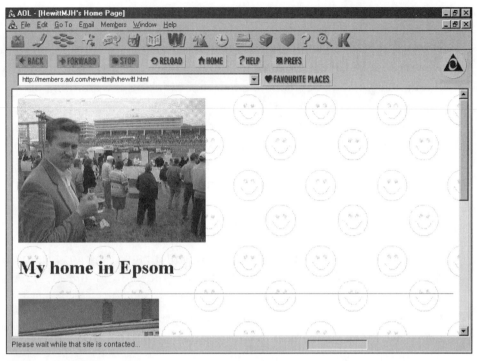

Figure 11.10
My Internet home page, resplendent on the Web.

What's In A Name?

I called my home page file HEWITT.HTML. The suffix stands for Hypertext Markup Language. Don't worry about this. Just as Word for Windows documents have a .DOC suffix and Excel spreadsheet files an .XLS suffix, so World Wide Web documents are saved with an .HTML suffix. One thing you should note, though: PC file extensions can't have more than three letters, so if you're saving an HTML document on your PC as opposed to on the Internet proper, the suffix will be abbreviated to .HTM. It makes no difference to how it works.

But here's how it works. The text proper of my home page, together with its formatting information—fonts, type colour, type size, justification, Web link addresses, and so on—is saved in a single .HTM (or .HTML) document. However, images are saved separately from this main document and are only called into it when you actually access the page on the Internet. The HTML codes tell the page which images are to be incorporated and where on the Net they're stored. This is why, when you open a typical Web page, the text appears first and then the images are pulled in and assembled together with that text.

AOLPress

Personal Publisher can produce respectable, pleasing results in a comparatively short time. One drawback to it is that you have to be online throughout your act of creation. So all that tweaking and shuffling of page elements is costing you, if not on your AOL bill (if you've selected unlimited access pricing), then certainly on your telephone bill. Therefore, you might consider using an alternative: AOL's very own AOLPress, which works offline. It's slightly more difficult to use than Personal Publisher, but the results are well worth the effort.

The following description of how it works is just that—a description, and a deliberately brief one. If you want to learn the nuts and bolts, I would advise you to send off for the documentation or download it from the AOLPress area (Keyword: **AOLPRESS**), shown in Figure 11.11. At 28,800bps, AOLPress takes just over 15 minutes to arrive. Once everything is saved to your PC's hard disk, decompress the file and install it. I don't have to tell you about software installation, do I? Read your Windows manual if you have any doubts.

I'm now assuming you're installed, up, and running. So let's compose a home page.

First, go to the AOLPress File menu and select New Page. A hi-tech *tabula rasa* (see Keyword: **OXFORD DICTIONARY**) then appears

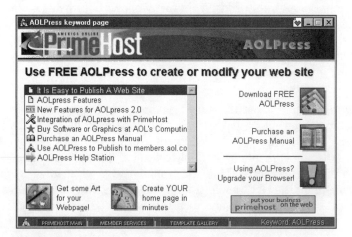

Figure 11.11
AOL's very own home-page creation program, AOLPress.

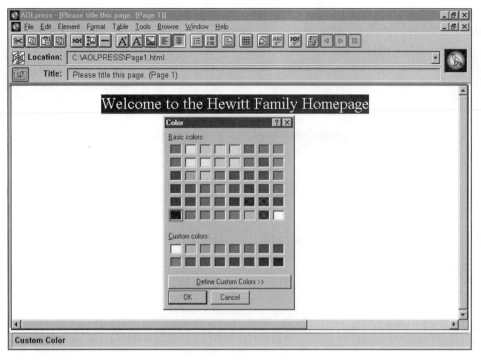

Figure 11.12
Using AOLPress is much like using a word processor.

(Figure 11.12). "Welcome to the Hewitt Family Homepage", I type. I'm not satisfied with just plain text, though. I want it written large and coloured blue. So I go to the Format menu and change the type style, size, and colour until I arrive at what I require.

Yes, it *is* just like using a word processor or DTP package, isn't it? Indeed, if you can use a program like Word for Windows, you're already 80 per cent of the way toward knowing how to construct a home page.

At this point, I insert a table by double-clicking on the table icon on the toolbar. Why a table? Because I want a multicolumn appearance with side-by-side graphics and accompanying text beneath them. The difficult way of doing this is to define precise page coordinates for those individual graphics and pieces of text. But why be hard on yourself? Create a table and you can simply drop the individual text and graphic elements into the separate cells in a couple of seconds. Here I define the table as six rows deep and two columns wide (Figure 11.13). Having clicked on

Figure 11.13
Inserting text and graphics into a table simplifies things enormously.

OK, I then see it sitting there on the page, pretty vacantly, my cursor blinking away in the cell in the top left (Figure 11.14).

I intend to insert a photograph into this first cell. So I click on the Insert Graphic icon and the Image screen appears (Figure 11.15). You're presumably used to how this works by now. Using the Browse button, I seek out the required file, hewitts1.jpg, from the Upload folder. In the Description window, I type "The Hewitt Brothers". The description is for the benefit of people—and there are still quite a few of them—who are using nongraphical Web browsers; in other words, browsers that can display text but not pictures. So my description tells them what they *would* be seeing if they sorted themselves out and used a proper Web browser. Then I press Return or click on OK. Thereupon, the cell becomes host to a picture of the three Hewitts (Figure 11.16). (I'm the handsome one in the middle, by the way.) When you insert graphics (and text) into the table, the cells obligingly expand to accommodate the insertion, so you don't have to define size or positioning.

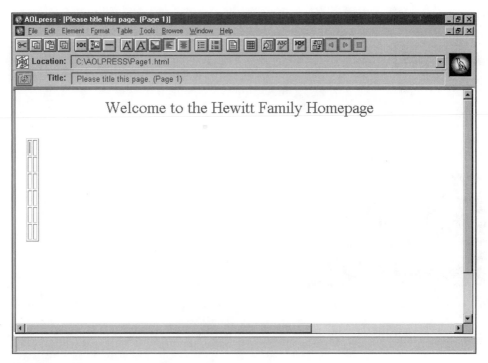

Figure 11.14
My table is created. Now what shall I put into it?

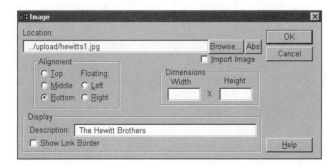

Figure 11.15
Use the Image window to choose the graphics file you want to insert into
the page.

> *Note: By default, the gridlines on a table created in AOLPress are visible. But
> if you're using the table simply for the purpose of positioning text and graphics,
> as I am, you might prefer to turn the gridlines off. This is best done at the end
> when all the page elements are in place. Go to the Table preferences under the
> Table menu.*

Figure 11.16
The Hewitt brothers somewhere in Greece.

Next, I do likewise with the second cell. Except into this one, I insert a picture of the oldest surviving member of our family, my Great Aunt Lilly, still going strong in her late 90s (Figure 11.17). You'll note, too, that I've captioned both graphics. This I did by typing directly into the cells—3 and 4—beneath the graphics. And you can't have failed to notice the Email Link window.

By now, during your Internet browsing, you'll have frequently encountered the legend "To email me, click *here*", or something similar. When you do click on "here," the Write Email screen appears, automatically addressed. There's nothing complicated or technically whizzy about this, though. Simply highlight the word or section of text you want to render clickable—in this case, "here"—and select E-mail Link, which is found under the Elements menu. This causes the aforementioned window to appear, into which you type the required email address and click on OK.

You can create a hypertext link almost the same way you create an email link. Highlight the word or words you want to click to reach your link

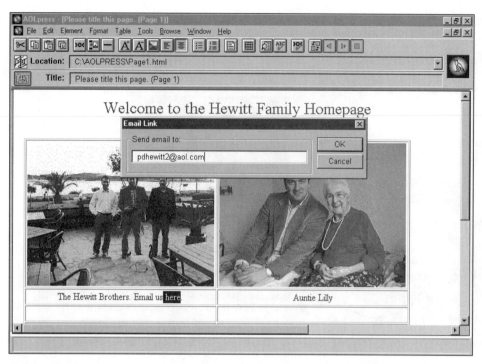

Figure 11.17
A picture of my Great Aunt Lilly, with an email link in mid-creation.

and then go to Link in the Elements menu. Type the URL, click on OK, and you're in business. To prove it, the previously highlighted text turns blue (assuming you've left blue as the default link colour).

Next, I insert a picture of my brother Peter and his wife, Pam, into cell number 5 and a small picture of their cat, Benjamin, into cell 6. And just to show what a hotshot home-page creator I am, I decide to insert some text into that cell, too, and flow it around the cat (Figure 11.18). This is done by positioning the cursor next to Benjamin, choosing Import from the File menu, and locating the desired text by following the usual prompts. Once you've done so, it simply flows in and around. You can only import raw ASCII text (i.e., a file with a .TXT extension), by the way, because text saved in a word-processor format (such as Word for Windows) contains lots of control and formatting characters in addition to the text itself. AOLPress doesn't take kindly to these.

I've also decided to prettify the page a little more (Figure 11.19). From the Page Attributes window (select Page Attributes from the Format

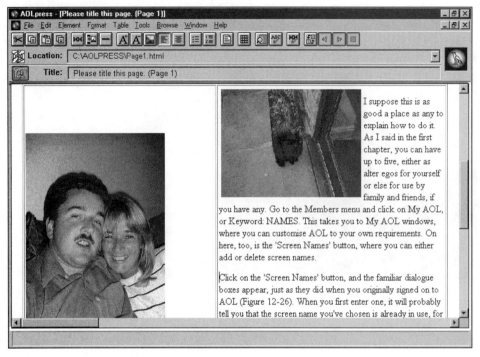

Figure 11.18
Flowing text around Benjamin.

menu), I can, among many other things, select a background colour or image, change the text and link colours, and even assign a censorship rating to the page (I talked about this in Chapter 10—you can determine whether your page is the Internet equivalent of U, PG, or 18). I'm content to set the background colour to light blue. And I'm done.

So much for that. Currently, however, my page is still on my PC. It isn't much use there. To publish it on the Internet, AOLPress and AOL must be running simultaneously. Once you've signed on to AOL, select Save As from the AOLPress file menu (Figure 11.20).

I enter the page name "http://members.aol.com/hewittmjh/hewittf.htm". The hewittmjh bit is particularly important because the area of AOL specifically designated as my private territory corresponds to my screen name. If I don't specify it, or if I try to save the page in someone else's directory or in one that doesn't exist, I'll get an error message. In this case, though, all goes to plan. I click on OK and the page and its separate

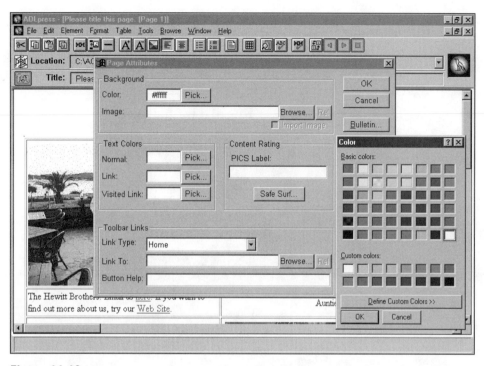

Figure 11.19
Setting various page attributes, including background colour and accessibility ratings.

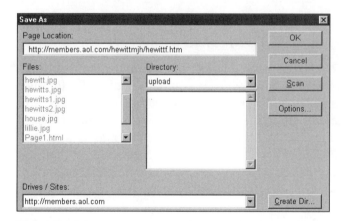

Figure 11.20
In AOLPress, publishing a page on the Internet is identical to saving a file on
your computer.

text and graphic elements are all sent up to AOL and stored there. To
prove it, go to Keyword: **http://members.aol.com/hewittmjh/hewittf.htm**
(Figure 11.21).

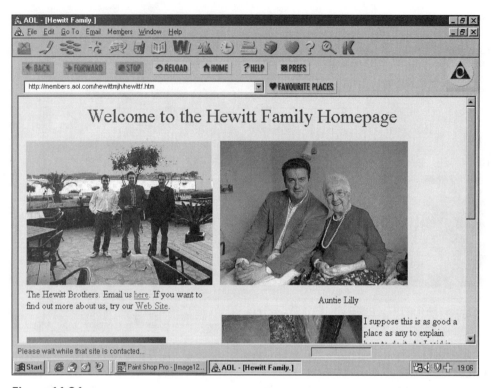

Figure 11.21
My home page in all its glory.

TIP — *Keep An Eye On Your Size*

You can store up to 2MB of text and graphics per screen name for your home page. So this, effectively, gives you a maximum size of 2MB. However, that's actually quite respectable. You can fit a few hundred pages of text and a large number of pictures into a space that big. Of course, there's nothing stopping you from conglomerating the Web space for the other four screen names that you get with your account to beef your capacity up to 10MB. But if you're the kind of person who needs a 10MB home page, you're almost certainly the kind of person who already knows how to do this!

Obviously, I've just scratched the surface here. AOLPress is a flexible and impressive home-page creation program. As I said, order the manual if you want to find out how to use its facilities to the fullest. Or use the online help, which is very good. To access it, you'll need to be running AOLPress concurrently with AOL. And for further information, I warmly recommend—especially because it has AOLPress and lots of other useful Internet utilities on the accompanying CD-ROM—a book called *Build a Web Site in a Day*, by Thomas Wrona and Elisabeth Parker, published by Ventana (ISBN 1-56604-514-2).

And now we move on from home page creation to Chapter 12, where we'll be looking at AOL for the Macintosh.

Chapter 12

AOL On The Macintosh

This chapter is intended for Mac users—you know who you are—and details some of the ways in which your version of AOL differs from the PC version described throughout this book so far. Most of the differences are in the email features of the AOL software, so this is what we'll be concentrating on.

The Email Menu

You Mac users out there have far fewer menu choices than your PC counterparts as far as email is concerned. They go like this:

▲ *Compose Mail*—The Compose Mail option is the same on the Mac as it is on the PC.

▲ *Read Mail*—The Mac user has no need for Read New Email because both old and new email messages are listed in parallel within a single, convenient Mailbox. There's more on this feature later in this chapter.

▲ *Address Book*—The Address Book is a more graphic-style address book than the PC version and is explained in greater detail later in this chapter.

▲ *Offline Email*—Offline Email is a Mac-style file/folder screen with click-down lists of the following items: Incoming FlashMail, Outgoing FlashMail, and Sent Mail. You simply click on the little arrows next to each title and the list of email files appears underneath. Mac owners will be familiar with this as it apes the usual Mac folder (what PC owners might call directories) style. You can drag email messages between folders just as you can in any other Mac folder window. The Offline Email screen contains the following buttons:

▲ *Delete*—You guessed it; deletes a file/email.

▲ *New folder*—Adds other/new folders to the list in the window.

▲ *Find*—Opens a dialogue box enabling you to find a filed email message.

▲ *Open*—Click on one of the email messages listed, click on Open, and the Compose Email screen with the selected email appears just as you wrote it.

▲ *Set Up FlashSession/Auto AOL*—This option is similar to its counterpart in the PC version of AOL (but you activate it via the Preferences box, as we'll see in the next section). Auto AOL sets up FlashSessions as it does in the PC version of AOL, so we won't spend any time on that here.

▲ *Email Centre*—The Email Centre option sends you to the Post Room screen.

▲ *Email Controls*—This option takes you straight to your email controls so you don't need to access them via the Post Room screen (unless you want to).

Email Preferences On The Mac

In the Mac version of AOL, select Preferences from the Members menu and then click on Email (not Mail, as you would on the PC). The email preferences boxes are different, too. For example, to save copies of the messages you send, you need to check the Save The Email I Send In My Filing Cabinet box.

While we're on the subject of preferences, there are many more Preferences settings here and they are different from the PC as follows:

▲ *AOL Link*—This feature allows Mac users to run TCP/IP applications over their AOL connection (Figure 12.1), which means you can

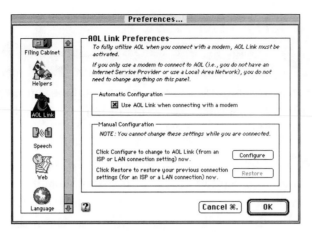

Figure 12.1
If you feel so inclined, you can run TCP/IP applications.

always keep up with the latest browser releases, use Telnet programs, and chat with Internet users on Internet Relay Chat (IRC).

▲ *Speech Preferences*—Here you can alter the Chat room speech capabilities of your AOL software on the Mac (Figure 12.2). For instance, you can select Allow Text-To-Speech and then select the kind of voice you wish to hear.

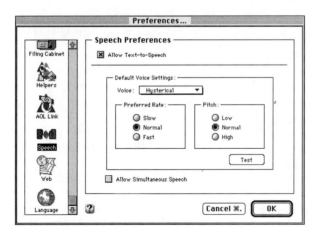

Figure 12.2
Alter the chat room speech capabilities of your software.

Sending Email On The Mac

You do not get a Write Email screen on the Mac; instead, after you click on the pencil icon or go to "Compose email" under the Email menu, you'll get an untitled window. It has no name on it unless you save the email to your Offline Email folder or Personal Filing Cabinet. In many ways, it is like the PC Write Email screen.

Click the Attach Files button and you'll get a typical Mac dialogue box asking you which file you want to attach. In the Mac version of AOL, you can attach numerous files to one email message and send the lot in one go as opposed to the one-file (zipped or otherwise) limit the PC version of AOL imposes. The Mac software compresses all the files ("stuffs" them) and sends them all at once. The Mac automatically uncompresses the "stuffed" file and shows the individual files when they are opened by the recipient of the email message.

If you try to close the email screen without sending the email or saving it for later, you will be prompted with a dialogue box asking you if you are sure you wish to do so. Incidentally, on this topic of saving emails, one of the nice things about the Save Email feature on the Mac software is that, unlike the PC version, when you save a message, AOL saves the address sections as well as the message part. This is especially useful if you need to transfer email messages between different copies of AOL (at home and at work, for example).

If you want to send the same email message to more than one person, you don't list them with a comma and space as in the PC version of AOL; you simply type the first name and press Return. A new To line instantly appears underneath, and you can then enter another recipient for the message (Figure 12.3).

Copying Your Email To Other Recipients

There is no CC box on the Mac version of the AOL software. Instead, in the Address To box, you will notice that there's a tiny arrow next to a little envelope icon. If you click on the arrow, the CC and BCC lines appear, or you can double-click on the envelope and you will get a

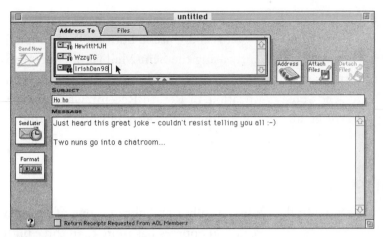

Figure 12.3
Just type the first name and press Return.

separate dialogue box that lets you add in a CC or BCC. There are a few other things that are worth noting here.

In the PC version of AOL, you cannot leave the Subject field blank—if you try, the email will not be sent. With the Mac you can, in fact, leave your email without a subject line. Another feature of the Mac software that you won't find on the PC version is that you can use the Tab button to format the message part of your email. This can be useful in many instances—most especially if you wish to send text in columns, as in a mini-spreadsheet. On the PC, clicking on the Tab button within the message field actually moves you between fields and onto the buttons, so Mac users have a useful advantage there.

Reading Email

The Read Email screen is really three screens in one with a tab system across the top to enable you to switch between them. Anyone who uses the latest Mac MS Word package will know what this is like. It allows you to move between New Mail, Old Mail, and Sent Mail screens with just a mouse click. Just as in the PC version of AOL, if an email message has a file attached to it, the little letter icon that starts the email description line has a computer floppy disk icon attached to it.

Different buttons become active when you switch between New Mail, Old Mail, or Sent Mail—the Status and Unsend buttons, for example, become active when you're currently using the Sent Mail view. For really important messages that you send to other AOL members, you can actually ask AOL to send you a notification, or Return Receipt, when your recipient has read the email. So there's no need to even click on a button to find out when your latest missive has been digested (Figure 12.4).

Replying To Email

When you go to the Online Mailbox and click on one of your newly arrived missives, the screen that appears has more than three buttons. You'll get a Delete button too. To complicate things just a little further, there is a little arrow next to the From/To window that switches between two different versions of this screen.

The first version has a large From/To window that tells you who the email was from and who it was to. You can grab these names and drag them elsewhere. You can also pull down the bottom of this field if there are many more people included in the list. And you can scroll up and down the list. If there is a file or files attached to the email, there will be a floppy disk icon next to the Files tab at the top of the screen. Click on the Files tab or the floppy disc icon and it will show you what the file(s)

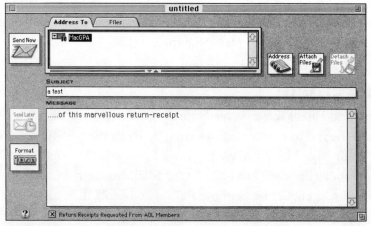

Figure 12.4
You can get AOL to tell you if the mail has actually been received.

is/are. Click on the actual file icon and it will save the file after opening a dialogue box that asks you where you want to put it. Subject and message windows are much the same as they are for when you compose an original email. Next to the Subject field, there is an icon of a letter over which some type tells you which particular email you are looking at, in what sequence it appears, and how many email messages there are in the Mailbox window. Clicking on it will send you back to the Online Mailbox.

TIP Automatic Address Book Entry

Worthy of mention here is yet another nice feature that the PC version of AOL doesn't include. When you're reading email messages, you may notice that the Address Book button changes so it has a plus sign over it. Click on the plus sign and the name of the sender is instantly added to your Address Book!

The second type of email screen is a little simpler. This one only tells you who the email is from. Subject and message windows (and a letter icon) are as before. Again, a floppy disk icon tells you a file is attached (but you'll note that there are no Download or Address Book buttons). Click on the disk icon and AOL will ask you where to download the file.

The Address Book

Compared to the PC version of AOL, the Mac's Address Book is totally different. For a start, it looks a bit like a proper ring-bound address book on screen (Figure 12.5).

Click on Edit Book and you'll get a list of the addresses you have inserted in your Address Book plus some buttons underneath to manage them: Delete, Edit, Group, New Person. There is also a separate Search Dictionaries button that searches the AOL member list for names like the one you're trying to remember.

Click on a name in your Address Book page and you can edit or delete it. Click on Edit and you'll get a screen that looks like a page out of a personal organiser, with fields for first name, last name, email address, and notes. You can change the information in these fields at will and

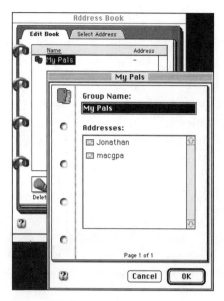

Figure 12.5
The Mac's Address Book actually looks like the proper ring-bound article.

resave the entry. Click on New Person and you'll get an empty personal organiser-type screen with the same fields to fill out for the new entry in your address book. Click on New Group and you'll find that you can input individual names underneath a group title, which is useful, for example, if you wish to keep friends, family, and business contacts in separate places.

Best of all, you can drag and drop an address from your address book directly into the To, CC, or BCC fields of the email you're writing. So, you simply click on the Compose Email pencil icon to bring up the window, click on the Address Book button, and drag the name of the person from the page of the address book straight into the To field. Alternatively, you can use the other tab at the top of the Address Book, Select Address, which gives you the option of using the currently high-lighted address book entry as a CC, BCC, or To entry in your email. So it's as easy as clicking on the name of the person and then clicking on the appropriate button; the field on the email message is filled in for you.

Livening Up Your Email

Unlike the PC version of AOL, where the text-formatting buttons are placed between the subject and text body areas, on the Mac AOL, there is a dedicated Format button. It brings up a window with all the formats for text: font, size, bold, alignment, colour, and so on (Figure 12.6).

You can also add text enhancements by using the Format button in the main AOL menu at the top of your screen. And on top of these features, you can specify settings for your font environment. You can also choose the fonts to use elsewhere—in Chat and text documents, for example.

The process of adding hyperlinks to email messages is slightly different on the Mac, too. You can click on the Link button and it asks which word you want activated as the link and the address to which you want the link to point. In the PC version, you can drag a Favourite Place heart from an AOL window or Web site and drop it straight into an email message to create a hyperlink. The same is true for the Mac version.

OK. That's just about all there is to say about email. There are a few other features of the Mac software to mention. One thing you'll notice straightaway is the familiar Mac-style "files and folder" way of organising information. This is the case all the way through from file-save dialogues

Figure 12.6
The Mac version of AOL has a dedicated Format button.

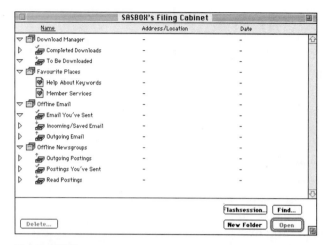

Figure 12.7
The Mac version of AOL has a somewhat more familiar way of organising files.

to your Personal Filing Cabinet (Figure 12.7). Another great thing is that the Web browser in Mac AOL is Internet Explorer version 2.7.

Big deal, you might say. Well it is; you can use Netscape plug-ins to your heart's desire with it. And over your AOL Link, you can use Internet Explorer 3.01. So you're not being shortchanged when it comes to your Web experience—not at all. Did I mention floating toolbars (Figure 12.8) and a more customisable interface for Mac AOL? I'll leave that one with you.

Figure 12.8
The Mac version of AOL's floating toolbar.

Chapter 13

A Preview Of AOL Version 4.0i

The focus of this book has been on the AOL version 3.0i software, but in this chapter, I'll give you a preview of AOL version 4.0i. This isn't just any old upgrade. In fact, AOL 4.0i represents a significant advance in AOL's functionality *and* performance. It's rather like going from a 486 PC to a Pentium Pro and then some. I'll list some of the major changes, but please bear in mind that this chapter is based on a beta version of the software. When it's officially launched (in late '98 or early '99), the genuine article may very well look different and boast even more features than those I'll describe here.

Installation

The installation procedure for version 3.0i doesn't really distinguish between existing members and new members, whereas the procedure for version 4.0i does (Figure 13.1). But that's not all. Existing members are also asked the following questions:

▲ Are you upgrading to a new version of AOL?

▲ Are you an existing member of AOL who's installing the AOL software on this particular computer for the first time?

▲ Do you already have an AOL account active on this computer, and if so, do you want to add an additional account?

Each option takes you through a slightly different installation procedure. And as the installation is taking place, you'll see a little animated graphic of a pair of legs in action. This gives you something to look at while

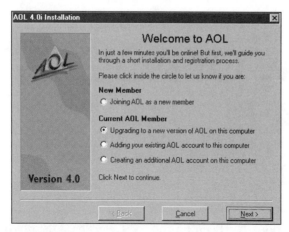

Figure 13.1
Are you joining AOL as a new member, or are you a current member who
is upgrading?

installation takes place, and also acts as a visual indication that the
program is actually working and hasn't frozen you out.

Once you've chosen the folder into which you want AOL installed, the
installation proper begins. It takes only a few minutes. During the
installation of this version, the software flashes up various messages
telling you what you can look forward to once you've signed on and the
sorts of features AOL and the 4.0i software have to offer.

Before you sign on for the first time, you're asked to select the country
from which you're dialing. Then you're prompted to choose at least two
access phone numbers (Figure 13.2) from those available. If your first
number is busy or unobtainable (which rarely happens), AOL will
automatically dial the second number. Once your selections have been
made, you can sign on. From the start, the new pastel-drawn designs on
the Connecting screen show you that this is not like any other version of
AOL you've ever used (Figure 13.3).

Navigation

You'll notice at once that version 4.0i *looks* very different from its predecessors (Figure 13.4). To begin with, all the Channels are now listed
down the left side of every AOL Channel screen. You'll be able to go
from Sports to Entertainment to Shopping with one click.

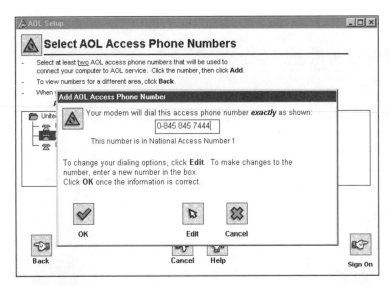

Figure 13.2
Selecting AOL access numbers.

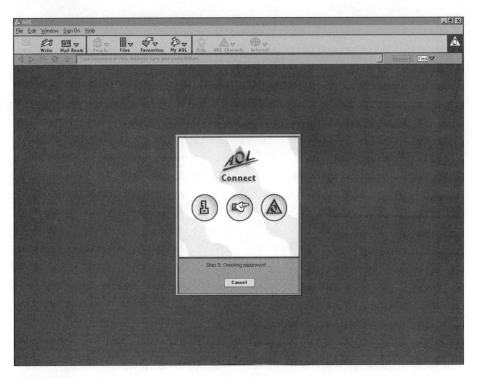

Figure 13.3
Even from the Connecting screen, you can see that AOL version 4.0i is a very different beast from its predecessors.

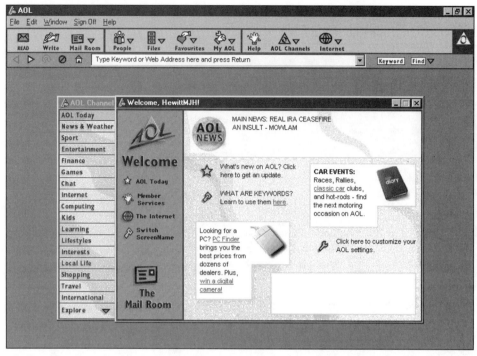

Figure 13.4
In version 4.0i, you can access all the Channels from every Channel screen.

The Toolbar And Keywords

The new Toolbar offers one-step access to the Web and AOL areas, as well as shortcuts to AOL's most popular features (like email, Chat, Favourite Places, and more). You'll likely use the Toolbar for almost everything you need to do online. Its main features include the following:

▲ It's customisable. You can add or remove buttons (if your monitor's set to 800×600 or greater) or collapse the Toolbar to display only text labels.

▲ The Keyword field is incorporated into the Toolbar. Enter any AOL Keyword or Internet address (as you would into a Web browser), click on Go, and you're taken directly to the online area you've specified.

▲ The Toolbar tracks the areas you visit and provides a "history trail" (Figure 13.5). Just click on the down arrow to the right of the input box to see a list of the last 25 places you've visited.

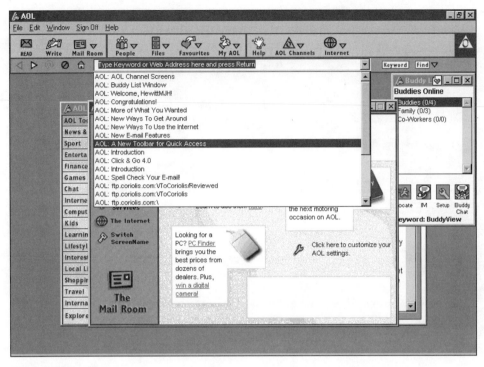

Figure 13.5
The Toolbar tracks where you've been on AOL and provides a history trail.

▲ The Web browser controls are incorporated into the Toolbar, which means you can use the Forward and Back buttons to navigate through AOL areas, too.

▲ The new drop-down menus take you right to AOL's most popular features and areas (Figure 13.6).

▲ The Files drop-down menu provides easy access to your Personal Filing Cabinet, Web page, Download Manager, and more.

Favourite Places

Favourite Places are now displayed both in the conventional Favourite Places window and in a drop-down menu. In addition, when you click on the heart icon to designate an area as a Favourite Place, you're prompted as to where you want to insert it: in the Favourite Places window, in an Instant Message, or in an email message (Figure 13.7). You can even add a few of your Favourite Places right onto the Toolbar for super-quick access.

Figure 13.6
New drop-down menus speed your way around AOL.

Figure 13.7
Where do you want to place your Favourite Place—in the Favourite Places window, in an Instant Message, or in email?

Email

There have been some major changes to email. For example, you can now insert photographs and graphics directly into your messages (Figure 13.8). Provided the person on the receiving end is an AOL member using version 4.0i software, he'll be treated to your graphical delights.

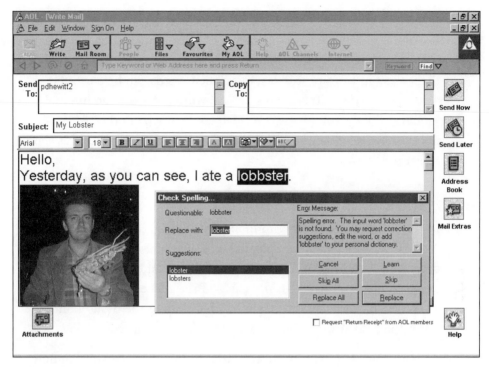

Figure 13.8
Graphics can now be inserted into email, and your outgoing messages can
be spellchecked.

Before he is, though, he'll receive a warning message informing him that
the incoming email contains an embedded graphic. This is for security
reasons, to guard against receipt of objectionable material.

In addition, you can insert specially designed letterheads into email,
either from AOL's default collection or of your own making. You can also
change text fonts from the default Arial. Again, only AOL members also
using version 4.0i software will be able to view your customized messages; those on version 3.0i or earlier will see the default Arial font.

You can now send multiple file attachments with email, too. Previously,
you could only attach one file per message. If you needed to send more
than one file, you either sent multiple emails or you had to compress the
files using something like WinZip. With version 4.0i, however, you can
attach as many files as you like and AOL will automatically zip them for
you. One caveat: the total size of the zipped file must be less than 16MB
or AOL won't send the mail.

You can also now spellcheck your email messages. You can have AOL perform the spellcheck automatically each time you click on Send, or you can spellcheck your missives manually, as and when you choose. As with spellcheckers in word processors, misspelled words can be corrected onscreen, and "specialist" or nonstandard words added to an internal dictionary. Finally, you can ask AOL to confirm when other AOL members have read the message by sending you a return receipt as soon as they do so.

Address Book

The new Address Book now stores entries alphabetically as opposed to sequentially (I can hear your applause now!). You also have the option of adding notes to entries and, if your stomach can take it, pictures of addressees, too (Figure 13.9). You can add the addresses of people who send you email to the Address Book with a click of the mouse. Simply click on the Add Address button when you're reading the email.

Another useful improvement to the Address Book is that you can now copy and paste entries from and to it.

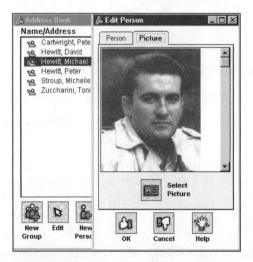

Figure 13.9
The new Address Book stores entries alphabetically and includes space for notes and pictures.

Chat

One of the most challenging things about Chat is infusing mere text with your wit, personality, and emotions. Smileys are all well and good, but 4.0i allows you to add text enhancements—change of font, font size, and style, for instance—to your Chat (Figure 13.10). Another use for this feature will be to help distinguish one person's chat from another's, especially in very busy rooms. Of course, only those using compatible software will be able to view your prettifications. You can also insert your Favourite Places directly into chat, where they'll show up as Keywords other members can check out.

Switch Screen Names On The Fly

If you have more than one screen name on your account, you can now change from one screen name to another while you're online, without hanging up the phone (Figure 13.11). Previously, to use a different screen name, you had to sign off, change the name, then sign on again—incurring the cost of a new phone call only to find out you had no email waiting. The best news is, before you do switch names, you can check to see whether your other screen names have email waiting for them.

You can switch screen names by selecting Sign Off from the menu bar or by clicking on the Switch Screen Names button on the Welcome screen.

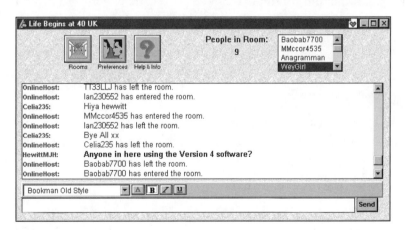

Figure 13.10
You can now add text enhancement to Chat messages.

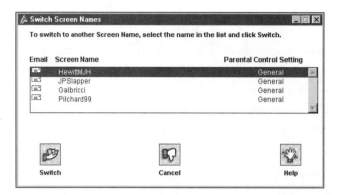

Figure 13.11
If your account has multiple screen names, you can now switch between them without having to sign off first.

The Best Of The Rest

Here are some of the other new features to look out for:

▲ You can switch locations (the Internet or an AOL access point abroad, for example) via a drop-down menu on the Sign-on screen, rather than having to navigate multiple setup screens.

▲ You can now set a default font and type colour to use when you're online. The default font will show up in your email, Instant Messages, Chat, and so on. Those viewing your IMs, email, or Chat must have the same font on their computer to get the benefit, however. If they don't, your message will show up for them in the default Arial font.

▲ You can password-protect your Personal Filing Cabinet to stop other people with access to your computer from prying into your private correspondence.

And that's my taster for you. As I said, when the software eventually goes live, there should be quite a lot more. All I can do here, like a trailer at the Odeon, is preview it as a "Coming Attraction." I'm certain it will be worth waiting for!

Next, I do my equivalent of "My Way." It's time to face the final curtain with Chapter 14 and a look at—amongst other things—the AOL community and online etiquette.

Chapter 14

Member Services
And Help

In this, the final chapter, I'll be looking at the community aspects of AOL and the way in which it does its utmost to provide assistance and advice to the members of its community. This includes regular updates on what's new, handy hints and tips, and one of the most comprehensive help sections of any online service. Then I'll be talking about how to comport yourself online, rules of the road, and that sort of thing. Finally, there are details on how to use AOL as a guest from someone else's computer and how to sign on over the Internet while travelling abroad.

What's New And Grand Tour

Trying to write an up-to-date guide to an online service—*any* online service, not just AOL—will usually be a bit like attempting to hit one of those plastic ducks at a fairground rifle range. AOL is always going to be improving and expanding through its members' input and because of periodic software and hardware upgrades. Therefore, don't regard what I've said in the preceding chapters as gospel. This book is intended primarily as a guide rather than an instruction manual. The only proper way to find out how everything works and to learn about any enhancements and additions to the service is to actually use AOL.

Usually, when new content and features are first introduced, they're advertised via promotional text and an icon on the Welcome screen when you sign on. Just click on that icon and you'll go straight to that new content. But if you haven't signed on for a while and you're worried you might have missed something, the best place to find out what's new is, perhaps unsurprisingly, to go to Keyword: **NEW**. Or click on the Toolbar's

What's New icon. This lists all of the most recent contents and features (Figure 14.1).

Another good guide to AOL—one that's far more up-to-date than mine could ever be—is the AOL QuickTour (Figure 14.2). Go to Keyword: **TOUR** and you'll see highlights of current offers (grouped by topic) and any major new developments.

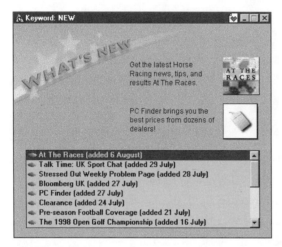

Figure 14.1
What's New is the place to go to find out the latest developments on AOL.

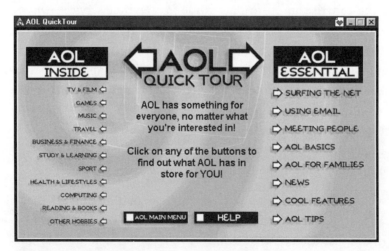

Figure 14.2
The AOL QuickTour takes in all the sights of AOL.

Help!

AOL is, as you've discovered by now, an extremely intuitive and easy-to-use service. This will be especially apparent if you've ever used rival online systems. Nevertheless, regardless of how user-friendly AOL is *intended* to be, because of its very nature, size, and scope, and all the different computers, modems, and phone connections its members use, there will occasionally be some problems. After all, accessing and transmitting text and visual data over a global network isn't exactly something that comes naturally—to anyone.

If you have a question, you can, of course, call the freephone number 0800 279 7444 and they'll sort out any difficulties very quickly. But before you do, you might care to go to Keyword: **QUESTIONS**. This takes you to the Frequently Asked Questions area (Figure 14.3). Here, AOL has compiled a list, organised by category, of answers to the most common queries. Whether you need to know more about email, your account, the Internet, or whatever, likely as not, you'll find your answer here.

Another place you can try is All About AOL (Keyword: **AAA**). In addition to links to Frequently Asked Questions and the AOL Grand Tour, All About AOL includes an A-to-Z glossary of AOL and the Internet, as well as information on email and Keywords. If you still can't

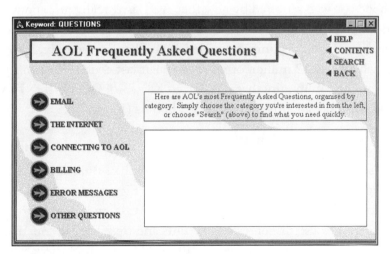

Figure 14.3
Keyword: **QUESTIONS** will probably have your answer.

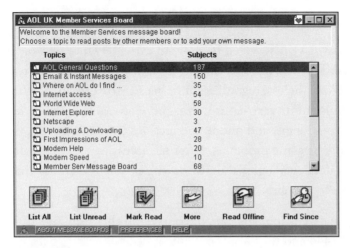

Figure 14.4
Ask fellow AOL members in the UK Member Services Board.

find answers, try posting your question in the UK Member Services Board (Figure 14.4). There, other AOL members, as well as staff, will be more than willing to help you out.

And, finally, please remember: There is no such thing as a stupid question.

The AOL Community

I hope you've discovered by now that AOL isn't really just about computers and the Internet. True, there wouldn't be an AOL without them. But they're not the most important elements. The members are. It's you, the members—all 12 million or more of you at last count—that make AOL the online community that it is. Go to Keyword: **COMMUNITY** and find out more about your online neighbours (Figure 14.5).

In this section, you'll find:

▲ *Jonathan's Letter*—Every two weeks, Jonathan Bulkeley, AOL's Managing Director, addresses the members (Figure 14.6). He discusses topical issues and events, new areas in AOL, and changes to existing areas. He also dispenses handy hints and tips. To read Jonathan's Letter, simply go to Keyword: **JONATHAN**. From there, you can also subscribe to get Jonathan's Letter via email and read an archive of past tips. Otherwise, go to Keyword: **AOL TIPS** (Figure 14.7).

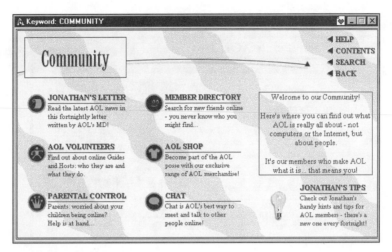

Figure 14.5
AOL is one vast, global online community.

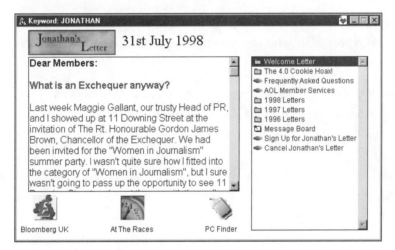

Figure 14.6
Jonathan's regular fortnightly letter to AOL members.

▲ *AOL Volunteers*—Find out about online Guides and Hosts: who they are, where to find them, and what they do. Have you got what it takes to join them?

▲ *Parental Controls*—Restrict your children's access to certain areas of AOL, newsgroups, and the Internet.

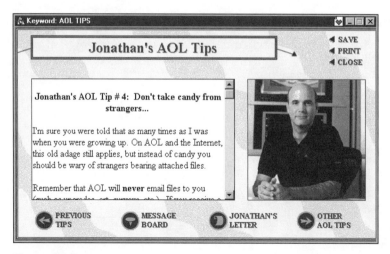

Figure 14.7
Jonathan's handy tips.

▲ *Member Directory*—Looking for someone online? Or looking for an AOL member who can provide a service in your area? Then search the Member Directory.

▲ *AOL Shop*—The online store where AOL members can buy an exclusive range of branded AOL merchandise.

▲ *Chat*—Make friends online in AOL's numerous Chat areas.

And, of course, as in any community, there are certain rules of conduct that you should try to follow to ensure that *everyone* gains maximum benefit and no one feels ill at ease.

Online Etiquette

Generally speaking, AOL is a very friendly place. Members usually take great pains to make it so. However, there are—inevitably—going to be occasions when people disagree about something or stir up problems. In a discussion about football, for example, someone based in SE14 might find it hard to accept the proposition that the world's greatest team is actually Manchester City and not Millwall. Jehovah's Witnesses and Muslims are unlikely to see eye to eye, either.

You mustn't let differences of opinion cause arguments. It spoils it, not just for you, but for everyone else on the message board or in the Chat room. Pretend instead that you're taking part in a debate in the Oxford Union or talking to your boss (or your granny). In other words, keep it civilised, keep it friendly, and remember that you have an audience.

Emoticons

It doesn't help, of course, that raw ASCII text is somewhat impersonal, which can sometimes lead to misunderstandings. Because there's no eye contact, voice inflection, or any other way of conveying mood and intent in an online message, it could be that you take offence from something that was, in reality, meant to be quite innocent or even friendly. This is where emoticons can help.

Emoticons—or *smileys*, as they're also known—are supposed to clarify the intention of a message where it might otherwise be misinterpreted. They're appended to the end of your sentences. This is a smiley :-) Turn your head 90 degrees counterclockwise and you'll see a little smiling face.

Here's a list of some of the more common ones:

▲ :-) Happy face

▲ :-(Sadness, frowning, or disapproval

▲ ;-) Winking

▲ :'-(Crying

▲ 8-) A smiley with glasses

▲ :-D Said with a broad grin

▲ { Alfred Hitchcock

Acronyms

These are often used in combination with emoticons or just for brevity's sake. You'll pick them up as you go along, but here are some of the more common examples:

▲ *AFK*—Away from keyboard

▲ *BAK*—Back at keyboard

▲ *BRB*—Be right back

▲ *BTW*—By the way

▲ *FWIW*—For what it's worth

▲ *GMTA*—Great minds think alike

▲ *IMHO*—In my humble opinion

▲ *IYSWIM*—If you see what I mean

▲ *LOL*—Laughing out loud

▲ *ROFL*—Rolling on floor laughing

▲ *TTFN*—Ta-ta for now

▲ *WB*—Welcome back

▲ *WTG*—Way to go!

You can get more detailed lists of emoticons and acronyms at Keyword: **SMILEYS** and Keyword: **LOL** respectively.

Basically, online etiquette just comes down to common sense. Be courteous and people will be courteous to you. To sum up, here are a few basic rules that will help you avoid misunderstandings:

▲ In the main, it's probably best to avoid personal attacks, or *flames*, as they're called. If you disagree vehemently with another person, or if you feel offended by what he's said, tell him (politely) by email rather than going public with it on a message board. If this situation arises in a Chat room, engage with the subject matter and not the person who's raising it. Life's much simpler and less troublesome this way.

▲ Keep your messages as short as possible. People don't like having to wade through reams and reams of text. It can irritate. In Chat, don't send reams of nonsense to the screen either—it's disruptive and not likely to endear you to your fellow AOL members.

▲ Keep to the subject. If the message board header says "Kayak sailing in the Bosphorus," don't start talking about coracle rowing in the Wash. Don't post messages or send Chat text composed entirely of capital letters. IN ADDITION TO BEING HARD TO READ, IT GIVES THE IMPRESSION THAT YOU'RE SHOUTING.

▲ Don't criticise other people for typos or misspellings. You're just as likely to make them yourself. In any case, online correspondence is supposed to be spontaneous, like a conversation. Would you criticise people for a regional accent or for being slightly ungrammatical?

▲ If someone in Chat is really making a nuisance of herself, use the Ignore function to block out her chat rather than attempting to shout her down. Double-click on her name in the list of people in the room and choose Ignore. That way, you don't even have to see what she's sending to the room.

▲ If things really get out of hand in a Chat room, summon a Guide or report the problem to the Conditions of Service staff. If the trouble is in a Chat room, use Keyword: **NOTIFY AOL** and click on the Page A Guide button in the upper right, making sure to accurately fill out the form that appears. A Guide or COS staff member will be there to assist you as soon as possible. Alternatively, copy the text of the chat that is causing the problem and click on the Chat button at Keyword: **NOTIFY AOL** and provide the information required.

For a roundup of security tips and online safety advice, go to Keyword: **SECURITY** (Figure 14.8). There's Parental Controls, advice on what to do if you encounter trouble, and so forth. You'll also be directed to an

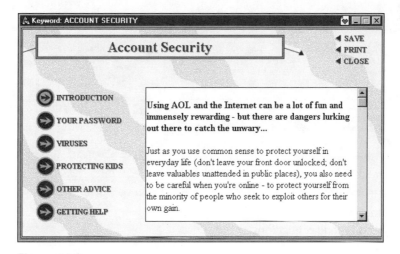

Figure 14.8
AOL's Account Security area provides security tips and gives you access to anti-virus software.

anti-virus area where you can download the latest hi-tech inoculations against computer viruses.

For the definitive last word on rules and regulations, go to Keyword: **RULES** and you can read AOL's Member Agreement (Figure 14.9). In a nutshell, it says that you use AOL at your own risk and you promise not to defame or disrupt people or transmit obscene material. Furthermore, you guarantee that you will *not* try to use AOL as any sort of online car-boot sale for flogging your instant baldness cures, steamy XXX-rated videos, and dodgy investment advice—unless you want your account terminated pretty swiftly, that is.

Changing Your Password

AOL recommends that you change your password regularly. If you suspect that someone else has obtained your password, change it straightaway. You can do this from several areas of AOL, such as My AOL and Member Services. But the quickest way is just to go to Keyword: **PASSWORD**. You'll then be prompted to select a new one (Figure 14.10). Make it something memorable, but not obvious. And *don't* forget it.

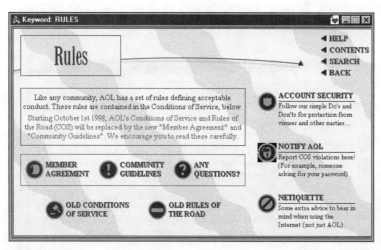

Figure 14.9
AOL's rules and regulations.

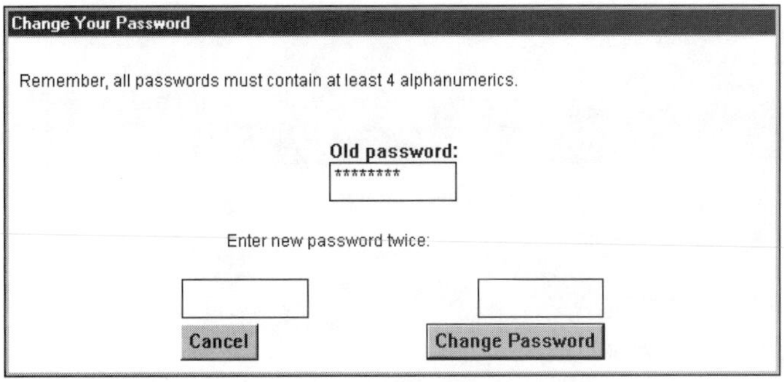

Figure 14.10
Do you think someone may have got hold of your password? If so, change it immediately.

AOL Pricing And Billing Information

AOL has three pricing plans. In most cases, by default, when you first sign on, you're on the Light Access plan. At the time of writing (September 1998—so it might have changed slightly by the time you read this), the Light Access plan costs £4.95 per month, which buys you three hours of online time. For each additional hour you spend online over this during the month, you pay £2.35.

If all you ever do is send an occasional email message, the Light Access plan is probably sufficient. If, however, you use the Internet a lot or are heavily into Chat, or if your monthly bill exceeds £15, then one of the other two plans would probably suit you better.

The Unlimited Access plan costs just £16.95 per month. For this, you can stay online as long as you like without paying another penny to AOL (although your phone provider might have other ideas).

The Annual Access plan also gives you unlimited online time. Here, you pay an up-front fee of £179.40, which covers you for a full 12 months. This is probably the most cost-effective option for those with several family members using AOL.

To find out exactly which pricing plan you're on, and to change it, if necessary, go to Keyword: **BILLING**. Here, all will be revealed (Figure 14.11). Two of the most frequently used items on this page are the Current Bill Summary and Detailed Monthly Bill.

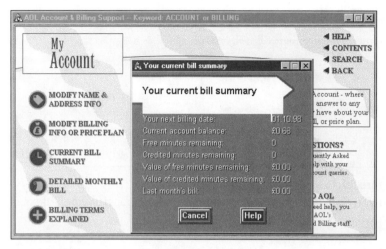

Figure 14.11
My Account allows you to check your monthly bill, change your pricing plan, update your billing information, and more.

Current Bill Summary

The current bill summary is most useful for those on the Light Access plan, but all members will find it useful as a snapshot of where you stand with AOL. It includes the following features:

▲ *Your Next Billing Date*—The next date you will be billed for your online usage. Your billing date is based on the monthly anniversary of the day you first registered with AOL. The date is currently shown in the American format of month.day.year. So 09.02.98 means September 2, 1998.

▲ *Current Account Balance*—The total amount due for your online usage as of today's date. Note that this amount only includes the amount you owe for this month's online usage. Charges still owed from earlier months are not listed.

▲ *Free Minutes Remaining*—The total amount of monthly free time remaining in your current billing cycle. (Only applicable if you are currently on an hourly price plan, such as the Light Access plan.)

▲ *Credited Minutes Remaining*—The amount of credited time you have remaining from time issued as a result of various online events (games, contests, or quizzes) or as a refund from AOL. (Only applicable if you are currently on an hourly price plan.)

▲ *Value Of Free Minutes Remaining*—The monetary equivalent of your monthly free time. For example, if the hourly rate is £2.35, 180 monthly free minutes is worth £7.05. (Only applicable if you are currently on an hourly price plan.)

▲ *Value Of Credited Minutes Remaining*—Similar to Value Of Free Minutes Remaining in that your credited time is also displayed as its monetary equivalent. (Only applicable if you are currently on an hourly price plan.)

▲ *Last Month's Bill*—Represents the amount you were charged for your previous month's online usage. This includes your monthly membership fee.

If you are on a flat-rate pricing plan (such as the Unlimited or Annual plan), your billing summary is updated at the end of each online session after you sign off from AOL. If you are on an hourly pricing plan (such as the Light Access plan), your billing summary is updated at the end of each online session after you sign off from AOL while you're within your monthly free time. Once your monthly free time has been used, your billing summary will be updated every 24 hours instead.

Detailed Monthly Bill

Here you can look at both the current month's billing detail and the previous month's complete billing detail. Each line represents one of your online sessions. The list of sessions is arranged in reverse chronological order (most recent sessions at the top). For each session, the following details are listed:

▲ *Time On*—The date and time your online session began. The time is given in Greenwich mean time (GMT). The date is shown as month.day.year, so 09.02.98 means September 2, 1998.

▲ *Name*—The screen name used during that particular session. This is useful information if, for example, you use one of your screen names for business or you want to check to see how much time the kids are spending online.

▲ *Free*—The number of minutes that were spent in a free area, such as Member Services (members on hourly pricing plans such as Light Access don't incur AOL bills for time spent in free areas).

▲ *Paid*—The number of minutes that were spent in normal paid AOL areas.

▲ *Charge*—The charge incurred. This is based on the number of minutes listed under Paid and the current AOL online hourly charge.

▲ *Credit*—Credit issued. If you still have some of your monthly free allowance remaining, this credit will equal what's listed in the Charge column, and hence, the total charge to you will be zero. If 0.00 is listed under Credit, you have used up your monthly allowance of free time and you will be charged as normal for your online time.

▲ *Total*—Total charge incurred for each online session. This is equal to the value in the Charge column minus the value in the Credit column. The totals for each column are shown at the bottom of the screen. The figure shown at the very bottom of the Total column is the total amount due to AOL.

Sign-On Options

If you want to use AOL from someone else's computer, over the Internet, or while you're travelling abroad, read on.

Signing On As Guest

Suppose you want to check your email or message boards but you're not at your own computer? If you have a friend or colleague who has an AOL account or you're at an Internet café, you can sign on from that computer as Guest. Your online session will then be billed to your own account.

To sign on as Guest, go the Sign On To AOL screen and select Guest from the list of screen names. Then click on the Sign On button. The software will dial in to AOL and, when you're connected, prompt you for your screen name and password (Figure 14.12). Thereafter, it's almost like using AOL on your own computer. There are just a few differences.

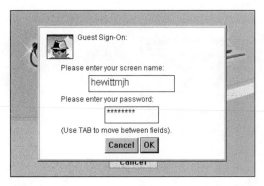

Figure 14.12
Signing on to AOL as Guest.

You can't use FlashSessions, basically for the sake of security. Your friend wouldn't want you to inadvertently download a virus to his precious PC, would he? Also, any mail that you do read won't be stored to your Personal Filing Cabinet because you're not using your own computer. So if the email is particularly important, mark it as unread and retrieve it again when you get back to your own PC.

Here are a few other things you can't do while you're signed on as Guest: You can't access your Favourite Places list or your Address Book (because they are stored on your own computer), and you can't add screen names to your account (nor can you delete them, for that matter).

Using AOL Over The Internet

You might choose to access AOL over the Internet rather than dialing in directly. It could be, for example, that you're running several different online services on your PC: AOL, CompuServe, and Demon, say. Rather than dial in to each separately, it can be quicker and somewhat less expensive (especially if one of your online services is based abroad) to just dial up your main Internet service provider (ISP) with a local call and use that connection to sign on to the others. In other words, you access them remotely via the ISP.

If your ISP allows such piggyback connections—and most do—then connecting to AOL is perfectly straightforward. At the Sign On To AOL screen, click on Setup, which takes you to the Network & Modem Setup area (Figure 14.13). Here, select Create Location and you're

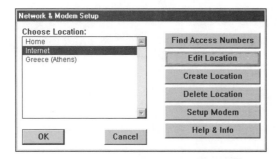

Figure 14.13
From your Network & Modem Setup screen you can create and edit different
locations and configure your modem.

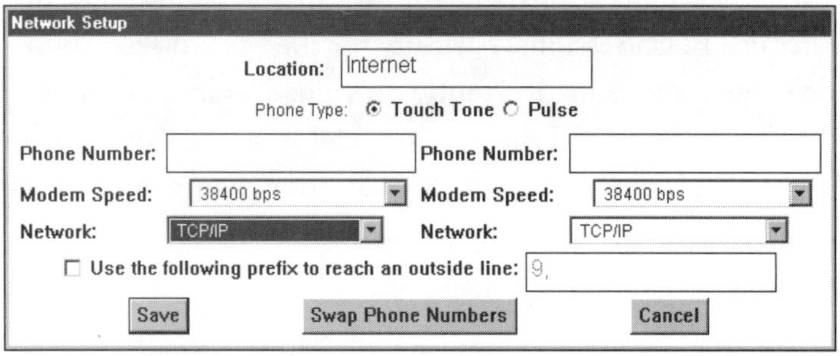

Figure 14.14
Setting up the AOL software to sign on over the Internet.

deposited in the Network Setup screen (Figure 14.14). In the Location
window, type "Internet". You don't need a phone number because your
ISP will be doing the dialing. Nor is it necessary to bother with the
modem speed because your ISP is doing the connecting. So just leave the
modem speed at whatever appears by default in the window. All you
need do is select TCP/IP (Transmission Control Protocol/Internet
Protocol) from the Network window and click on Save.

Thereafter, to access AOL via the Internet, first log on with your ISP.
Next, while your ISP is running in the background, start up AOL. Then
click on Sign On as you normally do, and in short order, you should be
connected. AOL will probably run slightly slower this way, especially
when it comes to uploading and downloading files, but there's unfortunately not much you can do about this. Blame the Internet.

Signing On From Abroad

If you're equipped with a laptop, you can sign on to AOL from most countries of the world, either directly or via an intermediate network. All you need is the correct phone number and the right sort of phone plug.

Let's start with the phone plug because, without the right one, you won't even reach first base. For those who revel in such trivia, the British telephone plug—the one dangling from your modem right now—is called a BT631A. Unfortunately, it's only welcomed by sockets in New Zealand, Malta, and a few remnants of the British Empire. If you delve into the matter a little, you'll discover that the world is actually served by a collection of incompatible phone plugs whose number and variety would put H. J. Heinz to shame. Some look like the U.K. version; others look more like those mains-powered mosquito killers or drill bits.

So what do you do? The answer is, you'll need to find an adapter.

First, find out what sort of socket is used in your intended destination. A good place to start is a U.K.-based company called TeleAdapt. Check out their Web site at **http://www.teleadapt.com**. You'll find a whole lot of advice for the laptop-equipped traveller, as well as pictures and descriptions of every single telephone plug in the world. You can order a suitable adapter online from this site. Or failing that, go to your local Tandy. Some of the larger stores have foreign telephone adapters in stock.

Your next step is to find out your local AOL access number abroad. Go to Keyword: **GLOBAL** and you'll find international numbers listed by country (Figure 14.15). Double-click on the name of the country and you'll get details of the regional telephone numbers, their maximum modem speed, and any other information, such as what sort of network is used and if there's a surcharge for using that network..

Having made a note of your access number, set it up as a separate location in your Network & Modem Setup screen. Just as we did when we set up an Internet location earlier in this chapter, click on the Create Location button. In the Setup Screen shown in Figure 14.16, I'm entering the connection details for AOL's Athens node. Then I go through the following steps:

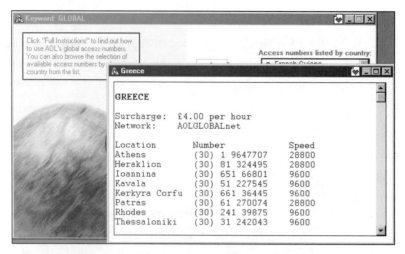

Figure 14.15
You can access AOL from over 100 countries worldwide.

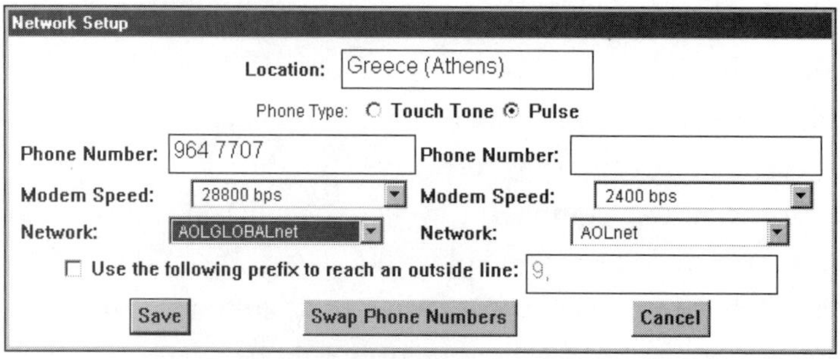

Figure 14.16
Setting up AOL to connect in Athens.

1. I choose pulse dialing, because—at the time this book was written—this area of Athens could not handle digital tones.

2. I enter the local phone number: 964 7707.

3. I leave the modem speed set to the maximum that Athens can currently handle: 28,800 bps.

4. I choose the network. AOL's list of countries includes the correct network for each country. To access AOL in Greece, you need to use one called AOLGLOBALnet. Basically, you dial into AOLGLOBALnet, which then connects to AOL's proprietary network, AOLnet. Not that you need to worry about any of this. It all happens automatically

and transparently in the background. The only thing that might concern you is that you'll incur a surcharge for using AOLGLOBAL.net, which varies with the number you use. This surcharge will be added to your regular AOL bill.

5. I click on Save.

Thereafter, you just sign on as you normally would. The only indication that you're doing so from abroad is a message alerting you to the fact that you're incurring surcharges.

Help! No Dial Tone!

Some modems are a bit like a minority of English holidaymakers: They expect the whole world to speak their language. But as anyone who's ever travelled abroad and used a foreign telephone will tell you, different countries can have their own unique dial tones, which will be completely unintelligible to many fresh-off-the-boat, visiting modems. If these modems can't detect a U.K. dial tone, AOL will display the error message "No dial tone" and will just sit there.

If this happens, go to the Network & Modem Setup screen and select Setup Modem. Then choose Edit Commands and you're presented with Modem Profile, which looks like a whole lot of gibberish (Figure 14.17). Try to ignore it. In the Setup Modem String window, simply insert "X1" before the ^M at the end, and click on OK. The X1 tells your modem to ignore the foreign dial tone and dial out regardless.

Custom Modem Profile	
Setup Modem String:	AT&F&C1&D2&K3&Q5E1V1Q0X1^M
Restore Modem String:	AT&F^M
Dial Prefix:	ATD
Dial Suffix:	^M
Disconnect String:	ATH^M
Escape String:	~~~+++~~~
Reset String:	ATZ^M
	OK Cancel

Figure 14.17
Instructing your modem to ignore foreign dial tones.

For more information on using a laptop abroad, you might care to check out a book called *Travels with a Laptop*, published by Thomson Computer Press (ISBN 1-85032-164-7) and written, if memory serves me correctly, by one Michael Hewitt.

Ave Atque Vale

So, that is it. As I said at the beginning, this book can only be a rough guide. AOL is continually growing and improving. In the near future, for example, you'll be able to send letters and faxes over AOL. Using Iphone, AOL members will be able to conduct conventional telephone conversations over the Internet. Chat will be upgraded and enhanced. Internet access will be faster. You'll be able to drop your holiday photographs off at the chemist and then have them sent, digitally, directly to your PC via AOL—amongst many, many other things.

But don't take my word for it. Sign on and find out for yourself.

Appendix

AOL Keywords

Most online areas have their Keywords noted on their main pages, but please note that not all U.S. Keywords will work for U.K. members, and vice versa.

These Keywords are accurate as of our August 1998 press deadline. Just as AOL's content is regularly updated, so are its Keywords. Therefore, Keywords added after our deadline won't be listed here, whereas some listed here may now be inactive. For the most current Keyword information available, please check at Keyword: **KEYWORD**.

Codes:

▲ (UK)—Only AOL U.K. members can use the Keyword as indicated. (For example, a U.S. member using the Keyword: **FINANCE** gets taken to the U.S. Finance area, not the U.K. Finance area.)

▲ (ALL)—The Keyword will take any AOL member to the area.

▲ (US)—Denotes a U.S.-only Keyword to a U.K. content area.

The Keywords area also contains a link to the U.S. (American) Keywords area. While much of this content is available to U.K. and other international members, some is not. (Hey, they can't use some of our Keywords, either.) Your best bet is to simply try using those Keywords that interest you.

System-Wide Keywords

BILLING	Online billing summary
BUDDY	Set up a Buddy list to track when your friends are online
CANCEL	Cancel AOL membership
CHAT HELP	The how-to's of Chat
DOWNLOAD101	Everything you need to know about downloading files
FLASHSESSION	The setup screen for FlashSessions
GUIDE APPLY	Information on becoming one of our volunteer Guides
HELP	Go to our free Member Services area
KEYWORDS	A list of AOL Keywords
LOGGING	Record onscreen text to file
MEMBER DIRECTORY	Find other AOL members online
MY ADDRESS	Check your email address
MY PAGE	Build your very own home page on the Web
NAMES	Create and delete screen names on your account
NETFIND	AOL's search engine
NEW HELP	Help file for new members
NEWSGROUPS	Read or subscribe to Internet newsgroups
PARENTAL CONTROL	Restrict access to specific areas and features
PASSWORD	Change the password for your account
PROFILE	Create or edit your online profile
QUESTIONS	The most frequently asked questions about AOL
QUICKFIND	Search AOL's online file libraries
REPORT	Report a technical problem to AOL
SHORTHAND	Information about the "smileys" and acronyms commonly used in chat
TROUBLE	Page an online guide or report Conditions of Service violations
URL	Keyword direct to sites on the World Wide Web

UK-Accessible Keywords

3D CARDS	Computing Forum (UK)
451	Science fiction area (UK)

A

AAA	All About AOL (UK)
ACCESS	UK local access numbers (Free, UK)
ACCOUNT MANAGEMENT	Account Management (Free, UK)
ALLSPORT	Allsport Photo Gallery (ALL)
ANYWHERE	Mystery Tour page (ALL)
AOL CARDS	Send a virtual Web card (ALL)
AOL FOOTBALL	AOL football area (ALL)
AOL RADIO	Online radio service (UK)
AOL SHOP	Official UK merchandise area (UK)
APPLE	Apple Mac areas on AOL (UK)
ARENA THE	UK Sports area (UK)
ASTROLOGY	Astrology links area (ALL)
AT THE RACES	Horse racing news, tips, results (UK)
AUTOSPORT	Autosport Magazine (ALL)

B

BIL	Business in London (ALL)
BILLING	Instant online billing summary (UK)
BLABBATORIUM	Nickelodeon chat room (UK)
BLOOMBERG	Financial news, data, and charts area (UK)
BLUE AQUARIUS	Astrology newsletter (ALL)
BOOKS	Books area (UK)
BOYS TORQUE	Members talk area of Car Channel (ALL)
BSH	Custom motor bike magazine (ALL)
BUYING COMPUTERS	Computer Buying Forum (UK)

C

CAMPING	Camping information (UK)
CAR	Motoring Channel (ALL)

CAR CLASSIFIEDS	Classifieds area for new and used cars (ALL)
CAR EVENTS	Motoring industry events area of Car Channel (ALL)
CAR NEWS	Latest motoring news (ALL)
CAR SHOWROOM	Major car manufacturers and latest models (ALL)
CAREERS	Careers and recruitment area (UK)
CDN	Daily computing news wire (UK)
CHARTS	CIN UK music charts (UK)
CHAT HELP	Tips for chatting (UK)
CITY NEWS	UK financial pages (UK)
CLASSIC CARS	Classic car area of Car Channel (ALL)
CLEARANCE	University entrance scheme (UK)
CLIP CLOP CLUB	Kids pony area (UK)
CLUBS	Clubs & Interests channel main screen (UK)
COMICS	UK comics area (UK)
COMPUTING	Computing channel main screen (UK)
COMPUTING CHAT	Hosted UK computing chats (UK)
COMPUTING NEWS	CDN daily news wire (UK)
COMPUTING UPGRADE	Computing Upgrade Forum (UK)
COMPUTING WEB	Digest of computing Web sites (UK)
CONTESTS	AOL Competitions area (UK)
COS	Conditions of Service (Free, UK)
CRAFT CORNER	Craft Corner main screen (ALL)
CREDIT	Online time credit requests (UK)
CRICKET	The Cricketer (ALL)

D

D&B	Dun & Bradstreet UK (ALL)
DEADLINE	Online cult magazine (ALL)
DIADEM	Diadem (ALL)
DON'T CLICK HERE	Unique Web sites (ALL)

E

EIU THE	Economist Intelligence Unit
EUROPE WEATHER	Europe weather main screen (ALL)

F

FACE OFF	Ice hockey (UK)
FAST LANE	Fast Cars area of Car Channel (ALL)
FAULT	To report AOL UK Software faults (UK)
FESTIVAL 98	Summer festivals and events guide (ALL)
FINANCE	Finance channel main screen (UK)
FINE FOOD	Gourmet food shopping online (UK)
FLASHSESSIONS	FlashSessions (ALL)
FOOLUK	The Motley Fool UK (UK)
FTSE	FTSE updates (UK)

G

GAME ON	Games reviews and contests (ALL)
GAMES	Games channel main screen (UK)
GAMES NEWS	The latest news and reviews (UK)
GAMESDOWNLOADS	UK download area for games (ALL)
GAMESPOT	Games content provider (UK)
GLOBAL	GlobalNet International Access numbers (UK)
GOOD HOTEL GUIDE	Good Hotel Guide on AOL (ALL)
GOOD TASTE	UK Food and cooking area (ALL)
GORILLAS	Mountain gorillas rescue project (ALL)
GRAND PRIX	Autosport magazine (ALL)
GREEN FINGERS	Gardening area (ALL)
GUIDE APPLY	Guide programme application (UK)
GUIDEPAGER	To report COS problems (UK)

H

HELICON	Hutchinson Encyclopedia online (UK)
HELP	Member Services area (Free, UK)
HIDLON	Hidden London (UK)
HOLIDAY REPORT	Members report on their holidays (ALL)
HOSTED CHATS	UK hosted chat schedules (UK)
HPUK	Hewlett-Packard UK Forum (ALL)
HTML	A beginner's guide to HTML (UK)
HUTCHINSON	Hutchinson Encyclopedia online (UK)

I

IM	Turn your Instant Messages on and off (UK)
IMDB	Internet Movie Database (ALL)
INSIDE SOAP	Inside Soap Online (ALL)
INTERFLORA	Online flowers service (UK)
INTERNET	Internet channel main screen (UK)
INTERNET BOOKSHOP	Online bookshop (UK)
INTERNET EXPLORER	Internet Explorer 3 area (ALL)
IRC	To download Internet Relay Chat software (UK)

J

JONATHAN	AOL UK's Managing Director (ALL)

K

KEYWORDS	Lists of AOL Keywords (UK)
KIDS	Kids channel main screen (UK)

L

LINUX	Linux Forum (UK)
LOCAL LIFE	Regional and local news area (UK)
LOCAL LIFE IRELAND	Local life regional and local areas (UK)
LOCAL LIFE MIDLANDS	
LOCAL LIFE NORTH	
LOCAL LIFE SCOTLAND	
LOCAL LIFE SE	
LOCAL LIFE SW	
LOCAL LIFE LEISURE	Local Life information areas (UK)
LOCAL LIFE NEWS	
LOCAL LIFE PEOPLE	
LOCAL LIFE SERVICES	
LOCAL LIFE TELL US	
LOCAL LIFE WEB SEARCH	
LONDON	Local Life London areas and information (UK)
LONDON ART	
LONDON CLUBS	

LONDON COMEDY
LONDON FILM
LONDON FOOD
LONDON GAY
LONDON KIDS
LONDON LEISURE
LONDON MUSIC
LONDON NEWS
LONDON PEOPLE
LONDON SERVICES
LONDON SPORT
LONDON THEATRE
LONELY PLANET   Down-to-earth travel area (ALL)
LOTTERY   UK Lottery Syndicate (UK)
LOVE SHACK   UK personals (ALL)
LURVE   Love Shack (ALL)

M

MACFORMAT   Mac Format magazine online (ALL)
MACHELP   UK Mac help forum (UK)
MACOS   Mac OS 8.1 download (UK)
MARKETING PREFS   Mailing list controls (UK)
MIME   About Internet mail and MIME files (UK)
MONEYFACTS   Moneyfacts (UK)
MONEYWISE   Moneywise Magazine (ALL)
MOTORBIKES   BSH custom bike magazine (ALL)
MOVIE BABYLON   Hollywood gossip (UK)
MULTIPLAYER   Multiplayer gaming on AOL (UK)
MUSIC   AOL's music magazine (UK)
MUSIC BOULEVARD   Online music store (ALL)
MUSIC DOWNLOADS   Band sound clips, pics and Web sites (UK)
MUSIC NEWS   Rock and pop music news from the NME (UK)
MY ADDRESS   What's my email address? (UK)
MYSTIC GARDENS   Mystic Gardens (ALL)

N

NAMES	Change or add names to your AOL account (ALL)
NEW	What's New area (UK)
NEW HELP	New members help (UK)
NEWS	News Channel main screen (UK)
NEWS CAPTION	News Caption (ALL)
NEWS DEBATE	News Debate (ALL)
NEWS SURVEY	UK News survey (UK)
NICK CHAT	Nickelodeon Online chat room (UK)
NICKELODEON	Nickelodeon Online (UK)
NME	Music news from the famous rock weekly (UK)

O

OBJECTS OF DESIRE	Cool gadgets and gizmos (ALL)
ON THE BOX	Entertainment channel TV area (ALL)
OUTEREDGE	UK Teen area (ALL)
OUTTHERE	Out There News (UK)
OXFORD DICTIONARY	The New Oxford Dictionary of English (UK)

P

PARAGON	Games console area (ALL)
PARENTAL CONTROL	Parental controls setup (FREE, UK)
PC FINDER	PC dealer search and free quotes service (UK)
PCZONE	PC games magazine (ALL)
PIN	Advice on computers and software for parents (UK)
PLANET EALING	UK movie forum (ALL)
POS GEN	Positive Generation (ALL)
PRACTICAL PC	Online computer magazine (UK)
PRICES	AOL prices (FREE, UK)
PRIMARY SCHOOLS	Learning Channel schools (UK)
PRIVATE ROOM	Make a private chat room (UK)
PROFESSIONAL	Professional forums (UK)
PROFILE	Create or edit your online profile (ALL)
PSK	PC Survival Kit (UK)
PUB	Virtual pub (UK)

Q

QUESTIONS	AOL FAQs (Free, UK)
QUIXELL	Online auction house (UK)
QUOTES	International company quotations (UK)

R

REFERENCE	Reference main screen (UK)
REUTERS PICTURES	Reuters news photos (UK)
RUGBY	The Rugby Club (UK)
RUSSELL GRANT	Russell Grant's astrology area (ALL)

S

SAFETY ONLINE	Safety Online (ALL)
SHAREWARE	Free software (UK)
SHOPPING	Shopping Channel main screen (UK)
SHORTHAND	Online smileys and acronyms (UK)
SIGN ON A FRIEND	Get your friends on AOL and win (UK)
SPORT	Sport channel main screen (UK)
SPRINGSOFT	SOHO software area (UK)
STATELY HOMEPAGE	Prizes for the best home page (UK)
STOCKS	Market reports (UK)
STORY MAKER	Kids Story Maker (ALL)
STRESSED OUT	Advice area for teenagers (ALL)
SUGGEST	Suggestion area (UK)
SURVIVAL	Survival (UK)
SYSTEM RESPONSE	System response problems (Free, UK)

T

TALK TIME	UK Sport Chat Channel (UK)
TALKINGPOINT	Internet Talking Point weekly survey (UK)
TANK GIRL	Deadline (ALL)
TECH CHAT	UK tech support (Free, UK)
TELEWORK	Telework Forum (Free, UK)
TELLY	UK TV Forum (ALL)
TERRIS	Terris role-playing game (ALL)

THE FEATURE	Planet Ealing film feature (UK)
THE LIST	Central Scotland guide to what's on (UK)
THIS IS LONDON	News, features, and information for London (ALL)
THIS IS LONDON BUSINESS	Daily business news (ALL)
THIS IS LONDON CLUBS	Clubs information (ALL)
THIS IS LONDON COMEDY	Comedy clubs information (ALL)
THIS IS LONDON FILM	Film news and reviews (ALL)
THIS IS LONDON FOOD	Food and drink features (ALL)
THIS IS LONDON KIDS	Kids features and information (ALL)
THIS IS LONDON THEATRE	Theatre information and tickets (ALL)
THORNTONS	Luxury chocolates online service (UK)
TICKER	UK news ticker (UK)
TIPSHEET	UK pop chart and forum (ALL)
TOE	The Outer Edge, UK teen area (ALL)
TOUR	Introduction to AOL Content Areas (UK)
TRAVEL FINDER	Travel bargains free email service (UK)
TROUBLE	GuidePager screen (UK)
TUNED IN	Driving Forum and community area of Car Channel (ALL)

U

UK CHARTS	CIN UK record charts (UK)
UK CHATS	UK hosted chat schedules (ALL)
UK HOTELS	Hotel guide (ALL)
UK TOUR GUIDE	AOL UK Tour Book (ALL)
UKLIVE	UK Live events and special chats (ALL)
UKMEETS	Upcoming events and meeting area for AOL members (UK)
UKSCHOOLS	UK Schools community (ALL)
UNIVERSITY	Universities online (UK)
UPGRADE	Upgrade your AOL software (UK)
UPGRADING FORUM	PC upgrade help area (UK)
URL	World Wide Web access (UK)
UTOPIA	UK Gay/Lesbian area (ALL)

W

WALES	Virtual Wales (ALL)
WEATHER	Weather channel main screen (ALL)
WEB BUILDING FORUM	Help with your Web page (UK)
WHATS WRONG	Check if there are any system problems (UK)
WIN95	Windows 95 files area (ALL)
WINDOWS 98	Windows 98 information area (ALL)
WINDOWS FORUM	Windows help area (UK)
WORLD PICTURES	Reuters news photos (UK)
WRITER	UK Writers Club (UK)
WSC	When Saturday Comes (football) (ALL)

Z

ZDUK	Ziff-Davis UK Forum (ALL)

Index